FOOD LOVERS' SE

W9-BPK-844

FOOD LOVERS'
GUIDE TO
QUEENS

The Best Restaurants, Markets & Local Culinary Offerings

1st Edition

Meg Cotner

gpp

Guilford, Connecticut

Copyright © 2013 Morris Book Publishing, LLC

Editor: Amy Lyons
Project Editor: Lynn Zelem
Layout Artist: Mary Ballachino
Text Design: Sheryl Kober
Illustrations by Jill Butler with additional art by Carleen Moira Powell and MaryAnn Dubé
Maps: Melissa Baker © Morris Book Publishing, LLC

ISBN 978-0-7627-8118-8

Printed in the United States of America
10 9 8 7 6 5 4 3 2 1

All the information in this guidebook is subject to change. We recommend that you call ahead to obtain current information before traveling.

Contents

Recipes, 347

Appendices, 359

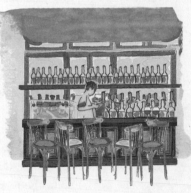

About the Author

Meg Cotner lives and works in Astoria, Queens. She is the editor of QueensNYC, a site about life in the borough of Queens. She is also a cofounder of *We Heart Astoria,* a popular blog focused on the communities of Astoria and Long Island City, where she writes about the arts, community, recreation, and, of course, food. She also writes about real, whole, nourishing food and related topics on her site, Harmonious Belly, which she founded in 2010. She also worked for About.com as the contributing writer for Astoria, Queens.

Additionally, she helps manage the Hellgate CSA as a Core Group member, working to bring local, organic, and sustainably grown and raised food to families in Astoria. In spring of 2011, she founded the Queens Swap, a food swap based in the borough of Queens.

She is a seasoned home cook and an avid backyard gardener, maintaining a thriving organic garden behind her apartment in Astoria. She also explores the art of food preservation on a regular basis, from lacto-fermentation to water-bath canning to pickling. She lectures and teaches workshops on food preservation and traditional food.

It also comes as no surprise that exploring Queens is also one of her passions and she loves exploring the borough's food scene, whether it's noshing on street food, eating at restaurants (fancy to divey), or meeting artisanal food producers and growers. Discussing food and food-related topics is one of her joys and she is happy to speak with anyone about this engrossing and entertaining subject.

Acknowledgments

First, I'd like to thank my number-one dude who supported me, challenged me, and came to enjoy foods he might not have tried on his own as a result of accompanying me to restaurants around Queens. He was a big help and tolerated lots of leftovers coming into our home. The rest of my family has also been supportive and encouraging of my work on this project, especially my parents, brother, and cousins.

Next, I'd like to thank John Roleke, my former editor at About .com, who connected me to this project with a recommendation of my work to Amy Lyons, my editor at Globe Pequot Press. I'm so grateful to her and the publisher for this amazing experience and opportunity.

I also must thank all my friends who accompanied me on the food adventures over the past few months—Anne, Betty, Bradley, Caitlin, Charlene, Dan, Dave, David, Dalena, Dayna, Denise, Harlan, Harris, Heather, James, Jennifer, Joseph, Judith, Kristin, Laura, Laurie, Mackenzi, Matthew, Maury, Michael C, Michael L, Missy, Rachel, Sajan, Sam, Shannon, Sue, Tom, Wayne, and Yan. Thank you for eating with me—I could not have done this without you. Many more have dined with me over the years while I've covered eating in Queens, and I am grateful to all of them, too.

Thank you to my friends and colleagues who submitted recipes for the book—Anne, Laura, Judith, and also Jen from The Queens Kickshaw. Many thanks to each of you for your contributions!

My writer and blogger friends in Queens have also been very supportive of me during this project, so thank you very much for all your good wishes and encouragement.

I have wonderful friends all around the world who cheered me on from both a distance and nearby. Thank you so, so much. All your support was deeply appreciated.

Finally, thank you Queens for having such kickass food. You are sweet, rich, spicy, and delicious.

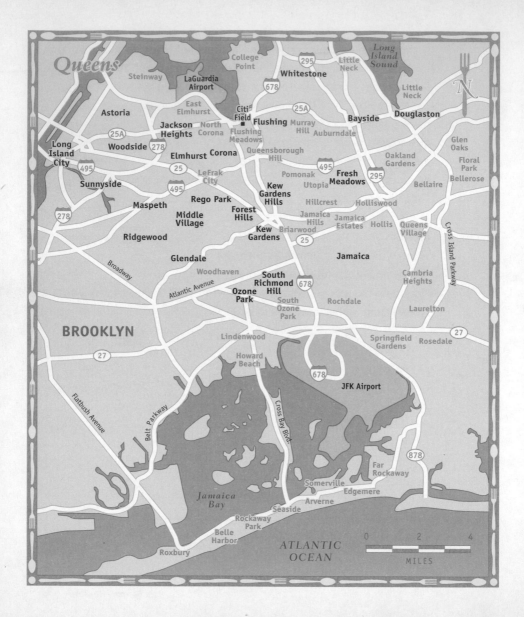

Introduction

Welcome to Queens! This fat comma-shaped patch of land is the largest of the five boroughs geographically, and the second most populous of the five. It is home to two major sports teams, the New York Yankees and the New York Mets; the impressive US Tennis Center, home of the US Open; New York City's airports, LaGuardia and JFK; two major parks, Forest Park and Flushing Meadows, home of the 1964 World's Fair (look for the Unisphere); and two robust film and TV studios, Kaufman Astoria and Silvercup Studios. The borough is the most ethnically diverse county in the nation, with more than 138 languages spoken here, and 100 countries represented. Scientists have found that certain parts of Queens are populated by people carrying genetic markers for almost all migrations that happened historically among the peoples of earth. And as you would expect, the food here is pretty diverse and varied, too, not to mention awesome.

One of the beautiful things about Queens is that despite the diversity and differences among cultures, people here really are more alike than they are different. Spend some time in Queens and you'll see that. Everyone really does want the same things, pretty much—a place to live, a safe environment for their family and friends, a way to make a living, time to relax and enjoy life. They also love to share their food with others, and delight in showing it off to those outside their culture—people are really proud of their culture's food. Everyone benefits.

Since Queens is so rich with immigrants, certain neighborhoods have become known for specific cuisines. This includes Astoria for Greek, Middle Eastern, and Brazilian; Woodside for Filipino; Jackson Heights for Indian and Colombian; Corona for Latin American; Flushing for Chinese and Korean; Rego Park for Bukharian/Uzbek; and Richmond Hill for South Asian and Caribbean. Of course, there are other cultures represented in each of these neighborhoods but these are the standouts.

On the other end of the spectrum is the whole "New American" food movement, which focuses on seasonal and organic ingredients as well as ingredients that are sustainably grown and meat from animals that are humanely raised. The majority of these restaurants are in western Queens in the Astoria/Long Island City neighborhoods—restaurants like Sparrow Tavern, Vesta, and Butcher Bar in Astoria, and Alobar and LIC Market in Long Island City. Brooklyn Grange, a large urban rooftop farm, also resides in Long Island City, producing vegetables for local residents and restaurants. CSAs (Community Supported Agriculture) have also popped up and are finding their way from western Queens (where there are seven CSAs) out into the borough. The first food co-op in Queens—the Queens Harvest Food Co-op—is in the planning stages, too.

Queens really is a massive place, and it would be unrealistic to include food from every single neighborhood, so we have focused primarily on the areas accessible by subway, with a few places here or there that require a bus ride or a car. All things considered, traveling by subway is the most convenient and economical sort of transportation in NYC, and that's the way most New Yorkers and visitors get around the city. We hope both Queens residents, adventurous eaters in greater New York, and far-flung visitors to our fair borough will find this guide useful, helpful, and inspirational, enough so to get you to explore Queens and uncover just how amazing and beautiful the food is here!

How to Use This Book

Queens, along with most of New York City, organizes itself by neighborhoods—neighborhoods are part of the identity of the City. So, after this introductory chapter, we've divided this book up by neighborhood, heading generally in a west to east direction. Each chapter is further divided into subsections, including:

Foodie Faves
This chapter is populated with restaurants we think you should check out, whether you're a local or a visitor.

Landmarks
Restaurants in this chapter have been around for a long time and have developed a multigenerational following.

Specialty Stores, Markets & Producers

Butcher shops, bakeries, markets, and more are included in this chapter. Some of the places listed here are where you can get some of the best ingredients to make a stellar meal, or where you can grab something delicious. We've also highlighted a few producers who excel at what they do.

Street Food

Some neighborhoods have a substantial street food community, so we've included them here. The biggest one is along Roosevelt Avenue in Jackson Heights, but you'll find street food throughout the borough.

Recipes

We've collected a choice handful of recipes from local chefs and food artisans, and they are included in this chapter.

Appendices

Additional content about food festivals, CSAs, and greenmarkets can be found in the last part of the book along with useful indexes of cuisine categories and special markets and dishes found throughout this guide.

Price Code

Each restaurant carries a price code to give you a rough approximation of what you will spend. We chose to base the code on dinner entree prices. As a general rule, double the figure to estimate the cost of a 3-course meal with a glass of wine. The codes only represent the majority of dinner entrees; most restaurants will have a few dishes that are less expensive and a few that are more expensive. The cost of lunch is almost always lower.

$	**under $15**
$$	**$15 to $25**
$$$	**$25 to $40**
$$$$	**more than $40 or prix fixe**

Navigating Queens

The best way to move around Queens is by subway; it's inexpensive, it goes where some of the best food is, and you don't have to worry about paying for gas or tolls. The borough is the home to four major subway transit hubs—Queens Plaza, home to the E/M/R lines; Queensboro Plaza, home to the N/Q and the 7; 74th Street/Roosevelt Avenue, home to the 7 and the E/M/R; and way far out east at Sutphin Boulevard/Archer Avenue, home to the E/J/Z lines, the Jamaica LIRR stop, and the AirTrain stop, which takes you to JFK airport. To orient yourself, pick up a subway map, free at any station. Google Maps includes all the subway lines, so that is helpful as well. There are also any number of smartphone apps that will help you navigate the system; the free NYCMate app for both the iPhone and Android phones is very good, as it includes both subway and city bus maps.

The LIRR, part of the New York metropolitan area's commuter rail system, also makes stops in Queens, including the communities of Long Island City, Woodside (major hub), Forest Hills, Kew Gardens, Flushing, Murray Hill, Auburndale, Bayside, Douglaston, and Jamaica. In some cases, it's much more convenient to take the LIRR to your destination than the subway. For instance, on weekends you can purchase a City Ticket, which allows you to ride the LIRR for about half the price of a regular one-way ticket, as long as you stay within the boundaries of the five boroughs. This ticket is valid only for the day of purchase, too, but if you're going for a day's jaunt to say, Bayside from Woodside, it's a real deal.

Some parts of Queens simply aren't practically accessible by using the subway. Some parts are much easier to get to by car or bus. We'll indicate these details if it is the case. Sometimes, the food is just so good you have to find a way to it, even if your MetroCard won't take you there.

Finally, I'd like to add a note about the address numbering system in Queens, which can be confusing even to native New Yorkers. Queens is unique, yet again, in that the addresses always consist of one number followed by a dash and then a second number. Most of the borough is laid out in a grid, too—avenues run east-west, with lower numbers toward the west, and streets run north-south, with lower numbers toward the north. The first number indicates the cross street and the second number indicates the placement of the building on a block. For instance, if you were at 21-33 27th Street, you would be on 27th Street near 21st Avenue about ⅓ of the way away from it. This can be helpful in knowing the general area in which an address is located, but as always, check your maps before venturing out.

Food News & Views

In a place like New York City, there is a plethora of food news outlets. It seems like everyone and his brother has a food blog these days. A lot of sites focus on Manhattan or Brooklyn, but Queens has an important place on the food news map; it's home to some of the most authentic food in the city.

Below is a list of food blogs, food-oriented websites, and a few that are a guide to Queens as a whole.

Astorians Community Food Forum (astorians .com/community). This is the place for the best tips on and discussion about the food scene in Astoria. Community members possess a collective eagle eye when it comes to witnessing what is new and/or upcoming on the neighborhood's food landscape. Go here for raw foodie news.

BORO Mag (boromag.com). This little monthly magazine has a well-written food column by Bradley Hawks, who also gets to show off his awesome photography skills in the articles. At least one feature focusing on the food world of western Queens is published each month. There are also coupons and discounts throughout that readers can use at local restaurants.

Chowhound's Outer Boroughs (chowhound.chow.com/boards/19). As expected from the name of this site, all four outer boroughs are discussed here, but Queens makes up a good portion of the discussions. Chowhound is known for its passionate and opinionated users, so feel free to take their comments with a grain of salt. It does serve as a great resource for rumors and gossip, but you'll also find thoughtful reviews of local restaurants.

City Spoonful (cityspoonful.com). Created by journalists Anne Noyes Saini and Clare Trapasso, City Spoonful covers food in the five boroughs; it's important to note that they have a special fondness for Queens. Intrepid explorers, they eat and write about Nepalese *momos,* Thai curries, Indian *chaat,* Mexican tacos, and more, all found in Queens. They'll tell you like it is and are skilled at helping the reader discover new and exciting tastes in the borough. See Anne Noyes Saini's recipe for ***Chana Dhal* with *Ghiya*** on p. 348.

Eater New York (ny.eater.com). Eater focuses primarily on "dining and drinking in the nation's most important food cities." Their beat is restaurants and the people behind them. Dining trends are also discussed. This is a great site for someone interested in more mainstream NYC restaurant talk.

Edible Queens (ediblecommunities.com/queens). This print magazine is part of the series of nationwide *Edible* magazines, which got their start in Ojai, CA. Published quarterly, *Edible Queens* covers food artisans in the borough, showcases notable restaurants, and highlights special culinary ingredients. They have an online presence, which includes the well-regarded World's Fare column, written and edited by Joe DiStefano.

Fooditka (fooditka.com). Judith Klein Rich has been writing this food blog for several years now, and covers the entire borough of Queens (as well as Manhattan, Brooklyn, and more). A former devoted resident of Astoria, she now resides in Great Neck, just over the Queens border into neighboring Nassau County. Her critical eye will never steer you wrong and pure boosterism is not her style—you'll be sure to know when something is truly great and when it fails to miss its mark. See Judith Klein Rich's recipe for ***Ceresnova Bublanina*** **(Slovak Cherry Cake)** on p. 351.

I Want More Food (iwantmorefood.com). Jeff Orlick writes this fascinating food blog about the lesser-known culinary delights of Queens, with his specialties being pizza, street food, and the food cultures of the interior of the borough. He also gives food tours, founded a food ambassador program, and created the Real Pizza of NY iPhone app. Jeff is passionate about authentic foods from Queens' immigrant population and has opened many people's eyes to the glory of eating fearlessly.

Jackson Heights Life Community Food Forum (jackson heightslife.com/community). Sister site to the above-mentioned Astorians Community Food Forum, this group focuses on the food world of Jackson Heights. Discussions on where to find the best eats in the neighborhood live here, and are a great resource to folks in west-central Queens.

Queens Love (queenslove.tumblr.com). This fun tumblr is written by a sizable group of Queens residents. While not all posts are focused on food, the majority are. They dive deep into Queens, unearthing choice eats that may have been overlooked before.

 Real Cheap Eats Queens (realcheapeats.com/nyc/queens). Another group blog by an even bigger contingent of writers, this site explores all five boroughs. The Queens section is substantial, and focuses on food that is $10 or less.

Serious Eats New York (newyork.seriouseats.com). This is one of the best food resources for New York City as a whole. Here, you'll find restaurant reviews, articles on food science experiments in The Food Lab, and behind-the-scene glimpses into some of the city's more interesting eating spots. You can go straight to articles specific to Queens at newyork.seriouseats.com/queens/.

We Heart Astoria (weheartastoria .com). This blog, rated Favorite Local Blog by the users of Why Leave Astoria?!, covers a variety of topics, including food, a topic beloved by its writers. Openings, closings, reviews, and opinions about the gustatory goings-on in Astoria and Long Island City are artfully expressed on this blog. Disclaimer: the author writes for this site.

Why Leave Astoria?! (whyleaveastoria.com). Astoria's own social network on the Ning platform, WLA?! provides a space for neighborhood residents to discuss food happenings in the area. A number of groups, such as the Astoria Foodies Network and the Starving Restaurant Brigade, are outlets for locals to congregate with one another and explore western Queens' ever-growing restaurant scene.

Astoria &
Long Island City

The neighborhoods of Astoria and Long Island City take up the western edge of the borough of Queens; they also occupy the western edge of Long Island. Both Astoria and Long Island City are generally considered to be the hip neighborhoods in the borough, with a vast range of restaurants, bars, and clubs situated throughout. Astoria is most famous for its Greek population, and has been the Hellenic center of Queens for many years. The Little Egypt area has also gained a bit of notoriety, thanks to the great restaurants, popular hookah bars, and a visit from Anthony Bourdain.

Long Island City is a case in contrasts. Its industrial past and present coexist with high-rise condos, apartment buildings, and glass office towers, attracting young urban professionals, some quite affluent. The bar and restaurant scene is most active along the Vernon Boulevard/Jackson Avenue corridor, but there are numerous bakeries and other wholesale food companies in the more industrial areas of the neighborhood. The range of restaurants in Astoria and Long Island City is so varied that you could eat food from a different cuisine every day for a month without repetition. Here, there is food from five continents represented—it's really remarkable and incredibly pleasing to those who love diversity in their food options.

The Greek influence is seen in the tavernas in the Ditmars and Broadway areas, the Greek cafes on 30th Avenue, as well as the butchers and Greek grocers from Broadway north. Italian restaurants and *salumerias* are dotted throughout Astoria. There's a Balkan and Central European presence on the eastern side of Astoria, in the form of restaurants, bars, and meat markets. The Czechs and Slovaks have a home at the Bohemian Hall and Beer Garden on 24th Avenue, which is one of the most popular spots in Queens. South Asians, including Bangladeshis, live in the more southern areas of Astoria, as do Brazilians; the Japanese have settled around Broadway; Little Egypt is on the strip of Steinway between Astoria Boulevard and 28th Avenue, and is full of Arab and North African restaurants and shops.

Astoria and Long Island City are easy to get to via subway as well. Most of Astoria is accessible via the N/Q elevated line, though the R train goes through the central and eastern parts of the neighborhood. Long Island City is conveniently situated on the 7 line, with the bustling Vernon-Jackson area just one stop away from Manhattan.

Alewife, 5-14 51st Ave., Long Island City, NY 11101; (718) 937-7494; Subway: 7 to Vernon/Jackson; alewifequeens.com; Gastropub; $$. This young spot in the Hunters Point section of Long Island City boasts a serious beer list, with many items that a true brew connoisseur will appreciate. Don't worry, though—many accessible and well-known beers are also available for those feeling less adventurous. Still, it's a great place to get to know a new one. The food is also excellent. A good choice is the burger, made from dry-aged beef and available with bacon ($2 extra). Be sure to order a side of fries, which are some of the best in the borough, served with a pickled garlic aioli. Seafood lovers will be happy with the Samish Bay mussels and Fishers Island oysters, fresh as can be. An artisanal cheese plate is available as lighter fare, perfect with a glass of wine from their small but focused wine list.

Alobar, 46-42 Vernon Blvd., Long Island City, NY 11101; (718) 752-6000; Subway: 7 to Vernon/Jackson; alobarnyc.com; New American; $$$. Home to dishes like Amish pig tails, roasted bone marrow, roast chicken, and Kentucky fried rabbit, Alobar reaches back into America's past, reinventing hearty comfort food for modern tastes. While this means a lot of meat-heavy dishes, there are comforting foods that don't focus on the fleshy side of eating. A great way to start a meal is with an order of one of their artisanal pickles (try the sweet carrot and tarragon). The pumpkin risotto is rich sans meat, and the wild mushroom toast combines umami-rich mushrooms, mild ricotta, and a duck egg on thick, rustic Italian toast. Like most restaurants of its kind in the area, it offers a burger, perhaps the most American comfort food of them all. Available on the burger is battered bacon, a decadent addition. And truly, anything they do with their locally sourced pork is sure to be a hit. Cocktails are also skillfully executed—try a Quince Cooler or LIC Lemonade for something refreshing and different. And the salted caramel bread pudding is a terrific way to end your meal on a beautiful sweet note.

Arepas Cafe, 33-07 36th Ave., Astoria, NY 11106; (718) 937-3835; Subway: N/Q to 36th Avenue; arepascafe.com; Venezuelan; $. The owners of this tiny spot in the southern end of Astoria found that their food was so popular, they needed room to grow; so they expanded into the adjacent space to make room for all their adoring and hungry fans. Arepas are a kind of sturdy pancake made from griddled corn-flour dough, and take different formats in different parts of South America. The ones at Arepas Cafe are prepared in a Venezuelan style—split in half and stuffed. One of the most satisfying of their arepa offerings is the Mami, stuffed with roast pork, avocado, and white cheese. The Reina is also fantastic—shredded chicken, avocado, and a little mayo. Apart from the arepas, there are a variety of appetizers, and a good way to get a good overview of them is with the Mini Platter—it comes with *tequeños* (deep-fried, dough-covered white cheese sticks), mini *cachapas* (corn pancakes), mini empanadas, and fried yucca (a starchy root vegetable reminiscent of potato). Be sure to have a squirt bottle of their delicious green sauce at the ready to add to whatever you are eating, too. Finally, consider a glass of *chicha* with your meal—it's a beverage that tastes like sweet, cinnamon rice pudding with a thick, smooth, viscous consistency. It's really excellent, and there really isn't anything else like it around.

Astor Room, 34-12 36th St., Astoria, NY 11106; (718) 255-1947; Subway: N/Q to 36th Avenue; astorroom.com; American; $$$. The Astor Room is an elegant supper club in the space that once was the old Kaufman Astoria Studios commissary. The place practically oozes with a classic movie vibe, and the food reflects a simpler time, too. The room is split into two areas—first, the Beaver Bar, where expert cocktails are composed, like the bourbon-based New Yorker and the gin-based Gatsby. On the dinner menu, you'll find old favorites like oysters Rockefeller, beef tartare, lobster thermidor, and a classic wedge salad, complete with iceberg lettuce and Thousand Island dressing. Don't forget to check out their raw bar, featuring oysters and clams from both Washington State and locally from Long Island.

Bareburger, 33-21 31st Ave., Astoria, NY 11103; (718) 777-7011; Subway: N/Q to 30th Avenue; 23-01 31st St., Astoria, NY 11105; (718) 204-7167; Subway: N/Q to Ditmars; bareburger.com; Burgers/Organic; $. This local chain has its origins in Astoria, and after much success expanded outward from the neighborhood to Mahattan and Brooklyn. The food overall is organic, from the meats to the fries to the milk in the shakes and beyond. They are also known for their selection of game meats for burgers, including bison, wild boar, and elk. Vegetarians have options as well, with both a veggie burger and portobello burger to choose from. Burgers come with a choice of breads—brioche and whole grain; you can even get it wrapped in a lettuce leaf if you are avoiding gluten or grains (gluten-free patrons can also order their burger on a tapioca rice bun). When it comes to the fries, Bareburger goes beyond simple ketchup (theirs is organic) and serve the fries with dipping sauces like chipotle mayo. The serving is quite large, so sharing is definitely the way to go. Other sides include onion rings, balls of sweet potato croquettes, and a selection of Rick's Picks pickles. Shakes are delicious, and come in a variety of flavors. The dining rooms are made from repurposed materials and each Bareburger is child-friendly, so bring the whole family to feast on the American classic meal, with a healthy revamp.

Basil Brick Oven Pizza, 28-17 Astoria Blvd., Astoria, NY 11102; (718) 204-1205; Subway: N/Q to Astoria Boulevard; basilbrickoven .com; Pizza; $$. This modest pizza joint makes some of the best Neapolitan-style pizza in Astoria. Their pies gained so much notoriety they decided to expand into the space next door—which is big and gorgeous—and expand their menu offerings as well to include pastas, fish, and poultry dishes. As for the pizzas, which number 40 different options, the star really is their Margherita pizza. Made with simple ingredients—tomato sauce, homemade fresh mozzarella,

Parmesan, extra-virgin olive oil, and fresh basil (which they grow out back)—it shines with clear flavors and exceptional taste. On the other end of the spectrum is the rich Pizzucca pizza, made with an herbed pumpkin walnut sauce and topped with fresh mozzarella and pancetta. All pizzas are baked in their brick oven fueled by cherry wood. On the salad side of things, their poached pear salad is a delight. Made with a sturdy selection of mixed greens, it's topped with a caramelized half pear, creamy goat cheese, and some candied nuts, tied together with a sweet balsamic vinaigrette. Their desserts are also made in house, including their light yet decadent tiramisu.

Bear, 12-14 31st Ave., Long Island City, NY 11106; (917) 396-4939; Subway: N/Q to 30th Avenue; bearnyc.com; Progressive European; $$$. Bear is one of a number of restaurants cropping up in western Queens that determine their menu by the seasons. This means a substantial portion of the menu changes throughout a year. They also use ingredients that are locally sourced, organic, and sustainable. Despite the menu changes, there are some items that remain static, including the Three-Shot-Vodka-Special, an ice-chilled vodka carafe with a trio of cured meats, pickled vegetables, and marinated herring on rye. Their mussels and *frites* are also available year round. Chef Pogrebinsky and the bar staff have also put time and energy into a thoughtful menu of cocktails, including the vodka- and tomato-based Firebird and tequila-based Maiden. They also offer 10 different kinds of vodka and an even larger selection of whiskeys. Their small but focused beer menu also indicates which dishes go well with each beer, which makes it easy to make a perfect pairing. Bear is also a popular spot for brunch, where you can get yourself a 32-ounce Bloody Mary—complete with a skewer loaded with a marinated mushroom, cherry tomato, pickled onion, olive, battered bacon, and a whole hard-boiled egg—to go with your omelet or scallops and eggs.

Bella Via, 47-46 Vernon Blvd., Long Island City, NY 11101; (718) 361-7510; Subway: 7 to Vernon/Jackson; bellaviarestaurant.com; Italian; $$. This is the home of coal-oven pizza in Long Island City. Bella Via turns out plenty of very thin crust pies each day—not the cracker-thin crust, but classic thin crust pizza. Lift up the pizza and check out the bottom of the crust—you'll see beautiful char under there, though it's not charred to an extreme. To get a really good sense of the magic of the coal oven, order the Margherita pizza, which is simple and straightforward with its fresh mozzarella and San Marzano tomato sauce. Bonus: This pizza tastes great the next day (if there's any left). Their pastas are very good, too—try the

light rigatoni with baby artichokes and sausage, decked out in a beautiful marsala wine sauce. And if you see *burrata* on the special menu, get it. It's wonderfully creamy and will often come with a plate of beautifully roasted red peppers and thin slices of savory salami, decorated in slivers of fresh basil. Everything goes well with a glass of Pinot Grigio or a Peroni, too.

Bistro 33, 19-33 Ditmars Blvd., Astoria, NY 11105; (718) 721-1933; Subway: N/Q to Ditmars; bistro33nyc.com; New American; $$. A wonderful spot for brunch in the summer, as they open all the windows and it's like being on vacation. A terrific light brunch meal is their apple taleggio salad, made with fresh greens, thinly sliced apples, crunchy potato sticks, a thick slice of taleggio cheese, and a wonderful yuzu honey vinaigrette. The truffled eggs and salmon in puff pastry are also wonderful. Their tasty burger is available at brunch and other times as well, and from 5 to 8 p.m. most

days, they'll make you a burger and a beer for $12. If you really want to fill your belly with extravagance, try the lobster mac and cheese, made with elbow pasta, fontina, gruyère, mozzarella, all baked with Maine lobster. This is one of their most popular dishes on the menu. The crawfish tempura, served with spicy mayo, is also another smash hit. They do have a full bar, and offer a nice selection of wine and beer, including Grimbergen, a beautiful Belgian Ale.

BZ Grill, 27-02 Astoria Blvd., Astoria, NY 11102; (718) 932-7858; Subway: N/Q to Astoria Boulevard; bzgrill.com; Greek/Mediterranean; $. One of the best pork gyros in the entire city is found at BZ Grill, a little hut of a space on the south side of Astoria Boulevard. The reason the pork gyro is so good is that they use actual pork, marinated to make it savory and juicy, instead of the

The Sunday Night Dinner—Queens' Underground Supper Club

Throughout the year, Tamara Reynolds cooks dinner for 20 people, some of them perfect strangers, at her home in Astoria. Their admission is cash and a bottle of wine in exchange for an amazing meal, either set in her living room or in her lovely backyard, complete with a vegetable garden. Tamara has been doing this for over 10 years, and is still going strong. She cooks seasonally, so you'll be able to enjoy the bounty of spring, summer, winter, and fall through her culinary creativity and kitchen skills. Often her menus have a theme, whether it's Georgian food (not the state but the country), Greek Easter, or a Thanksgiving oyster roast. For more information as to what Tamara does during these dinners, as well as her other food adventures, head to her website, oneasskitchen.blogspot.com.

pressed meat-like substance found at so many gyro and pizza spots in the city (you'll often find these two items served under the same roof). The guy behind the counter slices it off, and puts it in a grilled pita along with lettuce, tomatoes, and *tzatziki* sauce. BZ Grill also makes delicious fries that possess a ragged crunchy exterior that makes them irresistible. If you'd like to gild the lily with your fries, order the Greek fries, topped with feta, oregano, and olive oil. Don't worry if they're burned a tad in spots—that's a good thing! Their grilled halloumi is also delectable as well.

Cafe Triskell, 33-04 36th Ave., Astoria, NY 11106; (718) 472-0612; Subway: N/Q to 36th Avenue; cafetriskell.com; French; $$. This tiny—and by tiny we mean about six tables squeezed into the space—spot on 36th Avenue serves excellent French food from the region of Brittany, where Chef Phillipe Fallait is from. Breton food involves cider and crepes, and both are well done here. The hard cider comes in a beautiful *boule,* best sipped using both hands to steady the vessel. The savory crepes are made with buckwheat flour and are filled with things like goat cheese with herbs, seasonal vegetables, and ham and swiss cheese. Sweet crepes are made with wheat flour—the simple lemon and sugar crepe is beautifully simple, the sum greater than its parts. Apart from the crepes, classic French dishes like the *croque monsieur,* vichyssoise, escargots, and *foie gras* round out the menu.

Casa Enrique, 5-48 49th Ave., Long Island City, NY 11101; (347) 448-6040; Subway: 7 to Vernon-Jackson; Mexican; $$. Regional Mexican food has arrived in Long Island City, and that region is Chiapas and a little bit of Puebla. The space is casual and bright. Smaller tables populate the back of the dining room, with a long communal table up front. Their *aguas frescas* are fantastic—a light lemon, a tangy tamarind, and creamy *horchata* (you can actually taste that it has been made with rice, a rarity among *horchatas* in NYC). Guacamole is chunky and can be spiced to your liking. Tacos are delicious—try the *al pastor,* which arrives with lots of small pieces of marinated, grilled pork, complete with the traditional flavor of pineapple. A threesome of salsas includes a spicy orange-tinged smooth hot salsa, a medium-spicy green salsa, and a mild and chunky red salsa. Entrees come in the form of enchiladas, pozole, and braised lamb shank in chilies; the chicken mole is fantastic, served with dark meat chicken falling off the bone, over rice, which soaks up the delicious dark mole sauce. Best to leave room for dessert, too—their *tres leches* cake is spectacular, as is their warm chocolate cake with vanilla ice cream.

Cedars Meat House, 41-08 30th Ave., Astoria, NY 11102; (718) 606-1244; Subway: N/Q to 30th Avenue; Lebanese; $. Walk into this surprisingly large spot on 30th Avenue and you'll encounter a full sensory experience—the sizzling sound of the hot oil as it cooks fresh falafel balls; the sight and feel of the smoky, steamy air inside; the smell of grill as a beautifully marinated kebab hits it; and the taste of a warm, flavorful, toasted shawarma sandwich. The fresh and prepared food area is in the front and the grocery and halal meat counter is in the back. Up front, order a falafel sandwich or a shawarma sandwich for a crazy low price—under $5. Get everything on it for the full effect—lots of vegetables on the falafel sandwich and crazy savory accouterments with the shawarma—*toum* (a smooth garlic spread), a zingy hot pepper paste, bright pickled vegetables and tomatoes. It's truly spectacular. Other sandwiches containing eggplant, hummus, beef, and sausage can also be ordered. They will also grill meats by the pound—liver, rotisserie chicken, shish kebab. French fries can be ordered with your sandwich, and you can enjoy it either at the bar across from the grill, or take it with you—since it's wrapped in insulating foil, it will stay warm for a while. The bread they use—like a thin pita or lavash—kind of crisps up as they heat it. Enjoy a little bottle of mixed fruit drink, which manages to be both fruity and creamy (there's no dairy present), and goes really well with the sandwiches. The grocery area in the back has a lot of pantry items, like spices (including the thyme heavy zaatar), tinned favas with tahini, olives (both packaged and from an olive bar), and pickled vegetables. Check the refrigerated area for cheese, butter, and yogurt. Cured meats—*soujouk, basturma,* and the like are located near the food prep area, as are "alternative" products like beef bacon and turkey pastrami. On your way out, pick up a container (small or large) or their vegetable dishes or salads. The eggplant is simply sublime and the tomato and cucumber onion salad is nice and refreshing.

Cevabdzinica Sarajevo, 37-18 34th Ave., Astoria, NY 11101; (718) 752-9528; Subway: N/Q to Broadway; Balkan/Bosnian; $. Since 1976, a seasoned restaurant family has been serving up delicious Bosnian food to the masses, bringing the fresh, classic flavors of the Balkans to the multiethnic mix that is Astoria. *Cevapi,* which are Bosnian beef meatballs, is the specialty of the restaurant, and arrive hot, accompanied by a mound of raw onions and sweet *ajvar.* Eat them on their own or with *lepinja,* a ridiculously delicious, thick and soft bread that arrives at your table after you sit down. Made by an expert baker, the bread's flavor contains echoes of the grill, giving it deep flavor. Use it to carry the *cevapi* or eat it separately; either way, it's a must to try. The spinach *burek* is impressive, with a flaky pastry and a very light yet not skimpy filling of spinach inside. A serving of *shopska salat* helps balance things—iceberg lettuce, tomatoes, cucumber, and creamy goat cheese with a light vinaigrette. The stuffed cabbage leaves are also delicious, and contain a mixture of meat and rice inside. Visually pleasing domes of savory mashed potatoes accompany them. Consider washing down your meal with a bottle of orange-flavored Jupi, or Cockta, a carbonated beverage flavored with, among other things, dog rose hip, lemon, and orange. For dessert you can't go wrong with baklava, which is made with walnuts in this version, or a chocolate ball, dense, sweet, and heady with rum.

Christos Steak House, 41-08 23rd Ave., Astoria, NY 11105; (718) 777-8400; Subway: N/Q to Ditmars; chrislossteakhouse.com; Steak House; $$$$. Christos bills itself as an "American Steakhouse with a Mediterranean Influence," which is the perfect description of the restaurant. The Mediterranean influence is particularly appropriate for this neighborhood with a substantial Greek population. You'll see it particularly in the appetizers, like the hot *saganaki*, charred octopus served with spinach and capers, smooth taramosalata, as well as the beautiful, fresh *horiatiki* (Greek salad). The raw bar is an option, as is cooked seafood, like shrimp, wild salmon, and branzini. Of course, their meats are a great draw, this being a 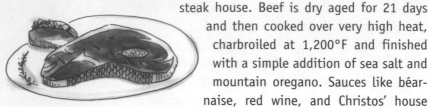 steak house. Beef is dry aged for 21 days and then cooked over very high heat, charbroiled at 1,200°F and finished with a simple addition of sea salt and mountain oregano. Sauces like béarnaise, red wine, and Christos' house sauce options, too. A number of sides are available, from the classic creamed spinach to lemon potatoes; the lobster mashed potatoes are a huge favorite among their customers. Desserts are delicious as well, especially the Baked Astoria, a riff off the classic Baked Alaska. A small selection of their meats is also for sale from their butcher, along with a handful of sides and salads. Their bar is also a great space, perfect for a pre-dinner drink or a place to meet with friends over a cocktail.

Creek & the Cave, 10-93 Jackson Ave., Long Island City, NY 11101; (718) 706-8783; Subway: 7 to Vernon/Jackson or G to 21st/Van Alst; creeklic.com; Mexican; $. **Aside from hosting its regular stand-up comedy shows and community events like Queens Green Drinks, Creek & the Cave puts out some tasty Cal-Mex–style Mexican food. Its menu is definitely influenced by the overstuffed burritos from the Mission District of San Francisco, beach eats in Southern California, and the liberal use of avocado in the kitchens of Mexican restaurants throughout the Golden State. Probably the epitome of the marriage of the above elements is the Baja Quesadilla—two**

flour tortillas filled with creamy goat cheese, avocado, and pickled jalapeños, a combination that is pleasantly spicy, tangy and smooth all at once. Burritos and tacos come with protein choices like chicken, pork, and seafood, and if you're feeling decadent, have them "chimichanga" it—deep fried and topped with sour cream and pico de gallo. As is the case in many restaurants in this part of Queens, a burger is available on the menu. The Creek Burger is unique, with the addition of grilled pineapple to the mix. Creek & the Cave is also one of the few spots in western Queens where you can grab a Sol, a far superior rival to that other Mexican lager. Be sure to start your order with the house-made salsa sampler, which includes pico de gallo, house salsa, and guacamole. When it's warm, their patio downstairs and in the back is one of the breeziest and laid-back spots in all of Long Island City.

Crescent & Vine, 25-01 Ditmars Blvd., Astoria, NY 11105; (718) 204-4774; Subway: N/Q to Ditmars; Wine Bar; $$. Adjacent to Astoria favorite Fatty's, Crescent & Vine is a small wine bar and craft beer haven on a quiet part of Ditmars Boulevard. Enjoy one of their 15 beers on tap—including Beyond Kombucha's Mava Roka kombucha ale—or a glass of wine in their dark, cozy space, either at a table or at the bar. They have a number of delicious though perhaps lesser-known beers, so if you have questions or are curious about something on the menu, just ask the staff and they will be more than happy to answer your questions. That

goes for the food, too, which consists of cheeses and charcuterie (try the *salsiccia*), panini (the "Big Guy with a Beard," made with *jamon serrano,* fresh mozzarella, ricotta, fig balsamic dressing, and fresh basil, is a winner), salads, and house bruschetta. They even do a banana and Nutella panini for dessert. There is a bit of seating outside in the front, which is a perfect spot on a warm evening. It's a particularly popular spot right after the fireworks above Astoria Park in late June (Astoria gets its own Independence Day show, just a bit earlier than everywhere else).

Djerdan, 34-04 31st Ave., Astoria, NY 11106; (718) 721-2694; Subway: N/Q to Broadway; Eastern European; $. There are multiple locations of Djerdan, but the Astoria location was the first. Serving up Bosnian food, the usual suspects of goulash, *cevapi,* stuffed cabbage, and *pljeskavica* are all available on the menu. Another delicious grilled meat option is the *ljute cufte sa rostilja*—spicy grilled meatballs (they resemble little flat sausage patties), accompanied by *ajvar* and raw onions, with a side of either rice or potatoes. Djerdan is particularly well known for their *bureks,* which can be purchased off-site at places like **Parrot Coffee Market** (p. 98) in Astoria. They range from a single spiraled *burek,* phyllo dough filled with potato or meat, to a large *burek* pie, which serves multiple people. Optional is the garlic yogurt sauce, which has the consistency of a loose sour cream, and is tangy and lightly garlicky—highly recommended, since it goes perfectly with the *bureks.* In addition to the meats, Djerdan serves soup, salads, and desserts. Give the *ledena kockta* a try, which consists of a mild chocolate cake soaked in light sugar syrup, topped with a generous layer of vanilla custard cream and finished with a thin layer of chocolate. It goes great with a cup of Turkish coffee, too. *Bureks* can be purchased frozen for takeout, so pick a few up to take home.

Dutch Kills, 27-24 Jackson Ave., Long Island City, NY 11101; (718) 383-2724; Subway: 7/N/Q to Queensboro Plaza or E/M/R to Queens Plaza; dutchkillsbar.com; Cocktails. This bar situated in the area known as Dutch Kills (northern Long Island City) serves up some of the best cocktails in Queens. A great way to try their cool cocktails is during happy hour—Sunday to Thursday from 5 to 7 p.m., and all evening long on Monday. Classic cocktails like the vodka gimlet, the daiquiri, and the whiskey fizz are all available during this time for $8. For just a few dollars more, you can imbibe one of their more elaborate cocktails. Take the Bayflower Cocktail for instance—made with Genever, St-Germain, fresh lemon and grapefruit juice, and simple syrup, all served over crushed ice—it is fresh and citrusy, and will bring light into even the darkest of days.

Duzan, 24-11 Steinway St., Astoria, NY 11103; (718) 204-7488; Subway: N/Q to Astoria Boulevard; Middle Eastern; $. In the few short years it has been open, Duzan has gained a fiercely loyal following from food-loving Astorians. The space is casual with bright green and red-orange colors throughout. Their chicken shawarma is moist and tender, with some of the meat showing bits of caramelization along the edges. It's available as part of platter with salad and hummus, or it can be stuffed in one of their excellent soft homemade pitas, especially delicious right out of the oven, when warm, toasted, and seemingly even fluffier than normal. To spice up your shawarma, use a bit of their lemony tahini sauce or their pickled ginger curry sauce (house recipe), which, according to the owner, is a common sauce in Palestine, Israel, and Iraq. It's a wonderful combination of tangy, earthy, and spicy. Their hummus is truly outstanding. The consistency is very smooth

and a bit nutty tasting. The Hummus Jerusalem consists of a base of hummus topped with warm fava beans (they'll put a little bit of spicy pepper sauce in with the favas if you like). The Hummus Abu Gosh—hummus topped with roasted garlic and pine nuts—is also very popular. You can get tabbouleh here, but a very tasty alternative is the *fattoush*, a salad of lettuce, tomato, cucumbers, and toasted pita, which softens as it absorbs the juices in the salad. On the drinks front, Mexican Coke is available in the refrigerator, as is the more elusive Mexican Sprite.

El*Ay*Si, 47-38 Vernon Blvd., Long Island City, NY 11101; (718) 389-8781; Subway: 7 to Vernon-Jackson; elaysi.com; New American/Comfort Food; $$. It's hard not to smile while looking at the El*Ay*Si menu, what with things like tater tots, mac and cheese, and pulled-pork tacos present. Comfort food really is the name of the game here, relying on classic approaches and quality ingredients. These ingredients are used to the best of their ability, which leads to a tasty result. Back to the tater tots—you can get them plain (ask for a bit of their chipotle mayo to go with them) or "disco" style, complete with white gravy and cheddar cheese on top ($3 extra). The burger is very good, and the veggie three-bean chili is a great lighter option while still under the guise of comfort food; amp it up by adding ground beef to it. The pulled pork tacos *al pastor* are wonderful, served with grilled pineapple and caramelized onions. Their cocktails are delightful, especially the "Jim Jam" made with bourbon and muddled blackberries and orange. For larger groups, there is a table in the back to accommodate six to eight people; booths on the right side are made for duos, and are very nice for a quiet rendezvous for both friends and lovers.

Fatty's, 25-01 Ditmars Blvd., Astoria, NY 11105; (718) 267-7071; Subway: N/Q to Ditmars; Cuban/New American; $$. This corner spot is one of the busiest places on this quiet stretch of Ditmars Boulevard; that's not surprising, thanks to the fun space, friendly staff, and quality food. The menu has a strong Cuban influence, so you'll find things on it like *maduros*, tostones, and the excellent Cuban sandwich. Their house chili is tasty and fresh, containing plenty of black beans, ground beef, and vegetables, topped with raw red onion and sour cream (which can be ordered on the side), and served with tortilla chips. There's a bit of cheddar cheese lurking in there, too, adding richness to this delicious dish. The aforementioned *maduros* (ripe plantain) are fried until they are golden brown and slightly caramelized, topped with a sprinkle of coarse salt. They are actually good dipped in Fatty's decadent garlic aioli, too. The burgers here are also excellent, and particularly notable is the Charity Burger, topped with avocado, cheese, sprouts, *añejo* rum ketchup, and more of that aforementioned garlic aioli. It's juicy and umami-rich, and $2 of the cost of the burger goes to help others. For $1.50 you can add fries, which is worth it. For dessert, your choices are flan or chocolate *tres leches* cake—the chocolate version of this wonderful Latin American dessert is a rare find. As for drinks, beer by the bottle and wine by the glass or bottle are available. A full bar is present, as are skilled bartenders, so your favorite cocktail is no doubt just a moment away.

5 Napkin Burger, 35-01 36th St., Astoria, NY 11106; (718) 433-2727; Subway: N/Q to 36th Avenue or M/R to Steinway Street; 5napkinburger.com/astoria-queens; Burgers; $$. 5 Napkin has a lot going for it—a great space with a bar (sometimes the game is on), comfy booths, and a separate space for private events; a great location, not far from the sensational Museum of the Moving Image; attentive staff; and great food and drinks that appeal to omnivores and vegetarians alike. Their signature burger, aptly named 5 Napkin Burger, consists of a 7-ounce or 10-ounce beef burger (the ground chuck comes from celebrated butcher Pat LaFrieda) topped with gruyère cheese, caramelized onions, and rosemary aioli on a white roll. Another terrific offering

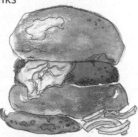

is their Avocado Ranch burger, topped with guacamole, pepper jack cheese, and ranch dressing. The simple cheeseburger is also excellent and the veggie burger—topped with 5N sauce, bread and butter pickles, lettuce, and tomato, and served on a multigrain roll—is one of the best veggie burgers in Astoria. Aside from burgers and fries, there is a whole other side to the menu—salads, appetizers like pork taquitos, fish tacos, a Kobe beef hot dog (topped with, among other things, pickled jalapeños), and even sushi. 5 Napkin also has a full bar, including wine and an extensive beer list. If milk shakes are your thing, be sure to give the salted caramel and peanut butter and chocolate shakes a go!

Gregory's 26 Corner Taverna, 26-02 23rd Ave., Astoria, NY 11105; (718) 777-5511; Subway: N/Q to Ditmars; Greek; $$. On a quiet stretch of 23rd Avenue lies a little Greek taverna, located on the first floor of an unassuming white house. There are about a dozen tables both inside and out, covered in red checkered tablecloths; everything here is unpretentious, casual, and rustic. The food is some of the best you'll find in Astoria, bar none. Start with a half liter of house wine (the rosé is particularly fruity and refreshing) and order a cold appetizer plate—it's filled with chunks of ripe tomatoes and cucumbers, and portions of garlicky *tzatziki,* salty and buttery taramosalata, savory eggplant dip and spicy feta spread. Toasted pita triangles come with it, used to scoop up these treasures. The flavors are wonderfully bold, making this a real winner. The *keftedes*—delicate meatballs seasoned with onions and spices—are quite large, and taste great with a squeeze of lemon.

The *loukaniko* are a great choice as well, with each sausage link sliced lengthwise and cooked cut side down, giving the sausage a terrific crust. The Greek salad comes in the more traditional configuration, with the feta in a big slice sitting atop the salad, which is nice. You can get a gyro here, too, the meat laced with plenty of oregano. Fish like sardines, tilefish, and porgy are available, some of which come from local fishermen. Little quail are also on the menu. Finish off your meal with a cup of Greek coffee and your meal will be complete.

Harissa, 34-05 30th Ave., Astoria, NY 11103; (718) 545-9595; Subway: N/Q to 30th Avenue; Mediterranean/North African; $. Hailing from Algeria originally, the chef has put together a menu featuring excellent North African cuisine. First, a cup of sweet mint tea is the perfect accompaniment to this food, and it arrives in a teapot just for you, so that you can pour your tea at your own pace during the meal. The *brik,* a large triangle of phyllo dough stuffed with tuna, capers, Parmesan, parsley, and an egg (it's beaten and added while raw, and the frying process cooks it) is a top menu item. The dough is light and crispy and the filling is wonderfully savory. Eat it with the spicy *harissa* that comes with every dish. Both the *chakchouka* (peppers, tomato, eggplant) and *zaaluk* (primarily eggplant) salad/spreads are delicious—the added egg to the *chakchouka* adds a nice richness to it. The *bourek* has a touch of sweetness in the steak filling, which is a delicious touch. If you are one for braised meats, the lamb tajine is for you—cooked to the point of the meat falling off the bone, it is extremely tender and rich. It comes with daily vegetables. For vegetarians, the vegetable couscous is wonderful, with big chunks of perfectly cooked vegetables sitting on a bed of light and fluffy couscous. Happily the baklava dessert comes from Al-Sham Sweets on Steinway Street, home of some of the most delicious Middle Eastern pastries in NYC. On top of this, Harissa uses Balthazar bread for its bread needs, and also sells their baguettes and morning pastries. The *pain au chocolat* is ridiculously good and a joy to eat.

Hell Gate Social, 12-21 Astoria Blvd., Astoria, NY 11102; (718) 204-8313; Subway: N/Q to Astoria Boulevard; hellgatesocial.com; Bar/Lounge. For a while, Hell Gate Social was about the only thing really hip or happening in this part of town, located in the western reaches of Astoria. For a long time, they were a bit mysterious, even forgoing signage outside this speakeasy-type bar; only a pair of red lights over a large dark vault-like door was the tipoff to its existence. They've come a long way since then (and they now have their name above the door), but haven't abandoned their original charming self. They offer some excellent cocktails, especially the vodka-based Hell Gate Lemonade; keep an eye out for seasonal cocktails as well. Their food options consist mostly of a few sandwiches, but most people come here to enjoy the excellent drinks and the relaxed vibe. Proprietor George does pull out all the stops on special occasions, like Easter and Independence Day, where he'll offer perhaps a spit-roasted pig, cooked outside on the back patio.

Hinomaru Ramen, 33-18 Ditmars Blvd., Astoria, NY 11105; (718) 777-0228; Subway: N/Q to Ditmars; Japanese; $. The housemade ramen noodles come in broths made of pork, chicken, fish, or a combination of the above, and vegetable. While all the ramen dishes have much to appreciate, the Nagoya, with minced pork, leeks, scallions, bean sprouts, and chili peppers, is tops. The Hinomaru is also a hit—a creamy pork broth with *chashu* (pork belly), *kikurage* (a kind of fungus, like wood ear), scallions, *menma* (fermented bamboo shoots), bean sprouts, monkey (not really a monkey, but a fish cake), nori, and fire ball (yes, it's spicy). Additional toppings can be added to your ramen, including corn, poached egg (this adds extra creaminess to your ramen—fantastic!), and cabbage. In addition to the fabulous ramen, a couple of sandwiches called *niku man* are on the menu. The pork belly *niku man* in particular is incredible—pork belly with lettuce, sprouts, and scallions on a big rice-flour bun and topped with a bit of hoisin sauce. Rounding out the menu are pork and beef *gyoza,* and various *donburi*—*ikura, oyako,* and *soboro.* A cold glass of jasmine tea is a very nice accompaniment to it all; Sapporo is also a good choice.

Il Bambino, 34-08 31st Ave., Astoria, NY 11106; (718) 626-0087; Subway: N/Q to Broadway; ilbambinonyc.com; Italian/Paninoteca;

$$. Il Bambino prepares consistently solid, interesting, and tre mendously tasty food, period. They have the whole package—an attentive, professional staff; a relaxed, friendly space both indoors and out; and delicious food and drink. The dark, cold days of winter are rescued by Il Bambino's soups—the celebrated smoked tomato bisque is something to look forward to on the weekend; anything with butternut squash is going to deliver a wallop of flavor, big time. In the warm, light days of summer, the back patio space is a wonderful spot to enjoy a meal. The menu is split into salads and tapas, crostini, and panini. Order the Bambino Antipasti, the items on which are not static, and change from time to time; the surprise is the delight. As for salads, both the chickpea panzanella and the baby green beans with shaved Parmesan and truffle oil have been mainstays on the menu, mostly because there would be a riot if Chef Darren Lawless took them off the menu. Crostini and panini take up the rest of the main menu. Popular are the longtime favorite truffle egg salad and shaved speck (a cured pork product) and newer combinations like the spicy avocado and goat cheese. As far as the panini go, their mozzarella with tomato *fresca* and basil pesto remains a big hit, and the prosciutto with *Gorgonzola dolce* and fig spread (a favorite of Chef Lawless) is also a good choice. The Il Bambino staff has also put a lot of time into choosing the wine and beer list—it's small but focused. A glass of the Rain Sauvignon Blanc is like a party in your mouth; the Borsao red is also a nice choice. And as for dessert—if

the chocolate truffle cake is available, have them heat it up a little bit and enjoy its almost unreal smooth texture.

JJ's Asian Fusion, 37-05 31st Ave., Astoria, NY 11103; (718) 626-8888; Subway: N/Q to Broadway, R. to Steinway Street; jjsfusion.com; Japanese/Sushi; $$. JJ's is a tiny spot full of big flavors, not to mention a dedicated following. Both Chinese and Japanese traditions are present, combined with the French Culinary Institute education of Chef-Owner JJ Lin. One thing to seriously consider is the specials, especially those that rely on the presence of sashimi/raw fish. No doubt the fish will be extremely fresh. By  far the most popular appetizer is the serving of steamed edamame dumplings, which contain a soft mixture of edamame with a touch of wasabi, making the whole thing light, creamy, and spicy. The fried potstickers are also very good. The menu's sushi and maki rolls are very fresh but the extent of the selection is fairly standard; again, look to the specials. However, their selection of sake is more extensive than at a lot of other places in the neighborhood. The unfiltered Snow Beauty Sweet is particularly lovely. Leave a little room for dessert, especially for the green-tea crepe cake—green tea–flavored crepes are layered with a touch of pastry cream, creating a light and unusual sweet finish to your meal.

John Brown Smokehouse, 10-43 44th Dr., Long Island City, NY 11101; (347) 617-1120; Subway: E/M to 23rd Street/Ely or 7 to 45

Rd/Court Square; johnbrownseriousbbq.com; Barbecue; $. **Serious** barbecue landed in Western Queens in 2011 and John Brown was leading the way with its Kansas City–style 'cue. Choose from meats like pulled pork, brisket, and decadent lamb sausage, and eat them either as a sandwich or part of a multiple meat platter (complete with sides). The burnt ends are particularly epic, succulent and savory. Notable among their remaining sandwiches is the PBLT, a modern twist on the diner favorite BLT—this time made with pork belly. As for the aforementioned sides, consider the pleasantly cheesy macaroni and cheese or the savory, pork-studded collard greens. John Brown also offers some salads, each topped with a different kind of meat, of course! But the twist is that you can order the salad sans meat—a possible option for your veggie friends. The house salad is probably the best choice in this case, due to the relatively extensive number of vegetables present. If you have room for dessert, it's worth it to end the meal with a little bit of sweetness. The pecan pie is just that—sweet—but not to the point of your teeth feeling like they're going to fall out. It has a pleasant caramelization going on with the top layer of nuts, which is a great foil to the softer filling below. Seasonal fruit cobblers are available, too.

La Rioja, 33-05 Broadway; Astoria, NY 11106; (718) 932-0101; Subway: N/Q to Broadway; lariojany.com; Spanish; $$. This is a great spot for a drink with friends, a few tapas, or a full-blown dinner. Their sangria has a great reputation, and can be purchased by the glass, half or full pitchers, in red, white, and champagne (not available by the glass) versions. By far, the red sangria is the most popular, full of wine and fruit, and it goes down smoothly and easily. The tapas are numerous, and ingredients range from fish and seafood, cured meats to cheeses, and more. The bacon-wrapped dates are a great choice to snack on, exhibiting that intoxicating mixture of sweet, salty, and smoky. The *patatas a la Rioja* tapa is a total winner, consisting of smooth mashed potatoes with smoked paprika mixed in, long pieces of savory chorizo sausage, all surrounded by narrow lines of smooth aioli. Spanish cheeses like Manchego and Tetilla, and the ever-present *jamón ibérico* are available as well. With a nod to the sea, the *gambas al ajillo* (shrimp in garlic) and the *croquetas de bacalao* are also classic. And as at any Spanish restaurant worth its salt, paella is on the menu—here, there are choices, including a classic seafood paella; a *paella de carne* containing chicken, sausage, and beans; as well as a tasty vegetarian paella. Dessert is something to consider well—along with the classic flan, the flourless almond tart is nice and light, accompanied by strawberries and whipped cream. They also offer several ice cream flavors imported straight from Spain and the ricotta, marcona almond, and honey ice cream is seriously good (also topped with a garnish of whipped cream and a strawberry slice). Their espresso is good and strong. Finally, if digestifs are your thing, don't miss the grappa-like liqueur from Spain the staff calls *chupito* ("little drink" in Spanish).

Leng Thai, 33-09 Broadway, Astoria, NY 11106; (718) 956-7117; Subway: N/Q to Broadway or M/R to Steinway Street; lengthai newyork.com; Thai; $$. **Neighborhood** favorite Leng's space is beautiful—including the bamboo-accented garden space out back—and the food is delicious. When you sit down, you're presented with a bamboo steamer of crispy, spicy rice noodles, which are pretty much irresistible. They offer a number of inventive small plates like duck rolls with hoisin sauce; Vietnamese "ravioli," which are rice crepes filled with chicken and shiitake mushrooms; and the very tasty *nuea dad-deow,* which is Thai beef jerky with sticky rice. It comes with a spicy sauce reminiscent of sriracha, and the whole thing is rather addicting. Soups and salads are great—the spicy *tom yom gung* (order it with chicken if you like) is made with aromatic kaffir lime leaf, which really sets it apart from the other soups. Noodles, meats, seafood, and vegetables make up the majority of the rest of the menu. Give their *larb* a try—it's made with chicken and is quite spicy. The mock duck dishes also get high praise. The desserts are quite nice, especially the sweet sticky rice with mango prepared with luscious coconut cream, which counters the earthy mango quite well. As for drinks, there are a series of cocktails made with sake, but on a nonalcoholic note, the sparkly and less-common and pleasantly sweet Vietnamese lemonade is a real treat.

LIC Market, 21-52 44th Dr., Long Island City, NY 11101; (718) 361-0013; Subway: 7 to Court Square; New American; $$. The menu here focuses on ingredients that are local, seasonal, and when possible, organic. Walk down the steps into the restaurant and you'll spy a collection of locally made comestibles for purchase (pick up some jam or pickles on your way out), and beyond that you'll find seating along the wall and a dining room in the back. The dining room can get a bit loud when it's full, but the seating up front is more manageable in the acoustics department. The food is delicious, and pretty much everything on the menu is terrific. For lunch, the Market BLT is a winner, in part because it includes avocado and is on excellent bread. The burger and roast chicken also get high marks. Dinner is served Wednesday through Friday with happy hour from 5:30 to 7 p.m., with individual drinks half off (excluding bottles and large-format beer). Brunch is on the weekend starting at 11 a.m., but the lines can get awfully long, so plan ahead. Because they choose to cook seasonally, the menu will change, so be aware. Often they'll display works by local artists, too, so check out the walls to increase your creative exposure.

Linn, 29-13 Broadway, Astoria, NY 11106; (718) 204-0060; Subway: N/Q to Broadway; Japanese; $$$. At Linn, home of some of the best sushi in Astoria, the fish is extremely fresh and delicious, and is prepared by Shigenori Tanaka (formerly of Manhattan's Masa). The space is simple—there are two rows of tables with a small number of purposefully mismatched chairs, with the sushi bar in the back. At the front of the dining room is a large screen showing silent moving images of professional surfers or Kurosawa films. The menu here is extensive—noodles, soups, salads, appetizers, fish and meat entrees, sushi and sashimi, and even dessert. When you sit down, you are offered an amuse-bouche of cold cooked tuna, which is a delightful and delicious way to start the meal. Choose from their small menu of sake, which can be served hot or cold (the house sake is a deal at $6 a glass). If you're trying to figure out what to order, perhaps start with the pork belly, which arrives in a bowl with a slightly sweet broth of soy ginger and sake. The fried oysters are also delicious, two pieces breaded in panko and served with a salty, savory dipping sauce. As for the sushi, it is excellent. The wild salmon is so fresh and flavorful, and the yellowtail is smooth and buttery—it's fish like this that will convince you of the appeal of sashimi. Get the warmed marinated shiitake mushroom for something a little different. And the eel is absolutely stunning, almost like fish candy with a little bit of sweet sauce on top. Linn's special rolls are also inventive—the Mach 3 is especially fun for those who love spicy food, what with a double dose of spicy tuna. For dessert, don't miss the *shira tama,* a dish made with a base of creamy vanilla ice cream, topped with sweetened red beans, and accompanied by gelatin cubes, Japanese rice cakes, and fresh berries.

Little Morocco, 2439 Steinway St., Astoria, NY 11103; (718) 204-8118; Subway: N/Q to Astoria Boulevard; Moroccan; $. This is one of the few Moroccan restaurants on Steinway Street's Little Egypt section, but they put out the best *merguez* sausage sandwich in the neighborhood, if not the entire city. The sausage, which is made in house, is cooked perfectly and placed in a hero roll with tomato, cucumber, onion, chopped green olives, and *harissa,* a spicy pepper sauce.

Astoria's Little Egypt

Another distinctive immigrant group—or, set of immigrant groups—in Astoria is the Middle Eastern and North African community, made of up Palestinians, Jordanians, Syrians, Lebanese, Egyptians, Moroccans, Algerians, and Tunisians. Their business and social hub lies in the Little Egypt area of Astoria, located on Steinway Street between Astoria Boulevard and 30th Avenue. On Steinway Street there is a vibrant world of men, women, and children practicing their faith, living their lives, and sharing their culture with each other and the larger community. Restaurants, cafes, halal markets, groceries, and a mosque are all here, and it's a great place to enjoy some serious choice eats.

To enjoy Little Egypt, start on the Astoria Boulevard end and head south (it's a short walk from the Astoria Boulevard N/Q station). For lunch, Little Morocco (p. 43) is wonderful (their *merguez* sandwich is amazing). Next door is Al-Sham Sweets (p. 80), which makes the best pastries in the area. Very popular on Steinway Street are the cafes where you can smoke shisha in a hookah and have some tea or coffee and food. Eastern Nights (25-35 Steinway St., Astoria, NY 11103; 718-204-7608), Jerusalem Nights (25-42 Steinway St., Astoria, NY 11103; 718-726-1444; jerusalemnightsnyc.com), and Layali Beirut (25-60 Steinway St., Astoria, NY 11102; 718-717-7730; layalibeirutnyc.com) all can accommodate your hookah-smoking needs. Stop by the Nile Deli (p. 97) and pick up some olives, preserved lemons, olive oil, Turkish delight, and fluffy pita. Dinner provides you with a variety of great options—the legendary Egyptian restaurants Kabab Cafe (p. 70) and Mombar (p. 72) just up the street; great seafood at Sabry's (24-25 Steinway St., Astoria, NY 11103; 718-721-9010); and Duzan (p. 29) makes incredible hummus, excellent falafel, and their chicken shawarma is also very, very good.

The mix of vegetables has an almost creamy consistency, and mixes perfectly with the *merguez*. It all goes very well with a cup of their sweet, hot mint tea, which contains a big leaf of fresh mint. On Friday, and Friday only, they serve couscous topped with either lamb or chicken, redolent of North African spices. Tagines are also available with a choice of chicken, lamb shank, baby lamb chops, or *kefta* (meatballs); tagine specials are available some days, too. This restaurant is halal, so no pork is served.

Lorusso's Pizza and Foccacia, 18-01 26th Rd., Astoria, NY 11102; (718) 777-3628; Subway: N/Q to Astoria Boulevard; Italian/ Pizzeria; $. Hidden along the edge of Old Astoria Village, originally a vacation spot for New York's rich and famous, lies Lorusso's, where some of Astoria's best focaccia is made. Pizza is made here, too, but the real draw is the focaccia. Smallish, round discs of this thick, savory Italian olive oil–rich yeasted dough are visible on the top shelf of the display case, minding their own business. Each one has different toppings—tomato and olive, chicken, sausage, spinach. Have them put some fresh mozzarella on your focaccia of choice and heat it up, too, for an extra treat. While you're waiting for that to finish, check out the taller display case on the right, which contains jars of homemade basil and sun-dried tomato pesto, both available for purchase. Crisp green salads and desserts—tiramisu and New York–style cheesecake—are also available. Before you leave, pick up a bag of their handmade black olive *taralli,* a southern Italian snack that is boiled like a bagel, and then baked or fried. It's so good and really outshines any other *taralli* in the neighborhood.

Manducati's Rustica, 46-35 Vernon Blvd., Long Island City, NY 11101; (718) 937-1312; Subway: 7 to Vernon/Jackson; Italian; $$.

Located well into the hip commercial strip of Vernon Boulevard lies Manducati's Rustica—part bakery, part market, part restaurant. As you step in you are greeted by a display case containing delicious Italian pastries, cookies, and cakes, as well as a selection of house-made gelato (try the hazelnut). Ahead and to the left are shelves containing pastas and sauces, among other things. There's restaurant seating in the main room and also off to the left. Order a pizza or calzone—made with Italian 00 flour, which gives it an amazing texture. The pizzas are perfect for two people or one very hungry pizza lover. Service can be a little slow, so patience is a virtue here—and the food is definitely worth it.

Melting Pot, 36-01 Vernon Blvd., Astoria, NY 11106; (718) 606-2670; Subway: N/Q to 36th Avenue or Q69 Bus to 36th Avenue; Jamaican; $. A bit off the beaten track lies this Jamaican restaurant serving up truly delicious plates of Caribbean home cooking. They offer foods for breakfast, including codfish fritters, porridge, and egg and cheese on a roll (hey, it's still New York City). Lunch and dinner dishes are more elaborate, and they offer things like curry goat and chicken, jerk chicken, oxtails, roti (filled with chicken or goat), and Golden Krust brand beef patties. Pastries like carrot cake and black cake are also on the menu. For lunch or dinner, when you order anything that has "(meal)" after it, that means you get a plate with the main item, plus rice and peas/beans, cooked cabbage, and plantains. The plantains in this case are sweet, and they fry them up until they start to caramelize; they are fantastic. The chicken roti is very good ("slammin," in the words of a fellow customer), and the jerk chicken is also fantastic—it's moist, savory, and spicy, and comes with the skin on. Quarter, half, and whole jerk chickens can also be ordered. Be sure to get a glass of their expertly made sorrel, too, which sits on the counter in a very large decorative glass container. Their sorrel is nicely balanced between tangy and sweet, is very refreshing, and a great foil to spicy food. The dining room is open and airy, with exposed brick walls and big windows letting in lots of light. The view onto the 36th Avenue bridge to Roosevelt Island is also stunning in its industrial glory.

Michael Angelo's, 29-11 23rd Ave., Astoria, NY 11105; (718) 932-2096; Subway: N/Q to Ditmars Boulevard; michaelangelospizzeria astoria.com; Italian/Pizza; $$. Sometimes you just want to dive right into a big plate of comfort food; Michael Angelo's excels in the Italian-American version of just that.

Familiar Italo-American dishes like penne alla vodka, fettuccine Alfredo, and veal piccata grace the menu, and are all deftly executed. Particularly well done is the gnocchi sorrentino, potato gnocchi settled

in a sauce of marinara elevated by melted bits of fresh mozzarella. Mushroom ravioli is also a decadent and satisfying option with its rich, fresh cream sauce. Anything cooked in the francese style—sole or chicken—is wonderful, too. The light sauce is smooth and slightly thickened, with a bright tang from the lemon, and the egg-based crust is never heavy. And then there is the pizza, which is some of the best in town when it comes to traditional New York–style pizza. Round pies come with a choice of regular or extra-thin crust, and their Sophia Loren pie is especially good with the extra-thin crust. It's a real winner, and comes topped with simple ingredients—fresh mozzarella, fresh tomatoes, garlic, and extra-virgin olive oil. For dessert, the usual suspects are tiramisu and amaretto cake, both very good. If you dine in, you might be lucky enough to be gifted a little glass of anisette to end your meal. Also note that during the warmer months, their backyard patio is open and it's a lovely, spacious spot to have a great Italian meal.

Ornella Trattoria, 29-17 23rd Ave., Astoria, NY 11105; (718) 777-9477; Subway: N/Q to Ditmars; ornellatrattoria.com; Italian; $$. Proprietor Giuseppe Viterale is the genius behind so many of the exciting and inventive items on Ornella's menu. He relies on his sense memory of the foods from his home region of Italy—the Cliento region of Salerno, on the Amalfi coast. His most notorious menu item is probably the *sanguinaccio,* a chocolate pudding thickened with pig's blood. On a tamer level, his *pasta di castagna* is wonderful and unusual because of the use of chestnut flour. The resulting chestnut pasta is combined beautifully with arugula and cherry tomatoes, all in a garlic and oil sauce. Often there will be a *burrata* appetizer, not listed on the menu—if it is available, snatch it up. Likely it will be paired with prosciutto and melon. In a related vein, their *caprese con pepperoni* salad is a lovely choice—it's made with buffalo mozzarella and served with roasted peppers. The *gnocchi alla Gorgonzola* is lovely—light and airy and swimming in the most decadent cream sauce flavored with a sweet Gorgonzola cheese. The king of the menu, however, is the *imbustata*. This magnificent display of pasta and meat is in the form of an oven-baked pasta envelope, stuffed with roasted veal and chicken, with wild mushrooms, spinach, fresh mozzarella and mascarpone, and topped with fresh tomato sauce. It is a dish for the ages. On the flip side, vegetarians and vegans are more than welcome at the restaurant, as Giuseppe has formulated a menu just for those who reject meat. As far as dessert goes, the Italian-style cheesecake is a sure bet—it's light and sweet and a perfect ending to any meal at Ornella. Ornella prepares a number of specials on different nights, too. One night will be chicken, one night steak, etc. Giuseppe is constantly pushing the envelope and experimenting with flavor and ingredient combinations, so no doubt new items will find their way onto the menu, so be sure to keep an eye out.

Ovelia, 34-01 30th Ave., Astoria, NY 11102; (718) 721-7217; Subway: N/Q to 30th Avenue; ovelia-ny.com; Greek; $$. **Ovelia** lies in the heart of 30th Avenue and provides a full menu of inventive

Greek food, and then some. In addition to their comfortable seating in their dining room, when the weather warms up there's seating outside, which makes for great people-watching along 30th Avenue, one of the most diverse streets in the nation. Ovelia makes an effort in their menu to accommodate omnivores, vegetarians, and vegans alike. Their ingredients are fresh and locally sourced when possible. Hot and cold meze choices start off the menu, including the big three of *tzatziki,* taramosalata, and *skordalia;* however, the *kafteri*—sautéed spicy peppers with feta—is a great choice, too. As far as warm meze goes, if you haven't tried it yet, grilled halloumi is a real treat. This is cheese that doesn't melt when heated. Ovelia's version involves prosciutto and red peppers, too. The fried feta cubes are also spectacular—cubes of feta are coated in a sesame-seed batter, deep fried, and drizzled with honey. But what shines even brighter is the house-made *loukaniko,* a traditional Greek pork sausage flavored with orange and fennel. Beyond these appetizers are salads and traditional *psistaria* (a Greek grill house) specialties like grilled lamb, pork, and organic chicken. The Ovelia menu goes on and on with dishes like the creatively titled Lamburgini (a ground lamb burger topped with cremini mushrooms and a feta sauce on a house-baked pretzel bun), the pastitsio (a kind of Greek lasagna), and the delectable *monastiraki bifteka* (ground beef and lamb kebabs). There's plenty of seafood on the menu, too, both grilled and raw. The dessert menu is extensive, and embraces traditional Greek pastries such as baklava, *galaktaboureko,* and *loukoumades,* as well as Western desserts like cheesecake and chocolate mousse. Coffee and liqueurs are also available to help round out the meal.

Pachanga Patterson, 33-17 31st Ave., Astoria, NY 11103; (718) 554-0525; Subway: N/Q to Broadway; pachangapatterson.com; Mexican; $$. Pachanga Patterson is brought to us by the brilliant minds behind the celebrated Astoria locavore restaurant **Vesta** (p. 65). And the locavore element is alive and well at Pachanga, too, evident in their partnerships with places like Long Island City's own rooftop farm, Brooklyn Grange, and the incredible corn tortillas at Corona's **Tortilleria Nixtamal** (p. 221). As far as cocktails go, the La Pachanga margarita is a well-executed version of the classic tequila and lime margarita, but theirs also contains P&H Soda Company's hibiscus syrup. The Tequila Mockingbird is worth trying. It's a mixture of tequila, lime, cucumber, and mint. If you are a gin and tonic fan, the Fizzing Out cocktail is right up your alley. The addition of P&H lovage syrup truly elevates this drink to serious fun in a glass. Not surprisingly, the guacamole is a great starter, and Pachanga's guacamole is nice and limey. The assertive flavors pair up with the sturdy chips, also made from the tortillas at Tortilleria Nixtamal. The portion is also pretty substantial; it's really a deal for $8. The cheese and kale empanadas are excellent, served with a robust tomato chili sauce. Tacos make up a small yet important portion of the menu and arrive in familiar to foreign flavor profiles—braised beef to battered fish, *queso fresco* to moo shoo duck. Their cheese enchiladas are served hot in a mini *cazuela,* and come with a rich mole sauce on top. For dessert, the El Diablito cake—counterpart to sister restaurant Vesta's Baby Jesus cake—satisfies, with its date-sweetened chocolate cake base, toped with a chili-spiked caramel sauce.

Petey's Burger, 30-17 30th Ave., Astoria, NY 11102; (718) 267-6300; Subway: N/Q to 30th Avenue; 46-46 Vernon Blvd., Long Island City, NY 11101; (718) 937-4040; Subway: 7 to Vernon Jackson; peteysburger.com; Burgers; $. If you're craving In-N-Out, but are all the way across the country in Astoria, Queens, Petey's has your number. They serve fast food–style hamburgers that are compared most often to that California mainstay of the burger world. Of course you'll find burgers—doubles and triples, to boot, with or without cheese, and grilled onions are an option as well. There's also a "Petey's Melt"—a patty melt with bacon, onions, cheese, and Russian dressing. Even vegetarians can get in on the action with a

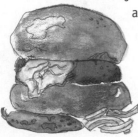

very respectable veggie burger, one of which comes in a Greek style, and contains spinach and feta, an obvious nod to the neighborhood. The orders of fries are plentiful and delicious—much better than the fries at In-N-Out, actually. In fact, you can order your fries as "California Fries"—topped with Petey's sauce, grilled onions, and melted cheese. The shakes are also thick and creamy—ask them to mix chocolate and strawberry for a real taste treat. The burgers, shakes, and fries come in various "Value Combos," which really do save you a good chunk of change.

Pita Hot, 25-15 30th Ave., Astoria, NY 11102; (718) 932-8282; Subway: N/Q to 30th Avenue; Mediterranean; $. Some of the best falafel in Astoria is found here, in a small little storefront with about four little tables inside. As you peruse the menu, which is posted above the counter, grab a crunchy zaatar-topped pita chip to snack on. While you wait for your food to be made, the man behind the counter might give you a taste of their smooth, delicious hummus on a piece of pita, too. The falafel is fried fresh as you order it; the thick, green falafel mix is visible right next to the stove. Be sure to get the tart, crunchy red cabbage on top—it adds amazing flavor to the sandwich, which also contains pickles and tomatoes. On the carnivorous side of things, both the chicken and gyro meat are moist and savory and can be eaten either in a sandwich or as part of a platter. The platters include rice, and if you're lucky you'll get some of the rice crust, which has a bit of a caramelized texture. Enjoy it all with a bottle of Sarkiz, a sparkly apple soda, or Ayran, a yogurt drink, both from Turkey. At the end of the meal, don't miss the baklava, sweet and full of pistachios, sprinkled at the last minute with rosewater. The spiced, aromatic orange blossom ginger tea—complete with a couple of green cardamom pods floating in it—goes perfectly with the baklava.

Queens Comfort, 40-09 30th Ave., Astoria, NY 11103; (718) 728-2350; Subway: N/Q to 30th Avenue; queenscomfort.blogspot.com; American Comfort Food; $$. Queens Comfort whips up comfort food that will appeal to both kids and the nostalgic kid at heart. On one hand you'll find a classic wedge salad with tomatoes and buttermilk blue cheese dressing, and on the other there's the chicken fingers coated in a Cap'n Crunch batter. The menu is rife with classic, stick-to-your-ribs foods; particularly good is the Three Leek Mac and Cheese, and the Ring of Fire burger (cue Johnny Cash) also gets good marks. They've also come up with an avocado sandwich that is simply awesome—it's battered in Korean fried chicken batter, yielding an extremely crisp exterior and a hot, creamy interior; chipotle mayo adds delicious heat to the sandwich, too. Robicelli's cupcakes have made an appearance, but just like the dinner menu, the dessert menu changes regularly, so keep an eye on the website.

Enjoy something sweet with a cup of coffee, courtesy of Stumptown beans—ask for heavy cream to make the coffee even more decadent than it already is.

The Queens Kickshaw, 40-17 Broadway, Astoria, NY 11103; (718) 777-0913; Subway: N/Q to Broadway or M/R to Steinway Street; thequeenskickshaw.com; Coffee/Sandwiches; $. The Queens Kickshaw is probably the only spot in Queens that specializes in grilled cheese sandwiches. Probably the most inventive one is the Gouda—it brings together black bean hummus, guava jam, pickled jalapeños, and Gouda cheese, all on Balthazar Bakery brioche bread. The combination of savory, sweet, and spicy along with the fatty cheese is just amazing. It also comes with a side salad with a zippy, spicy vinaigrette.

The classic pairing of grilled cheese and tomato soup is also on the menu—there's cheddar and mozzarella on buttery brioche bread alongside a bowl of some of the tastiest tomato soup you're going to find anywhere. Apart from the grilled cheese sandwiches, they offer a cheese plate made up of as many as five different kinds of artisanal cheeses (you determine how many you'd like), some salads, larger plates like knishes, snacks like crunchy curried *pepitas* and tangy lemon coriander olives, and several desserts. There's the brownie *affogato*—an intense walnut-studded brownie swimming in a mixture of strong coffee and cream, and the moist bread pudding, drizzled with an orange caramel sauce. The Queens Kickshaw also brews some of the best coffee in Astoria, with beans from Coffee Labs Roasters, located up the Hudson in Tarrytown. Their talented baristas pull well-executed espresso shots, and pair them with some of the creamiest steamed milk around for cappuccinos and lattes. They also do pour-overs (a single serving of coffee brewed one cup at a time) with single-origin coffee beans. Another menu item that sets them apart from the rest is the shrub, a colonial-era vinegar-based fruit drink, in both blueberry and golden raisin flavors. On Friday night around 9 p.m., more often than not you'll be able to hear live music, too. See recipe for The Queens Kickshaw's **Gouda Grilled Cheese with Black Bean Hummus & Pickled Jalapeños** on p. 357.

Rocco's Italian Sausages and Philly Cheese Steaks, 50-10 Northern Blvd., Long Island City, NY 11101; (718) 204-0478; Subway: E/M/R to 46th Street or Northern Boulevard; Sandwiches; $. Hidden in plain sight is this sandwich stand, tacked to the front of the Home Depot, serving up Italian sausage sandwiches and Philly cheese steaks. The sausages are grilled while coiled up, cooked until they are caramelized outside and juicy inside, in both sweet and spicy versions. The guys then cut off the appropriate amount of sausage and put it in a hero with onions and peppers. The cheese steaks, while perhaps not 100 percent authentic, are 100 percent delicious. Thin strips of beef are griddled up, then placed in a hero with melted white cheese and perfectly cooked peppers and onions. There's also a very spicy hot sauce you can add to your sandwich.

Inside the stand are a couple of high tables (no chairs) where can eat your sandwich, or go out the side door to a few picnic tables. They also run a number of value meals, which include chips and a soda. The staff members behind the counter are really nice and happy to answer any questions you may have. And since you're already at the Home Depot, you can pick up that paint you've been meaning to buy, too.

Sac's Place, 25-41 Broadway, Astoria, NY 11106; (718) 204-5002; Subway: N/Q to Broadway; Italian; $$. Sac's, owned by Anthony and Domenico Sacramone, is the only place in Astoria where you can get a pizza cooked in a coal oven. Coal ovens are not common in New York City, so this is a big deal. The pizza crust gets a little char on it from the oven—if you want a crispier pizza, ask for it well done. The best way to have your pizza is just tomato sauce (they use San Marzano tomatoes) and cheese—cooked in that coal oven, you have a simple delicacy that's truly authentic NYC. A simple cucumber salad is a nice accompaniment to the pizza, or if you're looking for something more elaborate, try the Caesar salad. Their homemade gnocchi with marinara are fantastic—they are so light and pillowy, really a taste treat. Sac's prepares a number of specials each day, so be sure to ask about them.

Sage General Store, 24-20 Jackson Ave., Long Island City, NY 11101; (718) 361-0707; Subway: 7/G to Court Square or E/M to 23rd Street-Ely; sagegeneralstore.com; New American; $$. This place really does have a store in it, though it's quite tiny—more of a "store setting" in the words of the owners. However, a small selection of artisanal food items—McClure's pickles and Nunu Chocolates, both made in Brooklyn—is for sale, ready to take home with you. The food does have a local aspect in that the staff works with local farmers and purveyors to get the freshest ingredients. They prepare a lot of specials, which can change daily, so be sure to keep an ear out for those. They are open for breakfast, lunch, and dinner, as well as brunch on the weekend. Among their greatest brunch items are the *chilaquiles,* made with chicken, corn tortillas, tomatillo sauce, and *queso blanco* and topped with a beautiful fried egg. The BLT is made with Neuske's bacon and is one of the most flavorful

BLTs around. The cheddar biscuit is epic, also containing bacon—large and fluffy, it's awesome with butter. Try their raspberry lemonade to wash it all down, or a strong cup of coffee. Speaking of the coffee, it holds up well in iced form and is particularly good with one of their moist and delicious homemade cupcakes. The red velvet is topped with a tangy cream-cheese frosting, and the "Hostess cupcake" looks exactly like its namesake, and is fabulous as well (it tastes much better than what it's imitating, too).

San Antonio Bakery No. 2, 36-20 Astoria Blvd., Astoria, NY 11103; (718) 777-8733; Subway: N/Q to Astoria Boulevard; panaderia chilena.com; Chilean/Bakery; $. This unassuming little bakery has so much delicious food within, you won't regret stopping in for a bite. From the street, it looks like a generic spot with a few sweet things—but that's not all. Those sweet things are indeed crazy delicious, but the main attraction is the *completo*—a Chilean-style hot dog, nestled in a homemade bun, and topped with tomatoes, onions, avocado, and mayonnaise. *Pebre,* a vinegar and oil–enhanced Chilean salsa, goes perfectly with the dog, and it is an irresistable combination. Wash it down with a Bilz (cherry) or Pap (papaya) Chilean soda, to make the experience even more authentic. Apart from the *completo,* San Antonio Bakery makes some delicious sandwiches. The *lomito* is particularly good, made with roast pork topped with melted cheese in between one of their homemade sandwich rolls. You'll also find empanadas there, including cheese, beef, and

seafood. The cheese is a standout because
it uses a different kind of dough than the
others—it's very flaky and buttery. The other
doughs are more bready, but their savory fillings
are really excellent, and include elements like raisins and olives,
which are traditional. As for the sweet side of things, the pan cake
really stands out. It's made of alternating layers of cake and *dulce
de leche*—sweet and decadent. Then there are the *chilenitos,* a kind
of *alfajor* (sandwich cookie) with *dulce de leche* inside and meringue
on top. The tropical fruit *lucuma* also makes an appearance in a soft
cake layered with Chantilly cream.

Seva, 30-07 34th St., Astoria, NY 11103; (718) 626-4440; Subway:
N/Q to 30th Avenue; sevaindianrestaurant.com; Indian; $. Seva,
which means "an act of service" in Hindi, is Astoria's most popular
Indian restaurant, and it gets written up year after year in lists
of neighborhood bests. The food is consistently tasty, the service
attentive without being intrusive, and there is something for
everyone, from vegans (they do not use ghee) to omnivores. It's a
modestly decorated dining room, but cozy just the same. A half-
dozen or so kinds of naan appear on the menu, and the cilantro
naan is by far the most interesting. Their vegetable samosas are
spot-on and taste especially great with the mint chutney. And while
it's not something you might expect to find on an Indian menu,
their smooth butternut squash soup is superb. For vegetarians,
try the *saag paneer* and *channa masala.* Among the meats, green
chili chicken is outstanding and the lamb vindaloo is earthy and

wonderfully spicy. The chicken tikka masala is a very popular dish and the cooks at Seva have figured out the way to make this dish perfectly creamy. Desserts are simple, with a choice of *gulab jamun, kheer,* or *rasmalai,* all executed well. A particularly popular choice overall is the dinner prix fixe, which includes an appetizer, main, and dessert. The lassi goes great with all, and their iced tea is also excellent.

Sparrow Tavern, 24-01 29th St.; Astoria, NY 11102; (718) 606-2260; Subway: N/Q to Astoria Boulevard; thesparrowtavern.com; New American; $$. This bar was featured on the Food Network's show *Diners, Drive-Ins, and Dives.* It's neither a diner nor a drive-in, so that qualifies it as a dive, but it's not nearly as grungy as a lot of dive bars are. But it's dark and a little beat up–looking inside, and the furniture is endearingly mismatched, but the place serves fantastic food. Around the neighborhood, their burger is often considered one of the best in town—it's made from grass-fed beef and served with minimal fixings—just raw red onion—though cheese, bacon, and/or speck are optional additions. Honestly, the beef is so flavorful, you really don't need any condiments on it. The bun is fluffy and handles the meat well. It comes with salad or fries—herb or spiced; with the herb fries you get long leaves of deep-fried rosemary mixed in which are delicious to nibble on. The veggie burger, made mostly with actual vegetables (no soy) and served in a whole-wheat pita, gets high praise from local vegetarians, as well as from Guy Fieri in the above-mentioned television show. Also a great option for vegetarians is Sparrow's distinctive grilled cheese, made from fontina and manouri cheeses, with the addition of radicchio, herbs, and truffle oil. It is truly delicious. Back on the meat side of things, the pork tacos are awesome—very flavorful and topped with cilantro and avocado, all in a corn tortilla. They also do a very nice cheese plate. Desserts are good but what is really special is the *pain perdu*—this is a grilled chocolate croissant, drizzled with a toffee-caramel sauce, accompanied by a dollop of thick whipped cream. Divine.

Stove, 45-17 28th Ave., Astoria, NY 11103; (718) 956-0372; Subway: N/Q to 30th Avenue; stoveastoria.com; New American; $$. Located a bit of a distance from the nearest subway line, Stove is something of a neighborhood secret. Open the front door and you'll find a bar up front on the right with a few tables on the left; the restaurant seemingly narrows as it heads back, and the space is comfortable and cool. For dinner, solid dishes like hanger steak with shoestring potatoes, shepherd's pie, French onion soup, and trout meunière grace the menu. For Sunday brunch (reservations recommended), they do a version of eggs Benedict, called Poached Eggs Royale, made with smoked salmon in place of the ham/Canadian bacon, with a wonderfully lemony hollandaise sauce made from scratch. Their corned beef hash is savory, delicious, and light. A cocktail comes with brunch, and their mimosa is pleasantly balanced—not too much orange juice and not too much champagne. Desserts are available at brunch, and a great addition to the table is fresh strawberries topped with whipped cream. The Irish-style breakfast is the way to go for those with a big appetite—it's chock-full of Irish specialties (the chef at Stove is Irish) like black pudding, white pudding, sausage, eggs, and more. Pair it with an Irish coffee and you've got a spectacular meal.

Sweet Afton, 30-09 34th St., Astoria, NY 11103; (718) 777-2570; Subway: N/Q to 30th Avenue; sweetaftonbar.com; Gastropub; $$. In a town that is full of bars and burgers, Sweet Afton excels at each and prepares some of the best food—of any kind—out there. First, it's a gorgeous space—dark wood (reclaimed), a sturdy and artful bar, low lights, and a sweet patio out back. As for the drinks, the beer selection is modest yet focused, and full-on classy. They even offer seasonal cask ale—a naturally fermented beer—that is a rare find in the neighborhood. They'll let you taste any of the beers on tap (including the cask ale!) before you buy, and they'll do it with a smile. Their cocktails—some classic, some less so—are artfully crafted and full of flavor. You can't go wrong with the fresh lime margarita and the Moscow Mule; the Gin Basil, aromatic with an

elderflower element, is wonderful. Their wine selection is small, but good; the Oregon Pinot Noir is a winner. The food menu is also small but focused, and everything is a hit. Sweet Afton gained notoriety around town from their unique fried pickles—slices of spicy McClure's pickles are coated in a beer batter, deep fried, and served with a spicy mayo that is an out-of-this-world combination. Their salt and pepper ribs are also wonderful and meaty, and come with a tasty slaw. And their burger, made from Pat LaFrieda beef, is a perfect rendering of the pub burger—juicy and full of flavor; during brunch it's topped with a fried egg. Speaking of brunch, give the Irish breakfast roll a whirl—it's a meaty sandwich complete with black pudding from Butcher Bar in Sunnyside. Be sure to have a brunch cocktail with your meal—the blueberry muddle is perfection.

Sweetleaf, 10-93 Jackson Ave., Long Island City, NY 11101; (917) 832-6726; Subway: 7 to Vernon/Jackson; sweetleaflic.com; Coffeehouse; $. Sweetleaf brews the best coffee in Long Island City, hands down. They've been at it for several years, and were the first people to bring Stumptown coffee to Queens (and only the second place to bring it to all of NYC). Since then, they've incorporated the coffee of award-winning roasters Verve of Santa Cruz, CA, and at the time of this writing, they are the only espresso bar to serve this coffee, which is used primarily for pour-overs. Ritual Coffee, based out of San Francisco, also makes an appearance, and their coffee from El Salvador makes especially good iced coffee with milk. Espresso drinks are, of course, available, from the standard cappuccino and latte to the less familiar *cortado*. Mochas, made with Jacques Torres chocolate, are divine, and if you are looking for something to really get your motor running, try the Iced Rocket

Fuel, which is cold brewed coffee with chicory and maple syrup. For something perhaps a little less intense, their iced latte is phenomenal, and everything you'd want an iced coffee to be (including strong). A number of baked goods are prepared in house—you can see the kitchen through the window off the Laptop Room—and vegans, vegetarians, and omnivores alike will find something to nosh on. Particularly memorable are the cinnamon puffs, which are small balls of cake—which taste a bit like an old-fashioned buttermilk doughnut—rolled in granulated sugar and cinnamon. The carrot cake is very popular as well. The bakers are always experimenting and often come up with interesting new items, which are gobbled up by hungry patrons. Keep an eye out for their gluten-free baked goods, too.

Ukus, 42-08 30th Ave., Astoria, NY 11103; (718) 267-8587; Subway: N/Q to 30th Avenue; Bosnian; $. Astoria has a strong and long-standing Eastern European community, with a particularly robust Balkan population. There are a number of Balkan restaurants around town, and among them, Ukus serves up great Bosnian fare, from salads to *bureks* to meats. The *Ukus salat* is extremely flavorful, full of tomatoes, cucumber, and plenty of crumbled feta. Their potato roll is essentially a spiral potato *burek;* they come three to an order but you can always order just one (they are pretty big). To get a good idea of the different kinds of meats offered at Ukus, get the mixed grill. It consists of *cevapi,* their amazing smoked beef sausage, veal liver, chicken, and a long beef kebab, accompanied by *ajvar* and raw onions, as well as a scoop of *bryndza,* a soft sheep's milk cheese. It is very luxurious. A basket of soft *lepinja,* the traditional Bosnian bread, accompanies everything. Get a bottle or Jupi or Cockta to wash down your meal. End it all with one of their desserts, available under the counter up front; the rich, smooth chocolate walnut cream roll is fantastic.

Vesta, 21-02 30th Ave., Astoria, NY 11102; (718) 545-5550; Subway: N/Q to 30th Avenue; vestavino.com; Italian; $$. **Vesta** is one of the most popular restaurants in Astoria, part of the newer generation of neighborhood eating establishments focusing on clean flavors, sustainability, and local ingredients. The food is delicious, the staff attentive, and the space is elegant and comfortable at the same time; who could ask for more? Their menu changes with the season, so what you get in January won't necessarily be exactly the same in June. But some things on the menu do move from season to season, including the rich, meaty lasagna, and the Margherita pizza, which has a very thin, almost cracker crust (also available in a whole-wheat version). This same crust can be found as the base for the Hangover Pizza, which contains potato, pancetta, sausage, spicy tomato sauce, with a fried egg on top. Also notable on the brunch menu is A Warm Bankie, which has a base of creamy polenta, with asparagus, mushroom, truffle oil, and fried eggs. Going back to dinner, the pasta dishes are excellent, and any kind of braised or slow-cooked meat is going to be just incredible. At one point there was a dish of short ribs served over polenta and it was just magnificent—rich, hearty, and flavorful. Wine is also an important element at the restaurant, and their bar is comfortable to hang out at and enjoy a glass of two. They also have local Long Island wines on tap. As for dessert, nothing beats "La Torta del Piccolo Bambino Gesu Cristo"—otherwise known as the "Baby Jesus Cake." It's a date-sweetened cake with a toffee sauce and whipped cream on the side. It's Vesta's most popular dessert and absolutely delicious.

Via Trenta, 36-19 30th Ave., Astoria, NY 11103; (718) 545-2090; Subway: N/Q to 30th Avenue; viatrenta.com; Italian; $$. This newer spot on 30th Avenue is a nice break from the many Greek cafes that populate this part of Astoria. Their food is modern, fresh, and extremely tasty. One of the best parts of their menu is the selection of pizzas, which are cooked in a very hot wood-burning brick oven.  The simple Margherita pizza is fantastic, and the vegetable pizza sans cheese is also delicious. A dish of beet gnocchi is really nice, but the mushroom ravioli in a cream sauce is over-the-top good. They have a good wine selection and the staff is happy to guide you to something you're going to love.

Wave Thai, 2137 31st St., Astoria, NY 11105; (718) 777-6789; Subway: N/Q to Ditmars; wavethainyc.com; Thai; $. A local fave, Wave probably has the biggest set of protein options around—chicken, beef, roast duck, vegetarian chicken, vegetarian duck, tofu, shrimp, squid, scallops, mixed seafood, and grilled salmon. The chicken is very good and the vegetarian duck is an excellent option for those eschewing meat. The roast duck is great, too. They use it to prepare a very tasty crispy duck salad, a terrific light meal all on its own. On the appetizer menu, the curry puffs are a standout, with a buttery pastry surrounding a light curried chicken filling, accompanied by a little cucumber salad, which can also be ordered as a full-sized salad dish itself. It's hard to go wrong with the *ki mao,* which is a simple dish of meat/protein, wide noodles, and vegetables like string beans, cabbage, and tomato; there's a little egg in there, too.

Zenon Taverna, 34-10 31st Ave., Astoria, NY 11106; (718) 956-0133; Subway: N/Q to Broadway; zenontaverna.com; Greek; $$. Solid Greek fare is found at Zenon Taverna, and you'll find more grilled land animals than fish at this festive spot on 31st Avenue. One of the best deals on the menu is the Kypriaki (Cyprus) *mezedes—*16 small dishes are included for a little under $20 per person. They range from cold dishes like *tzatziki, pantzarosalada* (beet salad), and *skordalia,* to *keftedes* (meatballs), *loukaniko* (Greek sausage), and *ortikia* (quail). The total amount of food is astonishing, and whatever you don't finish, you can take home for an additional meal or two. Desserts are classic Greek specialties—the *bougatsa* is particularly good, and the baklava is delicious. Be sure to get a cup of strong Greek coffee to round out the meal.

Agnanti, 19-06 Ditmars Blvd., Astoria, NY 11105; (718) 545-4554; Subway: N/Q to Ditmars; agnantiastoria.com; Greek; $$$. This neighborhood favorite has one of the best views in Astoria—it sits right at the northeast corner of beautiful Astoria Park, a gem of a park along the East River shoreline. The rustic dining room has a lot of character, and in the warmer months you can sit outside and enjoy the view, all the while enjoying delicious, classic Greek cuisine. The menu does not focus on one single region, but on food from all over Greece. That being said, they do offer some dishes that were an important part of the Greek community in Constantinople, Turkey. You'll find things like *bureks,* which are very popular in Turkey, as well as the *pastroumali,* which is phyllo dough filled with pressed beef and cheese—it's sort of like a delicate calzone, complete with melty cheese goodness. The dips are very good—the taramosalata, *tzatziki, skordalia,* and *tyrokafteri,* which is a wonderfully savory and spicy cheese spread. The Greek salad is made with large chunks of summery vegetables and the feta comes on the side. Agnanti prepares food from both land and sea. A plate of meaty grilled octopus shouldn't be missed, and the sardines are also excellent. Greek cuisine features various kinds of ground meatballs (not always round but sometimes oblong), including *soutkoukakia,* which are very good here, cooked in a fragrant tomato sauce. Their Greek sausage is made from pork and seasoned with orange or leeks, giving the meat an amazing flavor. Retsina, a traditional Greek wine (and flavored with pine resin), is a great accompaniment to all this food, and can be purchased by both the glass and carafe (small or large); house red and white wines are also available. Desserts are modest yet authentic and tasty, and include Greek yogurt with sour cherries spooned on top, and a semolina cake sweetened with orange syrup.

Bohemian Hall & Beer Garden, 29-19 24th Ave., Astoria, NY 11102; (718) 274-4925; Subway: N/Q to Astoria Boulevard; bohemianhall.com; Czech/Slovak Beer Garden; $. This is one of the biggest draws to Queens, and people from all five boroughs love to travel to the Beer Garden to spend time there, especially in the warmer weather (though there are the die-hards that will hang out in the garden in the middle of a chilly winter). The garden itself is quite large and spacious, filled with plenty of long picnic tables, a grill, a bar, and a small stage for occasional live music performances—bands have ranged from traditional Czech ensembles to wizard rock band Harry and the Potters. The grill is great for a (relatively) quickly grabbed meal of burgers,

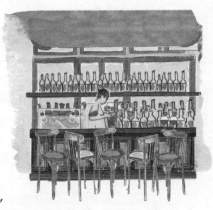

fries, and kielbasa (make sure you get the spicy mustard and sauer-kraut to go with it), but there is waitstaff to take your order off the menu. Try the *brynzové* (a potato dumpling pasta) with sheep's milk cheese and bacon; the potato pancakes with sour cream and apple-sauce; and *svickova,* which is a slow-roasted beef in a vegetable gravy—be sure to get the bread dumplings with it, which are great for sopping up all the delicious gravy. The beer here tends toward Czech beers like the well-known Pilsner Urquell and the perhaps lesser-known Staropramen. Krusovice Light is also good. Beer is available by the glass or the pitcher. If you're around in late May, stop by for the Czech and Slovak Festival, which features authentic food, music, and dancing all weekend.

Kabab Cafe, 25-12 Steinway St., Astoria, NY 11103; (718) 728-9858; Subway: N/Q to Astoria Boulevard; Egyptian; $$$. Chef Ali Sayed, who gained fame by both his brilliant cooking and later by being featured on Anthony Bourdain's *No Reservations* TV show, runs this tiny restaurant in the heart of Steinway Street's Little Egypt section; his food tradition comes from the northern Egyptian city of Alexandria. The consensus regarding the menu is to order the specials, but truth be told, the regular menu items are really good. Particularly the mixed mezze plate, consisting of spoonfuls of hummus, baba ghanoush, and *foul medamas,* a smashed fava bean dish; everything in the plate has at least a little lemon and garlic in it. The falafel balls—quite a bit smaller than your average falafel—are also excellent. The rabbit is also delicious. Ali likes to dust the plates with sumac and/or zaatar, which adds a lot of flavor to his dishes. He is also fond of cooking offal, so you'll likely find liver or sweetbreads, or perhaps some more daring sorts of innards on the specials menu. If offal isn't your thing, not to worry—other specials include vegetable-based dishes, and meats like goat, lamb, and chicken. Ali is a big presence in this restaurant, and the kitchen is fully visible, adjacent to the seating area, so you'll likely have a good chance to chat with him freely. Be sure to have a cup of mint tea while you're there, too.

Koliba, 31-11 23rd Ave., Astoria, NY 11105; (718) 626-0430; Subway: N/Q to Ditmars; kolibarestaurant.com; Czech/Slovak; $$. Koliba is arguably the home to the best Czech and Slovak food in Astoria. Both the food and drink are excellent and the space is warm and cozy, with a feel reminiscent of a private lodge with light wood paneling and even animal heads on the walls (the wild boar is the most interesting looking). Get a glass of Staropramen and listen to the specials, though the menu has many delicious items on it. The marinated herring are firm and wonderfully pickled. The spaetzle with tangy sheep's milk cheese and thick-cut bacon is excellent (the bacon is really out of this world scrumptious); the spaetzle comes with sauerkraut and bacon, too. The chicken schnitzel is perfectly breaded and comes with mashed potatoes alongside it. Anything with gravy, like the beef goulash, goes best with the fluffy bead dumplings, which are truly fabulous at Koliba. Dessert is a light affair, and the crepes with jam are an authentic way to end the meal. At the start of each year, Koliba holds its annual Venison Feast, so if you are around for that, it's definitely worth checking into.

Mombar, 25-22 Steinway St., Astoria, NY 11103; (718) 726-2356; Subway: N/Q to Astoria Boulevard; Egyptian; $$$. Mustapha El Sayed, brother to Ali who runs **Kabab Cafe** (p. 70) up the street, runs Mombar. The dining room at Mombar is more spacious and feels more formal compared to Kabab Cafe. Be sure to get a good look at the restaurant's highly decorated façade, complete with a giant stylized Egyptian eye. Everything here is good, particularly the tagines, such as the one with chicken and olives; lamb is great, too. The Egyptian molasses-glazed duck is also a winner. Mustapha also enjoys cooking offal, so if that is something you like to eat, you can be sure it will be expertly prepared here.

Piccola Venezia, 42-01 28th Ave., Astoria, NY 11103; (718) 721-8470; Subway: N/Q to Astoria Boulevard; piccola-venezia.com; Italian; $$$$. Fine, old-school dining is the name of the game at this northern Italian/Istrian restaurant in one of Astoria's quieter areas. The family has been cooking up great Italian food for close to 40 years and they show no evidence of stopping anytime soon. They prepare vegetables, fish, meats, and pasta extraordinarily well, which is a testament to their skill. Perhaps try the hot appetizer called Piccola Venezia—it's a combination of shrimp scampi, stuffed mushroom caps, and baked clams oreganata. This is a fantastic combination, full of flavor and great textures. Their pastas are homemade, so their cheesy, meaty lasagna or their signature pasta *fusi alla grappa* is a great choice in the pasta realm. This is made with bowtie-shaped pasta with saucy mushrooms, grappa and Parmigiano—really good and full of umami savoriness. The pumpkin ravioli are also awesome, dressed in a brandy cream sauce. Any of their gnocchi dishes are worth a try, too. If you are someone who loves braised meats, the osso buco is calling your name—rich, moist meat cooked at length until it falls off the bone. And get the gnocchi instead of the rice with it! As for meats and fish, the meats are grilled and a number of fish can be prepared to your liking. The restaurant stocks an extensive wine collection, so no doubt you'll find something that goes perfectly with your meal.

Sandwich Kings (Sal, Chris, & Charlie), 33-12 23rd Ave., Astoria, NY 11102; (718) 278-9240; Subway: N/Q to Ditmars; Italian Sub Sandwiches; $. This place is a beloved Astoria institution. They've been open for over 80 years, supplying monster sandwiches to the hungry masses. This is a place that is especially popular with construction workers, firemen, EMTs, and their brethren. It's also popular with those who simply love delicious, no-nonsense sandwiches for not a lot of cash. Perhaps their most infamous sandwich is The Bomb—it is packed to the hilt with meat (turkey, salami, pepperoni, ham, pastrami, and more) cheese (American, swiss, and provolone), and vegetables (roasted red peppers, tomato, onion, and lettuce). This gargantuan sandwich can easily feed you for two or more meals, or feed a few of you for one meal. Of course, there

are other sandwiches available (like the Italian combo), and you can construct your own. A particularly nice mix is lemon chicken, salami, and provolone, with lettuce, tomato, and sweet peppers. You can get a small container of spicy peppers for your sandwich as well. To go with your sandwich is a selection of chips (the jalapeño potato chips are really good) and drinks. You can also buy cold cuts here to take home—they stock primarily Boar's Head meats, but Alps Provisions salami is also available.

Stamatis, 31-14 Broadway, Astoria, NY 11106; (718) 204-8964; Subway: N/Q to Ditmars; Greek; $$. Stamatis is one of the heavy hitters in Astoria's Greek restaurant scene. The place is huge inside—there's a big dining room for large and small groups, as well as a smaller dining room in the back that is adjacent to an outdoor space. The food is solid, well-executed and tasty; this is classic, down-to-earth Greek food that is so satisfying to eat. Classic spreads—creamy taramosalata, lemony *skordalia,* earthy eggplant and tangy *tzatziki*—are delicious scooped up with the accompanying toasted pita triangles. The zucchini croquettes are also wonderful. Meat and fish are excellent here, and if you're up for it, the grilled octopus should not be missed, despite its high price point at $23. When it comes to actual fish, the fried whiting are just lovely. They are served deep fried in a light batter, arrive without the head but still with part of the skeleton, so be careful with the little bones. A squirt of lemon is welcome. This dish, with a side of *saganaki,* would make for a light and flavorful lunch. Or give the chicken souvlaki a try, which comes with a substantial serving of *tzatziki,* and some pita. A side of lemon potatoes goes well with this; with the whiting, the side of sautéed greens is a great match. Whole fish are also on the menu and are priced as the market dictates. Dessert is often on the house, so count yourself lucky if you are offered a piece of *galaktaboureko,* which consists of phyllo and custard—delicious!

Taverna Kyclades, 33-07 Ditmars Blvd., Astoria, NY 11105; (718) 545-8666; Subway: N/Q to Ditmars; tavernakyclades.com; Greek; $$. Kyclades is one of the best-known Greek restaurants in Astoria, and has a huge following with both locals and visitors alike. In the evenings, when you walk by the restaurant, you'll often see a line of people waiting to be seated, and this is with two dining areas full. If you can make it during the day, lunch is a great time to eat there, if only to avoid the crowds. A nice way to start the meal is with a plate of classic dips—taramosalata, *tzatziki,* and *skordalia.* The tarama is so light, it could almost float away, a nice change from the occasional gloppy texture this spread can have. The *tzatziki* has a lot of cucumber in it and less yogurt, giving it a sort of rustic feel. The *skordalia* is smooth, lemony, and garlicky. All dips go well with the bread they serve at the table, which arrives sitting in a little olive oil. The fish and seafood at Kyclades are excellent—fresh and delicious. A must order on the menu is the grilled octopus. This

WESTERN QUEENS WINE SCENE

Astorians like their wine, it's true. Whether it's Greek retsina at a local taverna, cold sake at a local Japanese restaurant, a playful Sauvignon Blanc from New Zealand to go with tapas, or a bottle of Astoria brand prosecco with which to celebrate, you can find it here. The wine scene includes, of course, wine at traditional restaurants, but also at wine bars and small wine shops. Crescent & Vine (p. 27) in the Ditmars area, Winegasm (31-86 37th St., Astoria, NY 11103; 718-932-3331; winegasmeatery.com) in central Astoria, and Domaine (50-04 Vernon Blvd., Long Island City, NY 11101; 718-784-2350; domainewinebar.com) in the Hunters Point neighborhood are all great places to enjoy a glass of wine and some nibbles—in lovely surroundings, to boot.

Astoria and Long Island City are fortunate to have some excellent wine stores. The youngest of the wine shops, Astoria Park

is not calamari (which is squid), but the meaty tentacles of the eight-legged sea creature. It is light, hardly fishy at all, and tastes great with a squirt of lemon juice. In fact, most everything on the menu is good with a squirt (or more) of lemon. The fried sardines are excellent—you can also get them grilled—and are eaten in full, including the crunchy tail but excluding the skeletal insides. Whole grilled fish of varying kinds are available, and are

Wine & Spirits (28-07 24th Ave., Astoria, NY 11105; 718-606-1142; astoriaparkwineansspirits.com), stocks a terrific selection, holds Friday evening tastings, and houses a section of affordable yet delicious, wines. Astoria Wine & Spirits (34-12 Broadway, Astoria, NY 1106; 718-545-9463; astoriawines.com) hangs local art at their shop and holds tasting events, too (look for their cute drawings on their outside sandwich board announcing tastings and other important news). Court Square Wine (24-20 Jackson Ave., Long Island City, NY 11101; 718-707-9911; courtsquarewine.com), one of the largest wine stores in western Queens, and Hunters Point Wines & Spirits (47-07 Vernon Blvd., Long Island City, NY 11101; 718-472-9463; hunterspointwines.com) are both great choices in Long Island City. All of these places stock an excellent selection of wines, and western Queens residents are fortunate to have such great stores in the neighborhood.

also a delight. Main dishes come with a choice of side, and both the lemon potatoes and the *horta* (dandelion) are great options. Dessert, often in the form of *galaktoboureko* (custard in between layers of phyllo), is not served at lunchtime, but it is at dinner, and is often presented gratis.

Tournesol, 50-12 Vernon Blvd., Long Island City, NY 11101; (718) 472-4355; Subway: 7 to Vernon/Jackson; tournesolnyc.com; French; $$. This small bistro on Vernon Boulevard serves up some of the best French food in the borough. On the menu, you'll find all sorts of classic French dishes—mussels and *frites,* French onion soup, escargots, and hanger steak (*avec frites*). Speaking of *frites,* they are fantastic. And if you see a lamb shank on the menu, don't hesitate to order it; they braise meats extremely well. Classic French desserts like crème brûlée and profiteroles anchor the dessert menu, and for something really extravagant, get the *marquise au chocolat,* a chocoholic's dream. Tournesol is also a great brunch spot, serving up various egg dishes, a brunch burger, and *pissaladière,* among others. You'll also get a great cup of coffee with your brunch. At certain times during the year they have special menus, like the winter holidays and for the restaurant's anniversary. Because of their popularity and small dining room it can seem a little cramped in there, but the space is lovely and the service is very good, so you'll no doubt have a wonderful time.

Trattoria L'Incontro, 21-76 31st St., Astoria, NY 11105; (718) 721-3532; Subway: N/Q to Ditmars; trattorialincontro.com; Italian; $$$$. Chef Rocco Sacramone's restaurant has attracted people from all over New York City, thanks to the delicious and well-executed Italian food that comes out of his kitchen. It's also well known for the numerous specials each night, which are recited to each table by the waiters. It really is a long list, so don't be afraid to ask about an interesting special you missed way back at the beginning. If you're going to look to the regular menu for your meal, you'll see an array of dishes—appetizers, salads, meat, fish, pasta, and risotto, not to mention pizza, which is cooked in a brick oven. On the subject of pizza, their Napolitano is fabulous, full of flavor from the olives, capers, tomatoes, and anchovies. To start off, though, consider their simple plate of gentle buffalo mozzarella, accompanied by olive oil and balsamic vinegar. This is one heavenly dish for mozzarella lovers. Their grilled escarole and white beans—*scarola alla brace*—is also excellent. All the homemade pastas are great—their signature pasta, mezza luna ravioli, is filled with mascarpone cheese and pesto, accompanied by an asparagus, brandy, and walnut sauce. Meats and fish are deftly prepared, though some dishes may take more time than others. For a decadent treat, try the rack of lamb or the *filetto di manzo*. This is a filet mignon topped with demi-glace, champagne, and Gorgonzola sauce. Simply fantastico! For dessert, the chocolate pizza is a fun option, and note that desserts, too, make their way onto the specials menu.

Specialty Stores, Markets & Producers

Alps Provisions, Astoria, NY 11103. This wholesaler, located on 23rd Avenue near 45th Street in the Ditmars area of Astoria, makes some of the most sought-after *salumi* (cured pork products) in New York City. They are well known for their sopressata and *cacciotorini,* which are made by hand, the way they have been made for centuries. Their fresh hot and sweet sausages are also excellent. Since they are a wholesaler, the average person can't buy direct from them (well, unless you're going to buy 30 pounds or more), but there are a couple of spots in Astoria where it can be had on a sandwich—the **Sandwich Kings** (p. 73) and **Dave and Tony Salumeria** (p. 87).

Al-Sham Sweets, 24-39 Steinway St., Astoria, NY 11103; (718) 777-0876; Subway: N/Q to Astoria Boulevard; Middle Eastern Bakery. This small shop on the north end of Steinway Street's Little Egypt section has connections to old-timer Laziza Bakery through their Jordanian baker, who spent many years working there. He prepares a variety of sweets, from the familiar baklava to the less familiar *gorayba,* a kind of shortbread cookie.  Their baklava, sticky sweet and stuffed with pistachios or walnuts, is cut in diamond shapes and comes in small and very small portions; the very small is bite-size and extremely cute. Their *gorayba* has the classic texture of slightly soft on the outside with a nice crunch in the middle. The *ma'amoul* comes stuffed with walnuts or dates, and the dough contains semolina, which makes the cookie's texture crunchy and pleasantly gritty. Their thin, sesame-encrusted cookies are only lightly sweet and full of toasty sesame flavor. Their *kanafe* comes in the more familiar combination of *kataifi* and cheese in a sugar syrup, but also comes with slightly sweet cream underneath a crumbly thin cake topped with cashews.

Artopolis, 23-18 31st St., Astoria, NY 11105; (718) 728-8484; Subway: N/Q to Astoria Boulevard; artopolis.net; Bakery/Patisserie. This bakery, tucked away in a little mall on an unassuming stretch of 31st Street in Astoria, is one of the best purveyors of Greek pastries in Queens. There, you'll find the classics—*melakamarona, kourabiedes,* baklava, and *galaktaboureko,* among many. Loaves of bread are also for sale; the six-grain bread is particularly good, as is the decorative olive oil flatbread and olive bread. *Tsoureki,* a traditional Easter bread, is available year-round. The cheese pies are also phenomenal. Additionally, western European pastries are available, like colorful French *macarons,* chocolate mousse, and tiramisu. Grab a cappuccino or latte while you're there, too, and if you have time, have a seat—they have seating both inside and out on the sidewalk.

Astor Bake Shop, 12-23 Astoria Blvd., Astoria, NY 11102; (718) 606-8439; Subway: N/Q to Astoria Boulevard; astor-bakeshop.com; Bakery/Cafe; $. This bakery, with a simple yet stylish dining room in the far western section of Astoria specializes in American-style baked goods, like chocolate cake with choco- 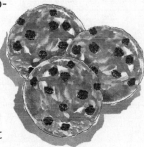 late buttercream frosting, carrot cake, red velvet cupcakes, brownies, and chocolate chip cookies. They also make a spectacular maize almond cake, unfrosted and lightly sweetened, and beautifully moist. Breakfast pastries include muffins and croissants. In addition to all the sweets, they make a great burger, a lentil-based veggie burger, and a really good chicken sandwich, flavored with *ras el hanout,* a spice mixture popular in Morocco. The french fries are also worth your time, complete with a crispy exterior and a fluffy interior. Wash it all down with salted lemonade or a refreshing mint iced tea. Coffee is also available as drip coffee or an espresso-based drink. Their iced coffee is excellent and provides an icy jolt, perfect during a hot New York summer.

Beyond Kombucha, 32-72 41st St., Astoria, NY 11103; (718) 274-2747; beyondkombucha.com; Kombucha Brewery. **Please note that this address is the factory location, and public tours are not given. Beyond Kombucha is a local business based in Astoria that produces artisan kombucha, a fermented tea with origins in China that has numerous health benefits, including probiotics. They make a number of flavors—yerba mate, vanilla rooibos, blueberry, just to name a few—and they also brew kombucha ale, and are the first ones to do so on the east coast. In fact, they are the first brewery in Queens since Prohibition. The name of their kombucha ale is *Mava Roka,* short for Maple Vanilla Rooibos Kombucha. They also make a honey-based kombucha called "Love Potion" (the SCOBY—Symbiotic Colony of Bacteria and Yeast—used to ferment the tea in this case is called a *jun*). Their kombucha is delicious and very easy to drink, and at the time of this writing is available throughout New York City. It's on tap in Queens at **The Queens Kickshaw** (p. 54), Cafe Bar, and **Crescent & Vine** (p. 27). It is also available in bottles at Vitality & Health in Astoria and the Food Cellar in Long Island City.**

Butcher Bar, 37-08 30th Ave., Astoria, NY 11103; (718) 606-8140; Subway: N/Q to 30th Avenue; butcherbar.com; Butcher Shop and Barbecue; $. This is the place for sustainable, humanely raised meats in Astoria. A relative newcomer to the neighborhood, they have been delighting compassionate omnivores with their meats since they opened their doors (which use a faux cleaver as a door handle). Meat, sourced from local farms, D'Artagnan, and Heritage Foods, can be purchased by weight, and they will also grind it for you if you like. Some items are already pre-ground, like the hamburger meat; the "Bob's Burger" is a big hit, made of 80/20 brisket. As mentioned above, they also serve barbecue, made from their locally sourced meats. The ribs are excellent, and the meat just falls off the bone; two kinds of barbecue sauce are available at your table, too. The burnt ends are fantastic, too—full of flavor and super moist, along with that delectable crusty element. Their sides  are well prepared, too. Try the macaroni and cheese, made with large, ridged macaroni and a saucy sauce, or the creamy, tangy coleslaw. They've also got a back garden area that is open during warmer weather.

Buttercup Bake Shop Outlet, 41-21 28th St., Long Island City, NY 11101; (212) 350-4144; Subway: N/Q/7 to Queensboro Plaza or E/M/R to Queens Plaza; Bakery. **Located just north of busy**

and frantic Queensboro Plaza lies the Queens outpost of Buttercup Bake Shop, one of New York City's most highly regarded cupcakeries. The shop is quite small, but for its size, it stocks a wide selection of baked goods—cupcakes, including their famous red velvet, Lady Baltimore, lemon, and Devil Dog, not to mention chocolate and golden (vanilla cake with chocolate or vanilla frosting); bars, including pecan pie, mango, and gigantic Rice Krispies treats; bundt cakes and layer cakes (see below for daily cake specials); and puddings, including their scrumptious banana pudding. They also have daily cake specials—amaretto bundt cake, Tuesday; chocolate sour cream cake, Wednesday; apple walnut cake, Thursday; and carrot cake, Friday. Note that this is not a "day-old" bakery, but the baked goods are discounted, compared to their Manhattan counterparts; they are baked on the premises in the bakery behind the retail outlet. Along with your classy cake, bar, or pudding, consider having a cup of coffee with it. They'll be happy to make you a cappuccino or latte, as well as a *cafe con leche;* iced coffee and tea, lemonade, and iced cappuccinos and lattes are all available. Please note that they have limited hours—they are open Tues through Fri from noon to 3:30 p.m.

Cassinelli Food Products, 31-12 23rd Ave., Astoria, NY 11105; (718) 274-4881; Subway: N/Q to Ditmars; Fresh Pasta. **This is the place in Astoria to get your fresh pasta straight from the source.**

It's a small retail space that stocks Cassinelli's popular pastas, both fresh and frozen, as well as tomato sauce and a few other miscellaneous items. They've been in business since the Depression, making all sorts of pasta, including fettuccine, penne rigate, and fusilli; they also make less common shapes, like orecchiette and trenette. Filled pastas like ravioli and tortellini (meat or cheese) are also available, as are simple pasta sheets, perfect for lasagna and the like. The hours are unconventional for a modern retail establishment, and they close early most days by about 2 p.m.

Chimney Cake, 10-50 Jackson Ave., Long Island City, NY 11101; (718) 786-1818; Subway: 7 to Vernon/Jackson; chimneycakenyc .com; Bakery. This spot in Long Island City focuses on *kürtoskalács,* a celebration pastry from Hungary's Transylvania region. It is normally prepared during special occasions like christenings and weddings, but here in Long Island City these "chimney cakes" are baked every day! The cake itself is made from a yeasted dough that is rolled out into a thin strip and then wrapped around a wooden cylinder, rolled in sugar, and baked in a hot oven. The resulting cake is in a cylindrical shape, with a crispy, sweet outside and a soft inside. Chimney cakes are then rolled in things like nuts and coconut, or eaten unadorned. You are given the option of a dip for the cake, in flavors like chocolate and butterscotch. Nontraditional variants are available, with savory additions of turkey, cheese, and the like. All sorts of espresso coffee drinks are also for sale, which complement the cake.

Croatia Meat, 44-10 Broadway, Astoria, NY 11103; Subway: M/R to 46th Street; Butcher. Apart from their beautiful kebabs, they are also known for their *cevapi,* little casingless sausages that come 18 to a box (about 2 pounds), and cost $10; this is a very good deal. Be warned that when you go to open the tray, you should flip them out on the counter upside down, otherwise you'll "mess them up" (they are not made with casings, so that's understandable). You can pick up a jar of *ajvar* while you're there, too, as well as some pita, and you're on your way to a fantastic meal. There are other cuts in the meat case, but it's really the *cevapi* that is the main draw. That being said, there is a modest selection of products on the shelves, including cookies, noodles, skewers (in case you want to make kebabs yourself), and a lovely orange syrup that contains simply orange juice, sugar, and citric acid.

D&F Italian Deli, 35-13 Broadway, Astoria, NY 11106; (718) 728-2422; Subway: N/Q to Broadway or M/R to Steinway Street; Italian Deli. Fresh bread and giant hanging prosciutti in the front window beckon you into this quality Italian deli on busy bustling Broadway. Inside, the clean space is easy to navigate, with a refrigerated display counter on the left and shelves on the right full of sauces, pastas, and other pantry items. In the refrigerated section, you'll find olives, salads, meats (prosciutto and sopressata, for starters), and a nice variety of cheeses (the list

of cheeses is displayed on the glass), including their own fresh mozzarella. Cured meats hang from the ceiling, including the aforementioned prosciutto in the front, and sausages in the back. D&F also carries not only Virgil's root beer but the more elusive orange cream soda and vanilla black cherry soda made by the same company. Their sandwiches are also excellent—give the eggplant parm a try. Before you leave, pick up some of their homemade prepared dishes like cheese stuffed shells and veal parmigiana, located in the freezer.

Dave and Tony Salumeria, 35-18 30th Ave., Astoria, NY 11103; (718) 728-4850; Subway: N/Q to 30th Avenue; Italian Salumeria. For over 50 years, Dave and Tony Salumeria has provided Italian specialties to the 30th Avenue area in Astoria. They still make their own fresh mozzarella, located up at the counter, and a kind of fresh farmer's cheese (displayed in plastic baskets) reminiscent of ricotta, but more rustic with a larger curd. Next to them on the counter is a big tin of salted, cured anchovies; you'll also find salt cod and other whole dried fish throughout the store. Hanging above the counter are cured meats, including some from Astoria's own Alps Provisions, and in the refrigerated case toward the back of the store are house-made fresh sausages (try the sweet version) and bulk varieties of Astoria's Cassinelli pasta. Dried pasta of all kinds lines the shelves in the back, along with jams and tomato sauces. There's even a box of carob pods for sale—that's something you don't see every day.

Euro Market, 30-42 31st St., Astoria, NY 11102; (718) 545-5569; Subway: N/Q to Broadway; European Market. One of the most noticeable things about this market is the smell of smoked meats that greets you as you enter the store. Look to the left and you'll see the edge of the meat and cheese area, which is the origin of this arresting aroma. There are big slabs of bacon hanging up above the refrigerated case, as well as some dry sausages. In the refrigerated case below are more imported cured meats packaged up, as well as softer forcemeat like liverwurst and braunschweiger. More sausages are piled up on the top of the case, almost haphazardly. In the middle of the refrigerated case are multiple kinds of feta, from the creamy French to the more crumbly Greek. You can also get a sandwich made there—62 different kinds are listed on the board, and you can also compile your own mix and match of meats and/or cheese. Another big draw to Euro Market is the magnificent beer selection. Seriously, it is epic. From Grolsch to lambics, stouts to pilsners, and everything in between can be found here. Apart from this, lots of packaged Polish, Balkan, German, Russian, Italian, and UK products are for sale, as well as tea, coffee, olives, legumes, spices, grains, flours, dried fruits, nuts, chocolates, juices, and jams. There's a selection of yogurts and butters, as well.

Family Market, 29-15 Broadway, Astoria, NY 11106; (718) 956-7925; Subway: N/Q to Broadway; Japanese Market. This is Astoria's only dedicated Japanese market, and it is a joy to explore. It's also open late, too, until 1 a.m. Walk in and you'll see a selection of prepared foods and snacks in a refrigerated case on the right and some Japanese periodicals on the left. The refrigerated case contains bento boxes, *onigiri* (rice balls, though they are triangle shaped—the *ume*/plum is particularly good), sponge cakes, myriad *daifuku* (the small pink unmarked strawberry *daifuku* is especially tasty), green tea drinks, and more. They also carry a nice selection of Kasugai brand gummies and plenty of varieties of Pocky stick cookies. Cooking implements and bento boxes are in the back corner. In the back left corner is a surprisingly extensive selection of Japanese DVDs. In the freezer are dumplings, gyoza, edamame, and the shelves in the center of the store hold curries, soba noodles (including some delicious organic buckwheat soba), Kewpie mayo, miso (organic and conventional), seasonings, green tea, dried squid, nori, *kombu,* and Japanese snacks. You can even find rice bran with which to make *nuka* bran pickles, a kind of fermented vegetable traditionally made in Japan. Additional candies are available, like the addictive HiChew. Family Market has a somewhat high ($15 at the writing of this book) credit card minimum, so be aware of this when you are shopping.

Fresh Start Organic Market, 29-13 23rd Ave., Astoria, NY 11105; (718) 204-7868; Subway: N/Q to Ditmars; fsorganic.com; Organic Market. Both freshly prepared and packaged foods are found at this small but well-stocked natural foods store in the Ditmars section of Astoria. Most of the prepared food—which is made at the store—is suitable for vegans, though they do have some things containing animal products. Particularly satisfying is the tuna sandwich, made with Vegenaise and slathered on slices of whole-grain bread. On the other hand, they also make a delicious seitan salad. Their cookies are also baked there and come in flavors like almond, chocolate fudge, and molasses cocoa (my favorite). Their juices are also delightful, both the fruit- and vegetable-oriented ones. One that is especially easy to suck down in mere minutes is the Cowboy, which is made with blueberry, banana, peach, and apple juices. Fresh Start carries a great selection of whole grains, flours (including sprouted and gluten-free), some legumes, cookies, and crackers, as well as produce, frozen foods, kombucha, canned beans, vinegars, oils, chips, and some bulk goods. They have a small selection of Japanese products like *ume* plums, *kombu,* and dried shiitake mushrooms. And for your cats and dogs, Fresh Start stocks a small selection of Organix and Wellness brands of pet food.

Gian Piero, 44-17 30th Ave., Astoria, NY 11103; (718) 274-8959; Subway: E, M, R, to 46th Street; Bakery. Located a few blocks east of Steinway Street, this is a true old-school New York bakery, complete with a dedicated following of both old timers and new arrivals to the neighborhood. And that following has come about because

the bakery puts out excellent baked goods, from pastries, to cookies, to breads. Consider getting a cannoli—freshly filled—and either plain or covered in chocolate; the pignoli cookies are excellent, as are the lemon and rainbow cookies. Their Italian cheesecake (made with ricotta, not cream cheese) also gets raves from the bakery's devotees. As for the bread, the *pane di casa* is a standout, with a crusty exterior and soft interior. The space inside is frills-free, but there are places to sit and enjoy your pastry or cookie with a cup of coffee, whether it's a shot of espresso or a latte. Bonus: You'll be right across the street from **Sorisso's** (p. 104), another gem in this part of town (hint: Get a ball of the fresh mozzarella to go with Gian Piero's *pane di casa*).

International Meat Market, 36-12 30th Ave., Astoria, NY 11103; (718) 626-6656; Subway: N/Q to 30th Avenue; Butcher. Only the best quality meat is offered for sale at this excellent Astoria butcher shop. This is the kind of place where the line of customers is out the door some days; holidays like Christmas and Easter are particularly intense, so be sure to take a number while you wait. The meat is fresh, prices are fair, and the staff is knowledgeable, helpful, and friendly. They'll cut anything to your specifications, whether you're looking for thick pork chops, a fully butchered chicken for frying, or pork pounded thin for schnitzel. Whole animals can be seen hanging in the windows, too. Game meats like wild boar can also be purchased here. International Meats also stocks D'Artagnan products, Despaña Food chorizo, and Boar's Head hot dogs, and you can pick up staples like olive oil, coffee, and Rao's tomato sauce.

La Casa Del Pan, 38-02 Broadway, Astoria, NY 11103; (718) 726-7946; Subway: N to Broadway or R/M to Steinway Street; Colombian Bakery. This little Colombian bakery is full of Latin goodies. Their *pandebono* (advertised as "Pan De Bono" on the sign outside) are excellent, exhibiting the sweet and savory balance, along with a definite cheesy element that makes a good *pandebono*. Their buñuelos are also delicious, nice and round with a crack along the top. They are a bit crustier than the *pandebono* (and made with wheat flour as opposed to corn and cassava), and less sweet, but good just the same. Their empanadas (baked, not fried) are also good and have a loyal following—the chicken is a favorite and has a touch of sweetness to it; the chicken meat is also substantial. There are a few seats at the bakery, and if you want to hang and you see one, grab it. Try a Manzana Postobón—a popular apple-flavored Colombian soda—for something a little different.

La Guli, 29-15 Ditmars Blvd., Astoria, NY 11105; (718) 728-5612; Subway: N/Q to Ditmars; laguli.com; Italian Bakery. La Guli sells traditional American cakes, Italian/Sicilian pastries and cookies, and homemade gelato. You'll also find some things here that aren't really available elsewhere in Astoria; one of those is the *cuccidata,* a Sicilian fig cookie reminiscent of a Fig Newton. St. Joseph's pastries, including *sfinge,* made with sweetened cannoli cream, and zeppole, made with pastry cream, are a popular treat around mid-March. La Guli's cannolis are very good, as is their Italian cheesecake, made with ricotta and lightly sweetened. Among the American-style cakes are carrot cake (best in the neighborhood), chocolate mousse, and red velvet cake, available both whole and by the slice, and the chocolate strawberry cake is an extremely festive way to celebrate an important day. Their gelato and Italian ices are made in house and have gained quite a following in the neighborhood. The La Guli Chocolate—chocolate gelato with a ribbon of thick caramel throughout—and the hazelnut gelato are real winners, and the spumoni, pineapple, and lemon ices are nice and refreshing on a hot summer's day. Their ices tend to be less sweet than a lot of the others on the market, too.

La Rioja Gourmet Store, 33-05 Broadway; Astoria, NY 11106; (718) 932 0101; Subway: N/Q to Broadway; lariojany.com; Spanish. In the back of this Spanish restaurant, where they serve tapas and sangria, is a small market where you can buy Spanish meats and cheeses, as well as olives, beans, paella rice, vinegars, marinated sardines, and spices (yes, pimenton is stocked). Hams and sausages hang from the ceiling, and cheeses and other items needing refrigeration, including Despaña meat products, are located in the display cooler straight back. Here, you can find necessary ingredients for paella and Spanish tapas. The ever popular *jamón ibérico,* as well as *jamón serrano,* are both for sale, too. This is a lesser-known gem in Astoria, but for those in the know, it's a terrific resource for authentic Spanish products.

Laziza of NY, 25-78 Steinway St., Astoria, NY 11103; (718) 777-7676; Subway: N/Q to Astoria Boulevard; Bakery, Middle Eastern. Laziza has been a mainstay on Steinway Street's Little Egypt section, and has been producing quality Middle Eastern pastries for many years. Looking through the storefront window, you'll no doubt spy some very un-Arabic sweets, but don't get discouraged; as you walk through the front door, it's a different story. Various kinds of baklava and other phyllo-wrapped pastries abound, in different shapes and sizes, from layered to rolled. Other delicious treats include *ma'amoul,* a lightly sweet cookie filled with dates or nuts; *ghraybeh,* a kind of butter cookie with a barely soft outside and crunchy inside; a honey-soaked almond and semolina cake; and *knefe,* a Lebanese dessert made with cheese and *kataifi,* a kind of shredded phyllo. The *knafe* is stunning—with a reddish orange layer on top, it is prepared in a large round pan and served in smaller pieces. It's best served warm.

Malu, 12-09 Jackson Ave., Long Island City, NY 11101; (718) 729-6258; Subway: 7 to Vernon/Jackson; G to 21st/Van Alst; amomand popshop.com; Ice Cream. **Named** after the owners' two children, Matteo and Luc, Malu was conceived as a fun family business that they, their friends, and all their kids could enjoy equally. The space is very child-friendly (the kid-size tables and chairs are adorable), and you'll see lots of families coming in and out. However, the taste of the ice cream is highly appealing to adults and that keeps them coming back as well. This is premium ice cream, rich and smooth, and incredibly creamy, not to mention tasting fabulous. The flavors come through clearly—this ice cream is a joy to eat. Be aware that because they use seasonal ingredients, their roster of ice cream flavors changes, sometimes daily. Excellent flavors they've offered at times are chocolate orange hazelnut; salted caramel; rocket fuel, made with coffee from neighboring **Sweetleaf** (p. 63); chocolate peanut butter; and The Princess, a strawberry ice cream embedded with edible silver glitter. They also make sorbets and frozen yogurts. All their ice cream, sorbet, and frozen yogurt can be purchased in hand-packed containers to take home to enjoy as well. They also offer a number of chocolate confections that will delight both kids and the kid at heart—you'll find packages of chocolate-covered corn flakes and Fritos, chocolate-covered pretzels, and various fruit enrobed in beautiful chocolate.

Mediterranean Foods, 30-12 34th St., Astoria, NY 11103; (718) 728-6166; Subway: N/Q to 30th Avenue; 23-18 31st St.; Astoria, NY 11105; (718) 721-0221; Subway: N/Q to Astoria Boulevard; Greek. Almost anything you'd need to make Greek food can be found at Mediterranean Foods. They have two locations—one in Agora Plaza, a small mall filled with Greek businesses; and one on 34th Street just south of busy 30th Avenue. Here you'll find wonderful olives, peppers, and pickled vegetables in their olive bar; a great selection of feta cheeses, including the creamy Dodonis, Parnassus, and Arahoya styles; homemade spreads like taramosalata, *skordalia,* and *kopanisti,* a spicy feta spread; various breads, some from local Parisi bakery; tinned foods like giant beans, eggplant spread, and favas with tahini; salted and oil-preserved sardines and anchovies, as well as salt-preserved fish; sweet things like jams, Syrian apricot paste,

honey, mastic paste, fruit syrups, and chocolates; dried legumes and grains; frozen spinach pies; Mythos, a Greek beer; and pita bread. Turkish coffee and the *ibrik* in which to prepare it are for sale, as well as stainless pots for housing olive oil (they keep the light out, which is a good thing). And if you're in the market for an evil eye, you'll find them there as well. While you're at the 31st Street location, you can visit the Greek butcher next door, the Greek bakery **Artopolis** (p. 81) one door down, and Omega Wines around the corner. It really is a little bit of food heaven right there in a 2-story mall.

Muncan Foods, 43-09 Broadway; Astoria, NY 11103; (718) 278-8847; Subway: M/R to Steinway Street or N/Q to Broadway; Eastern European Meat Market. Muncan Foods is essentially the center for cured meats in Astoria. When you open the door and walk in, the aroma of smoked and cured meats arrests your sense of smell, and then you see it—all the sausages and slabs of bacon hanging from the ceiling that are responsible for that heavenly bouquet. It really is impressive. Muncan is well known for their double-smoked bacon, which can be eaten raw. And while most of what Muncan offers is pork-based, there are a handful of products made from meats other than the pig. In particular is the pepper lamb salami. The duck pastrami is also a hit and has a smooth, gentle flavor; the duck prosciutto is nice and smoky. The pork rinds, aka *jumari,* are delicious nuggets of fat and pork and can be found at the back of the store. Bite into one and you'll experience both melt-in-your-mouth fat and the substantial crunch of the rest. They are great to snack on. There is just so much sausage, bacon, pastrami, ham, and other cured meats it would take quite a while to get through them all. Best thing is to find something that piques your interest and ask the friendly staff behind the counter what it is and how to use it. They'll also be happy to make suggestions, too, as well as give you samples of things you're curious about. Apart from the meats, you'll find some cheeses, including *brânză de burduf,* a soft sheep's milk cheese that they make there at the store, and isn't found elsewhere in the neighborhood. A variety of *bureks* are also for sale, filled with things like apple, beef, and cheese. Pantry items—cookies, jams, etc.—are also available on the shelves against the wall.

Nile Deli, 25-12 Steinway St., Astoria, NY 11103; (718) 278-6030; Subway: N/Q to Astoria Boulevard; Middle Eastern. There are a number of Middle Eastern delis on Steinway Street's Little Egypt, but this is a favorite. Outside are unmarked bags of thick fluffy pita that is fresh and soft. It's more luxurious than the rough-textured, bland, and almost flatbread-like pitas you find in the average super-market. They also carry many Middle Eastern staples and treats, including olives, rosewater, giant tins of roasted eggplant, dates, rolls of apricot paste (similar to apricot leather), various cheeses, beans, preserved lemons both plain and spicy, and Laziza drink. They also sell hookah supplies, so if you are looking to find a way to smoke shisha at home, they can hook you up.

Parisi Brothers Bakery, 30-17 Broadway, Astoria, NY 11106; (718) 728-5282; Subway: N/Q to Broadway; parisibakeryastoria .com; Bakery. It's easy to find excellent baked goods at Parisi. There, you'll find creamy cheesecake (available whole or in slices); lovely éclairs and cream puffs (the chocolate cream–filled ones are a 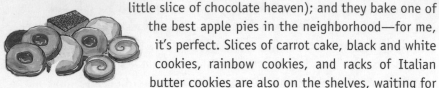 little slice of chocolate heaven); and they bake one of the best apple pies in the neighborhood—for me, it's perfect. Slices of carrot cake, black and white cookies, rainbow cookies, and racks of Italian butter cookies are also on the shelves, waiting for you to take them away. The cannoli are filled fresh, so the shell doesn't have the opportunity to get soggy; this is a very good thing. As for the bread, try the rustic ciabatta bread—crusty on the outside and soft on the inside, with a nice chewy crust.

Parrot Coffee Market, 31-12 Ditmars Blvd., Astoria, NY 11102; Subway: N/Q to Ditmars; European Market. This market, located on Ditmars Boulevard, just around the corner from 31st Street, is full of European delights, with a prime focus on food from the Balkans and Turkey. It's one of the best places in Astoria to find bulk nuts, some of which are already prepackaged in 1-pound bags; dried fruit is also available both in bulk and in bags. Coffee is also displayed in bulk and is self-serve. Chocolates—Milka bars, Kinder, and Ritter-Sport in particular, grace the shelves and the display under the checkout counter. In the refrigerated section you'll find various butters, a wonderful strained goat yogurt from Greece, as well as a Bulgarian whole-milk yogurt made from the milk of grass-fed cows.

You'll also find different kinds of Eastern European and Mediterranean cheeses, slab bacon, Eastern European sausages, and homemade spreads like the pepper paste *zacusca*. You can even get *boza,* a fermented wheat beverage, there. The freezer beyond that contains *bureks* (some from Astoria's own **Djerdan,** p. 28), *cevapi,* phyllo dough, and various sausages. In the back half of the store is a section of bulk olives and bulk European candy. Baklava and savory pies can be purchased, as well as a sweet Hungarian bread filled with nuts and chocolate. Parrot carries the best medjool dates in Astoria, too—huge, sweet, and soft.

Rio Market, 32-15 36th Ave., Astoria, NY 11106; (718) 728-4300; Subway: N/Q to 36th Avenue; Brazilian Market. This is a fairly large market specializing in products in demand by the Brazilian community in Astoria and beyond. Here you can find a selection of *dulce de leche,* yerba mate, coffee, cheeses, breads, frozen sausages, frozen *pão de queijo,* açaí drinks, dried herbs, an array of Goya products, teas, and Brazilian candies and chocolates. Pans and pots for cooking and baking can also be purchased here. Their prepared-food area consists of a small meat counter, a refrigerated dessert section, and a lunch buffet, and there's even a place for you to sit and enjoy your Brazilian meal. Apart from food, you'll find personal care products, CDs and DVDs, sports jerseys, and jewelry.

Rosario's Deli, 22-55 31st St., Astoria, NY 11105; (718) 728-2920; Subway: N/Q to Ditmars; Italian Deli. This is a true gem

in northern Astoria, full of delicious Italian foodstuffs. Their fresh mozzarella—made in house multiple times a day—is a huge draw. Be sure to ask for the freshest batch if you are planning to eat it within an hour of purchase. And speaking of cheese, they stock a number of imports—real Parmesan is available (ask for it grated if you prefer it that way) along with other imported Italian cheeses. They also make their own ricotta in-house. If you are curious about anything, ask for a sample, as they are very accommodating in this respect. They also carry a selection of cured meats—the sweet sopressata is excellent and the guys behind the counter will slice it really thinly for you. In the refrigerated counter, all sorts of prepared foods are available—large rice balls, rectangles of lasagna, tomato and mozzarella salad. Some olives are also available, including the meaty and buttery bright green Sicilian Castelvetrano. They stock a wide variety of dried pastas (including whole wheat and gluten-free pasta); some Cassinelli products—including pasta sheets—in the freezer; canned tomatoes; olive oils; coffee; and chocolates. Behind the counter there are espresso-brewing implements for sale, and they'll also make you a nice cappuccino in the store. Rosario's also makes a great NYC street slice; you'll find the pizza in the back. There are a couple of stools and a small counter where you can eat them, or just take your slices with you and eat them on the go.

Rose & Joe's Italian Bakery, 22-40 31st St., Astoria, NY 11105; (718) 721-9422; Subway: N/Q to Ditmars; Italian Bakery.

This popular Italian bakery in the Ditmars area of Astoria has it all—classic Italian cookies, muffins, black and white cookies, sandwiches, croissants, coffee, and even pizza. Their selection of Italian cookies is extensive—particularly great are the rainbow cookies layered with apricot jam; the lemon drops, a knot-shaped butter cookie covered in tangy lemon icing; chocolate chip orange cookies; and slightly chewy pignoli cookies. They make a variety of muffins—the pumpkin is particularly tasty. Chocolate croissants are an especially excellent treat hot out of the oven. Their breads are really good, too—you'll find Italian semolina bread, a round, braided sweet egg bread, savory black olive bread, and a French-style baguette (ask for "the baguette you make the sandwiches with"). Speaking of these sandwiches, up at the counter are some simple sandwiches—the tomato and fresh mozzarella is excellent. To feel really in the know, though, head back to the bakery to the pizza counter—Rose & Joe's makes the neighborhood's best "bakery pizza"—a thin Sicilian slice that is savory, satisfying, and absolutely delicious. Have them heat it up for you, or just eat it at room temperature; both ways, the pizza tastes great.

SingleCut Beersmiths, 19-33 37th St., Astoria, NY 11105; Subway: N/Q to Ditmars; singlecutbeer.com; Beer. By the time this book is published, SingleCut Beersmiths will be up and brewing beer at their 5,000-square-foot brewery in an industrial area out in northern Astoria, not far from the historic Steinway piano factory. It takes about 15 minutes to walk there from the Ditmars N/Q station—and you'll want to go to experience their tap room and the beers within. In that room, you'll be able to taste their lagers (which they are really fond of), and there's a good chance you'll find IPAs as well. The brewery's owner and head brewer loves hoppy beers, so keep an eye out for those, too. The tap room will not be a bar, but a place to taste the different beers available at any one time and fill up a growler to take home. A stage for live music events is in the works as well. This brewery is a big deal for Astoria, and for beer lovers in NYC—their beer is brewed in Astoria and Astoria only.

Slovak-Czech Varieties, 10-59 Jackson Ave., Long Island City, NY 11101; (718) 752-2093; Subway: 7 to Vernon-Jackson; slovczechvar .com; Eastern European. Don't be fooled into thinking this is just a place for tchotchkes, because it is so much more than that. Its focus is on Eastern European foodstuffs as well as a small selection of nonedible items, like wooden toys and crystal. As you enter you'll see a couple of boxes of bread for sale, and at least one of them is likely to be a medium-sized boule of hearty wheat bread (made in New Jersey). Past that lies a refrigerator that contains *bryndza,* a sheep milk cheese from Slovakia. If you're lucky, there will be some bread dumplings inside for purchase. Along the right side wall is a large selection of cookies, chocolates, and novelties. The Milka bars are great, and the round, colorful hockey puck–shaped items are Fidorka brand wafer chocolates—the coconut flavor is particularly delicious. In the back are both hot and sweet sausages for sale. If you want one that is a bit drier, just ask; they hang a selection of them around the corner in the store to dry them out a bit.

Socrates Sculpture Park Greenmarket, 32-05 Vernon Blvd., Long Island City, NY 11106; Subway: N/Q to Broadway; Farmer's Market. This relatively new greenmarket fills a serious void for those desiring a venue to buy local produce, meats, cheeses, and the like. At the writing of this book, the number of farms is modest, but word on the street is that expansion of vendors would be welcome. Currently, one can buy a nice variety of products—bread, vegetables, fruit, juices, honey, duck products, fresh Mexican specialty products, and sometimes cheese. Cooking demonstrations also take place each weekend, with free tastings afterward. The market is set against the Socrates Sculpture Park—an open space for large scale artistic works—with beautiful views of the East River, Roosevelt Island, and the east side of Manhattan. The park has plenty of lawn space, so a picnic made up of your greenmarket bounty isn't out of the question.

Sorisso's, 44-16 30th Ave., Astoria, NY 11103; (718) 728-4392; N/Q to 30th Avenue; Italian Salumeria. Sorisso's is widely known as the spot for the best fresh mozzarella in Astoria, and it really is delicious. Made in house, it's creamy yet firm, and slices up really well for sandwiches. They make it multiple times a day, and you might even find some of it beautifully braided. They make the sopressata in house, too, flavored with combinations like red wine and garlic, porcini and truffles, olive and fennel, and they also make a spectacular spicy version, too. Samples are gladly given, so don't be afraid to ask (more likely, you'll be offered samples first). Other goodies include rice balls, meatballs, fish cakes, crab cakes, and chicken pot pies. Fresh pasta, both made in house and imported, is available. Give their fresh pasta sheets a whirl in your next batch of lasagna—fresh pasta will transform your dish. Canned homemade pasta sauce is also available to go with that fresh pasta—try the fra diavolo for the spicy treatment. Imported dry pastas are also available, including some gluten-free pastas. Other Italian provisions, like olive oils, vinegars, and fruit spreads are all there for your shopping enjoyment. And if that wasn't all, give the gelato a try; hazelnut is an excellent choice. Finally, their incredible sandwiches deserve a special shout-out. Choose from their great selection, be it the Italian combo, the eggplant parm, or the *rosino panino,* among others.

Terrizzi Pastry Shop, 3514 30th Ave., Astoria, NY 11103; (718) 726-9698; Subway: N/Q to 30th Avenue; terrizzipastry.com; Italian

Bakery. They've been around for close to fifty years, and they're still going strong. Come here for great Italian pastries, including one of the best cannoli in the neighborhood—the shells are crisp and the filling is fresh and sweet. They produce a whole line of Italian butter cookies, which are also excellent; the pignoli cookies are especially good, as are the rainbow cookies. Marzipan is a specialty here, made from Frank Terrizzi's secret recipe—they really are pretty in their delightful fruit shapes, and will no doubt satisfy even the most demanding marzipan fan (I am not in that camp, unfortunately). In the warmer months they offer gelato and Italian ices, which are also very good. There are a few tables at the bakery, perfect for enjoying your sweets with a cappuccino.

Titan Foods, 25-56 31st St., Astoria, NY 11102; (718) 626-7771; Subway: N/Q to Astoria Boulevard; titanfood.com; Greek. Titan is often referred to as the "Greek Zabar's" due to the excellent selection of Greek foods within. You can even find a modest selection of Greek Orthodox icons for purchase on the shelves. Walk through the aisles and you see a bounty of Greek foods—a solid selection of feta cheeses (be sure to ask for a taste as the various cheeses really are different in taste and texture), noodles and pastas, beans and whole grains, and spices. You can purchase either soothing Greek sage tea or mountain tea, each of which is a soporific (meaning, they will relax you). To counter that, you can find Nescafé coffee for both hot and cold frappés, one of Greece's most popular drinks (and high on the caffeine scale). Frozen foods include souvlaki and gyro meats, spanakopita, and *sfoliatakia* squares. They also stock a terrific selection of Greek sweets, like *bougatsa* and *koulouri,* as well as savory baked goods like *tiropita*. Western sweets like chocolate mousse and cheesecake are also available. Nearby is the bread, with a selection of Greek pita (thick with no pocket, and great for toasting or grilling). You can even pick up a Greek-language newspaper or magazine while you're there. Bonus for drivers: They have a small parking lot attached. Bonus for everyone else: They are conveniently located near the Astoria Boulevard subway station.

Triboro Beverage, 41-08 Astoria Blvd., Astoria, NY 11103; (718) 278-0620; Subway: N/Q to Astoria Boulevard; triborobeverage.com. This place is a craft beer lover's paradise—in their words, "odds are, we carry it." When you walk into the retail space, it's easy to get blown away by the selection. That inevitably leads to a serious moment of gratitude for such a place, then the excitement that comes with anticipating exploring their selection. On the shelves you'll see, for example, Crispin hard cider, La Chouffe golden ale, Rince Chochon blonde ale, Lolita Belgian-Style ale, little Reissdorf kegs, Rogue chipotle ale, Allagash Belgian-Style IPA, Maine Beer Company Pepper Ale, and Odyssey Ale; they do carry  a number of Belgian and Belgian-style beers, some in larger bottles. Along with the craft beer are more mainstream brews—"macrobrews" like Coors, Bud, Miller, Dos Equis, and Corona—as well as upscale beers from the bigger breweries such as Brooklyn Brewery, Saranac, Sierra Nevada, Six Point, and Blue Point. Growlers (see the staff for the current selection) and kegs are also available. In addition to their open retail space, they have a refrigerated beer cave, which is basically a big walk-in refrigerator. It's nice and chilly there—a glorious place to be on a hot August day. According to their website, they have over 400 beers, so no doubt you will find something to your liking. Finally, you can pick up ice (dry ice, a block of ice, or a bag of ice cubes), charcoal, and even propane while you're there.

United Brothers Fruit, 32-24 30th Ave., Astoria, NY 11102; (718) 728-7011; Subway: N/Q to 30th Avenue; Produce Market. Fruit and vegetables are pretty much all United Brothers sells, and they display them in a way that can literally stop you in your tracks. Gorgeous piles of apricots, peaches, peppers, beans, potatoes, squash, and citrus can't help but draw you in. You'll find conventionally grown fruit, not organic, but the quality here is quite good. You'll also find produce that is perhaps a little harder to find at your average Key Food or C-Town, too, like small Indian eggplants, cactus pears, fresh favas, Persian cucumbers, Indian spinach, savoy cabbage, callalou, and celeriac. In the middle of the store on ice there are plastic containers of cut-up fruits—melons and berries, mostly—which you can grab and go; containers of Fage yogurt are in the refrigerated case off to the side, which makes for a great pairing with that cut-up fruit. Off to the side of the main store is a narrow addition that houses mostly apples (and some melons), and there are at least a half-dozen different varieties at any one time. For those on a budget, around the corner on 33rd Street is a section of very ripe produce, on sale for 29 cents a pound. Some of the fruit are extremely ripe and can be skipped, but some are just ripe enough for something like jam and sauce-making, so keep an eye out for appropriate bargains.

Street Food

El Rey del Taco Truck, 33-01 30th Ave., Astoria, NY 11103; (347) 754-2966; Subway: N/Q to 30th Avenue; Mexican/Food Truck; $. When anyone thinks about food trucks in Astoria, El Rey is the first one that comes to mind, both because they prepare consistently delicious Mexican fare and because they were real food-truck pioneers in Astoria. They truly are "El Rey" around there. Their original truck has settled into a space on 30th Avenue in front of the Rite Aid, though they do shift east and west of that spot from time to time. Their success in the neighborhood spawned a second truck (and even a onetime restaurant), though it has a more intermittent pattern of attendance over on Ditmars Boulevard near 31st Street. Their menu is modest in its diversity, but what they do make they do very well. The tacos are the most popular menu item, by far. Meats include, but are not limited to, carnitas, *al pastor* (roast pork), chicken, and *lengua* (tongue), and  for $2 a taco, it's easy to try a variety of meats. A close second in popularity is the *torta,* a hefty Mexican sandwich made with a fluffy yet substantial roll, with toppings that include avocado, mayonnaise, and tomato. El Rey del Taco also serves *huaraches,* burritos, and quesadillas, all very good. The truck is out late, ready for your middle-of-the-night craving or path to sobriety after a night of drinking with your pals.

King of Falafel and Shawarma, 30th Street and Broadway, Astoria, NY 11106; (718) 838-8029; Subway: N/Q to Broadway; thekingfalafel.com; Halal Street Food; $. Freddy, the proprietor of this cart, has won the coveted Vendy Award twice—in 2009 and 2010—and shows no sign of resting on his laurels. He and his assistants are out there 6 days a week from 11 a.m. to 9 p.m., creating some of the best street food in all of Queens. Take your pick—awesome tubular shaped falafel, chicken and rice, beef and chicken kebabs, and shawarma. Be sure to get both white sauce and hot sauce, no matter what you order. And while you're in line, you might be lucky enough to be handed a freshly made falafel to munch on while you wait; his cart is extremely popular, so there is often a line of people waiting to order. Many of the dishes come with a side salad, which is made up of lettuce and tomato and their wonderful pickled vegetables—try the pickled turnip!

LIC Food Truck Lot, 43-29 Crescent St., Long Island City, NY 11101; Neighborhood: Long Island City; facebook.com/ LICfoodtruckLOT; Various; $. In the summer of 2011 the Rockrose Development Corporation, a local luxury real estate owner-manager-developer, donated one of their parking lots to serve as a safe home for NYC food trucks. At the time, food trucks were running into problems with the police and resistance from brick-and-mortar food establishments they were parked in front of, so a space dedicated just to food trucks seemed to make sense. It certainly is a popular spot in Long Island City, and local workers make a beeline to the trucks to sate their hunger at lunchtime. The range of offerings is extensive—you'll find trucks like Green Pirate (juice), Rickshaw Dumpling Truck (Chinese), Pera Turkish Tacos (Mediterranean), Coolhaus (ice cream sandwiches), and Mexico Blvd (Mexican). Trucks change from day to day, so keep an eye on their Facebook page for the week's lineup and also their schedule—sometimes the lot is closed for a day. The lot is not open on weekends.

Wafels & Dinges, 31st St. near Ditmars, in front of the Citibank, Astoria, NY 11105; Subway: N/Q to Ditmars; wafelsand dinges.com; Belgian Waffles; $. It was a happy day when the Wafels & Dinges truck appeared on 31st Street, a short distance from the northwest exit from the Ditmars subway station; they are there every Sunday morning and afternoon. The guys in the truck offer both sweet and savory Belgian waffles, and the waffles themselves come in two styles—light and crispy, aka the Brussels Waffle, and the soft and chewy, aka the Liège Waffle. Various toppings can be put on your waffle, the first one being free with subsequent ones costing $1 each. Try the *spekuloos,* which is a spread made of spice cookies popular in Belgium. Other sweet toppings include Nutella, real Grade A maple syrup, walnuts, strawberries, and chocolate fudge. In the summer they offer ice cream made by their friend Benoit Gerin (former Jean Georges pastry chef), in flavors including *spekuloos,* Tahitian vanilla, and framboise-lambic. Ice cream can be purchased on its own or as a topping for your waffle. On the savory side of things, the pulled pork is really tasty and comes with coleslaw and a "coolickle," which is a pickle mixed with Kool-Aid, making it bright red (it sounds unusual, but it's worth trying). Other savory toppings include bacon and maple syrup, and chili con carne with sour cream and cilantro.

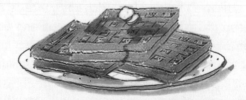

Sunnyside & Woodside

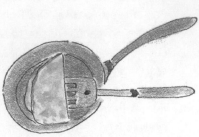

Sunnyside and Woodside are neighboring communities just east of Astoria and Long Island City. For a time, Sunnyside was part of Long Island City, but these days it is considered to be its own entity. Both neighborhoods are accessible by the 7 train, from 40th Street/Lowrey in Sunnyside to 69th Street in Woodside.

Sunnyside is a small area that is not terribly well known outside of Queens. The longtime Irish influence is especially evident in the strip of Irish pubs full of great food and drink along Queens Boulevard, not to mention the wonderful Butcher Bar, a local grocery full of Irish and UK products, and house-made Irish specialties like black sausage. Just before St. Patrick's Day, the St. Pat's For All parade marches along Skillman Avenue, highlighting Sunnyside's diversity while recognizing the Irish roots of the neighborhood.

Woodside is a primarily residential neighborhood, and also ethnically diverse. However, it once had the largest Irish population outside of Ireland. A lot has changed since then, but the area still retains its Irish flavor—it's a popular destination on St. Patrick's Day.

Asians also make up a large percentage of the population of Woodside, and that is reflected in restaurant offerings. One of the best—if not the best—Thai restaurants in all of New York City, Sripraphai, is located in Woodside, attracting people from all over the city. There is also a strong Filipino presence in Woodside, evident in restaurants and markets from about 63rd Street to 70th Street. Some of the best Filipino restaurants are in Woodside's Little Manila, including Ihawan, Engeline's, and Krystal's.

Foodie Faves

Aubergine Cafe, 49-22 Skillman Ave., Sunnyside, NY 11377; (718) 899-1735; Subway: 7 to 46th Street; auberginecafe.com; Cafe/Coffee Shop; $. Aubergine Cafe is one of the nicest spots in Sunnyside in which to relax with a cup of coffee or tea. They use Irving Farm coffee, roasted about 90 miles upstate from NYC in historic Millerton, a small Hudson Valley town. Coffee is brewed by either drip method or as espresso, so a cappuccino or latte is easy to obtain. Tea is also available. They offer a nice selection of baked goods, from a duo chocolate mousse cake, to cheesecake, to carrot cake, and more. They are rich, so a little goes a long way. Sandwiches are also on the menu—particularly nice is the smoked turkey sandwich, paired with brie, and served on a baguette with honey mustard. The fresh mozzarella, roasted red pepper, basil, and olive spread sandwich is also delicious. Sit along the Skillman Avenue side of the dining room for some good people-watching.

Claret Wine Bar, 46-02 Skillman Ave., Sunnyside, NY 11104; (718) 937-7411; Subway: 7 to 46th Street; claretwinebar.com; Wine Bar; $$. This is Sunnyside's only wine bar and attracts a variety of people, from university students to young professionals to neighborhood regulars. The wine list is well thought out and the food accompanies the wine well. As for the wine, both reds and whites are available, either by the glass, the carafe, or the bottle. On the lighter side of the menu are cheese and charcuterie plates, delicious citrus-marinated olives, and even a chef's tasting plate. More elaborate dishes include pizzas, tartines, and panini. There's even crème brûlée and molten chocolate cake to end your night on a sweet note.

De Mole, 45-02 48th Ave., Sunnyside, NY 11377; (718) 392-2161; Subway: 7 to 46th Street; demolenyc.com; Mexican; $. On a quiet corner on the southern side of Sunnyside lies De Mole, a modest restaurant serving up delicious Mexican standards of tamales, tacos, enchiladas, and the like. Pull back the thick curtain separating the dining room from the street entrance, and you'll see the simple and relaxing space, light on the decorations, with proclamations from the city for their positive contributions to the business environment in the local community adorning the wall. A bowl of the mild guacamole, composed of avocado, onions, and tomatoes and topped with fresh cilantro, is a great starter, and comes with yellow corn tortilla strips. The chicken dishes are worth passing over for the beef and pork, which are much more flavorful. The tacos are a particularly strong element on the menu, prepared simply with fresh ingredients. The *carne enchilada* (spicy pork) taco is pleasantly spicy, topped with cilantro and raw onions, and accompanied by a slice of lime that adds just the right amount of acid to the rich taste of the pork. Ask for the spicy red sauce in the squeeze bottle; it adds additional depth of flavor. This magical red sauce is good on the *carne asada* (steak) taco, too. The brisket quesadilla—slightly saucy meat in a hard shell—should not be missed. Larger plates are also available, filled with enchiladas, fajitas, and burritos. Vegetarian and vegan guests can also enjoy the food at De Mole, whether it's the seitan fajitas or the vegetable burrito. Special items like squash blossom quesadilla and the huitlacoche quesadilla are also available. Be sure to get something to drink, too—they offer bottled beer (including Corona), Pellegrino, Mexican soda and Coca-Cola, *aguas frescas* (hibiscus, tamarind, and lime), as well as a carafe of white sangria, flavored with thin slices of orange, lemon, and apple, which is very refreshing and the perfect accompaniment to the food on a warm day.

El Nuevo Izalco, 64-05 Roosevelt Ave., Woodside, NY 11377; (718) 533-8373; Subway: 7 to 61st Street or 69th Street;

Salvadoran; $. *Pupusas* are the national dish of El Salvador, and they're a tasty one at that. Masa is filled with ingredients like meat, cheese, or beans, flattened into a disc and panfried. Regardless of the filling, they must be eaten with *curtido,* a pickled/fermented spicy cabbage condiment. That, with the *pupusa,* is one of the most delicious combinations out there. For an extra indulgence, get the *crema* (a slightly looser version of sour cream) and the hot sauce. A side of sweet plantains is a great accompaniment as well. Suprema, a Salvadoran beer, is perfect for washing it all down.

El Sitio, 68-28 Roosevelt Ave., Woodside, NY 11377; (718) 424-2369; Subway: 7 to 69th Street; Cuban; $. One of the best Cuban sandwiches in New York City is found here—it's well balanced and extremely easy to eat, what with its combination of thinly sliced roast pork, ham, swiss cheese, pickles, mustard, and a garlic sauce called *mojo.* The bread is soft and the sandwich is pressed in a *plancha,* a heavy, square sandwich press. During the pressing process, they'll lift the lid of the press a couple of times and apply a little more *mojo* to the sandwich. The result is just fabulous—meaty, garlicky, and tangy. As for everything else, the food is homestyle Cuban and very good. Their rice and beans (they'll offer you black beans or red beans, but black beans are more authentic) are very tasty and satisfying. Their lunch special is a good deal, as well as delicious and filling—$6.50 (including tax) for a portion of meat, like garlic chicken, with rice and beans. Eat in their lovely dining room or take your food to go. When you stop in for takeout, you can order at the bar (the place is split into two rooms, a dining room and a bar/luncheonette) and wait for your food there, sitting on one of their seriously retro stools. While you're there, enjoy an *espresso cubano* or *cafe con leche,* both of which are well made and smooth.

Engeline's Restaurant, 58-28 Roosevelt Ave., Woodside, NY 11377; (718) 898-7878; Subway: 7 to 61st Street; Filipino; $. While the majority of Filipino businesses and restaurants are off 69th Street, just 10 blocks away, this Filipino spot is a nice addition to this part of Woodside. Walk in and you'll see a long case on the right full of beautiful baked goods, and seating on the right for all the hot savory foods on the menu. The staff is very friendly and happy to describe anything they offer, even if you have no famil-iarity with Filipino food. Their chicken empanadita is on the sweet side, with chicken mixed with carrots and raisins. The cupcake-size *macapuno* tart is delicious, with a sturdy yet not tough crust, a caramelized top, and delicious sweet *macapuno* coconut inside (the *macapuno* is a kind of coconut that grows in the Philippines). The *braso* is two layers of thick, sweet meringue with egg custard sandwiched in between—it is light and delicious. The *ensymada* is a lightly sweetened, enriched egg dough with a thin layer of butter and a little bit of sugar spread on top, and is great for breakfast with coffee or tea. They also serve traditional savory Filipino food—*lumpia,* noodles, meats, chicken, seafood—but I really like coming here for the baked goods, since they do such a great job with them.

Fresca La Crepe, 39-82 61st St., Woodside, NY 11377; (347) 768-1488; Subway: 7 to 61st Street; French Crepes; $. Walk by anytime this little creperie is open, and you'll spy owner and chef Patricia Chu hard at work creating crepes on her two large, round electric griddles. She is also the person who takes your order, which she does with a smile. Head back several steps to the dining space and hang for a bit, and when your crepe is ready, she'll deliver it, folded over into a triangle, right to your seat. Savory crepes include the classic gruyère and ham, and the Margarita—fresh tomato, mozzarella, and basil. Sweet crepes include a delicious simple sugar crepe or one filled with luscious Nutella; ask about the *speculoos* spread, too. Smoothies, coffee, and tea are available, and for something a little different, try a Thai iced tea with tapioca balls. Along the wall where the short bar is, there are cans of paper and colored pencils for the kids to play with.

The Haab, 47-22 48th Ave., Sunnyside, NY 11377; (718) 729-4838; Subway: 7 to 46th Street; thehaab.com; Mexican; $. This little cafe, right on the corner of 48th Street and 48th Avenue, is a great place for delicious Mexican food in the neighborhood. The majority of their clientele speaks Spanish, and the regulars seem to know each other—but everyone is welcome, no matter what language you speak. The place is extremely cheery—colorful bottles of Jarritos line the front window, colorful decorations hang from the ceiling, and the decorative lights are beautifully multicolored. Mexican popular music plays over the sound system, and *telenovelas* play on mute on the TV against the back wall. The staff is really friendly, too. *Aguas frescas* are a regular thing here, and they are delicious—not overly sweet and very refreshing. The pineapple is fantastic, and comes with chunks of real fruit in the glass. At any time of the day the huevos rancheros hit the spot, and they are expertly done—two thin corn tortillas topped with an egg each—perfectly cooked with a loose yolk, topped with a pleasantly spicy ranchera sauce, *crema*, and grated cotija cheese. It comes with some pan-roasted red potatoes, which are cooked well—not an undercooked potato in the bunch, and some of them even have a little bit of a crust on them. Red and green salsas—both with a little bit of a kick to them—are served along with your meal. The coffee is good diner-style brew, and goes well with one of their Mexican pastries, which are very fresh. You can order tacos, enchiladas, quesadillas, *chilaquiles* (recommended), and other classic Mexican dishes, too. They are open early in the morning until late at night, so you can easily satisfy your cravings there during most of the day.

Ihawan, 40-06 70th St., Woodside, NY 11377; (718) 205-1480; Subway: 7 to 69th Street; ihawan2.com; Filipino; $. If Filipino barbecue is what you're craving, look no further than Ihawan in Woodside's Little Manila neighborhood along Roosevelt Avenue. You actually enter the restaurant through the kitchen, then go up the stairs and turn left. The dining room opens up from there. Their pork barbecue skewers are a must order, and you can find a number of other delicious porky items, too. But start out with the Lumpia Shanghai, delicious tiny eggrolls of fried goodness. It's hard to go wrong with the *sinigang na baboy,* which features—yes—pork. The *sinigang na isda* is made with fish and is also very good. If you are a pork lover, the *lechon kawali* should be seriously considered—deep fried pork belly in all its crispy, fatty deliciousness has a wonderful buttery texture and the dipping sauce is a nice tangy foil to the richness of the pork. For a non-pork dish, the chicken adobo is worth a try, and the chicken skewers made from dark meat are also excellent, charred by the grill and slightly sweet. For dessert, try the *halo halo,* made with crushed ice, fruit, red and white beans, milk, and custard. It's a fun dessert, for sure. Other options are flan and the Filipino dessert *ginataang,* which is a rice pudding mixed with corn or beans. And if you are a bubble tea fan, get the *sago,* a sweet drink with a slight melon flavor, which contains large multicolored tapioca pearls.

I Love Py, 43-16 Greenpoint Ave., Sunnyside, NY 11104; (718) 786-5534; Subway: 7 to 46th Street; ilovepybakery.com; Paraguayan; $. It's not easy to find Paraguayan food in this city, so it's a real treat to eat at this little Paraguayan spot on one of Sunnyside's main drags. Callouts for fresh juices and empanadas (both are delicious) grace the front windows of this neat and clean restaurant. As far as empanadas go, they are simple and straightforward with minimalist fillings. The crust of the fried empanadas is crispy and the use of egg in the beef empanada is a nice touch. The ground beef is simply spiced inside deep-fried pastry goodness. *The empanada de choclo* is slightly sweet (just ever so), and contains creamy melted white cheese studded with corn kernels; the texture is luxurious. A popular item on the menu is the *chipa guazu,* which is a traditional, soft-baked corn pudding; it's also considered to be a casserole. Made from eggs, cheese, and corn, among other things, it has a pleasingly strong corn flavor and a texture that almost melts in your mouth—the softness on your tongue is wonderful. It is usually eaten with stew or some such thing, but it's so filling, flavorful, and satisfying, it can be eaten on its own. Add a little of their red hot sauce if you'd like to spice it up slightly. Daily soups are on the menu, and if you see that it's an option, be sure to try the *vori vori,* a traditional Paraguayan soup made with a rich broth, chicken, and little grape-sized balls made of corn flour and cheese. Their fresh juices are very good and definitely worth getting. Good choices are the orange, strawberry, or pineapple, and each drink is made from actual fruit, not commercial fruit puree. They are light and refreshing and go perfectly with all the Paraguayan comfort food you're enjoying at the restaurant. On your way out, consider perusing their desserts, found up front—there's rice pudding, flan, and some cakes. You can also buy round breadsticks (reminiscent of the Italian *taralli*), *alfajores,* and even a Paraguayan flag.

Krystal's Cafe and Pastry Shop, 69-02 Roosevelt Ave., Woodside, NY 11377; (718) 898-1900; Subway: 7 to 69th Street; Filipino; $. One of the best things about Krystal's is the all-you-can-eat lunch buffet that takes place upstairs via the stairs in the back on weekdays from 12 to 3 p.m. There's always a nice variety

Little Manila:
Woodside's Filipino Community

Get off at the 69th Street stop on the 7 line and you'll find yourself at the focal point of Little Manila, Woodside's vibrant Filipino neighborhood, whose boundaries are generally considered to be 63rd to 71st Streets. Here there are shops, restaurants, and bakeries catering to the Filipino community. The largest Filipino population in NYC resides in Queens, so you can expect there to be a good number of places to meet their needs.

Restaurants such as Krystal's Cafe (p. 121), Fritzie's Bakeshop (69-10 Roosevelt Ave., Woodside, NY 11377; 718-507-0205), Fiesta Grill (69-12 Roosevelt Ave., Woodside, NY 11377; 718-205-4010; fiestagrill.net/woodside), and Renee's Kitchenette and Grill (69-14 Roosevelt Ave., Woodside, NY 11377; 718-476-9002) are right around that 60th Street station, with Ihawan (40-06 70th St., Woodside, NY 11377; 718-205-1480; ihawan2.com) slightly to the east. They all put out good, classic Filipino food, with Ihawan having a reputation for excellent Filipino barbeque. Further toward Sunnyside is Tito Rad's (p. 130) and Engeline's (p. 117). There's even a Jollibee—the most popular fast-food restaurant in the Philippines—on Roosevelt near 62nd Street, complete with their giant bee mascot statue standing outside the restaurant, inviting you in. Across from that is Red Ribbon Bake Shop (p. 148), an extremely popular bakery in the local Filipino community.

of things in the buffet—*lumpia* (spring rolls), chicken cooked in white sauce (with tangy green olives!), *dinuguan* (my favorite), *pansit bami* (noodles), chicken adobo, fried chicken and tilapia, and *inihaw na baboy* (pork). Dessert is also part of the meal, and you might find flan, *ube* cake, or *ginatan mais* (a kind of loose tapioca pudding studded with sweet corn kernels). Drinks consist of American soda and water; beer is also available, including the Filipino brand San Miguel. And you can enjoy all of this for just over $8, which you pay after you eat; also note that you can't take any of the buffet food home. When you get downstairs after your meal, don't forget to stop at the baked goods counter, which is filled with a solid selection of Filipino pastries. The *mamon* is big and tasty, the *ube* cake light and sweet, and their *halo halo* is excellent. They also sell a lot of *pan de sal* each week. Bottom line—this is a great place in Queens to find Filipino comfort food, and at a great price to boot.

La Flor Bakery and Cafe, 53-02 Roosevelt Ave., Woodside, NY 11377; (718) 426-8023; Subway: 7 to 52nd Street; laflorrestaurant .com; Mexican Bistro; $$. This charming corner spot on Roosevelt Avenue is a local favorite all day, but it's particularly popular for weekend brunch. Evenings (every day except Monday) are also nice because of the presence of live jazz music. At breakfast, it's nice to stop by for a cup of American diner-style coffee and one of their homemade scones. They warm it up for you, which crisps up the outside a bit (the crunchy sugar topping helps in that department, too), while the inside is soft; the combination makes it kind

of crumbly, which is the mark of a quality scone. They offer a number of omelets, scrambles, and other egg dishes, including the classic huevos rancheros. It's served with refried black beans and two sunny-side up eggs. The red and green sauces present in the dish are not spicy at all; you'll have to doctor it up with Tabasco to make it spicy. In fact, most of the Mexican dishes are on the mild (but not bland) side. Popular dishes for later in the day are the crab cakes (served with a light chipotle aioli), pork loin stew, and the lamb shank. Mexican *tortas,* tacos, and quesadillas are also well done. There really isn't another place like this in Woodside, which makes it really special.

Mi Bolivia, 44-10 48th Ave., Sunnyside, NY 11377; (718) 784-5111; Subway: 7 to 46th Street; Bolivian; $. To tell if they are open, look for the neon "open" sign, and when it's lit, it's all good. When you are seated, you want to go straight for the *salteña,* which they do extremely well. This is the Bolivian version of the empanada, and it must be one of the tastiest things in Queens. It consists of a firm yet tender baked shell that is savory with some sweetness to it, filled with a thick meat stew of sorts. Mi Bolivia prepares both beef and chicken *salteñas,* though the chicken is especially good. The filling is made of very tender chicken, hard-boiled eggs, and a thick sauce. The combination is savory, meaty, and a little sweet. You can add some of their spicy green sauce, which tastes mostly of green chilies, called *llajua* (there is no vinegar bite as there is with so many hot sauces from Latin America, but it's very spicy).

On the empanada subject, they do make a *humita,* which is a sweet, corn husk–wrapped empanada containing sweet corn, some spices, sugar, and cheese, and it's a lovely kind of dessert. The menu at Mi Bolivia is extensive and offers dishes with chicken, pork, beef, and fish. A lovely, simple sandwich is the *sandwich de chola*—roast pork, pickled vegetables (carrots and onions), and crispy pork skin layered between a split toasted bun. It's porky, tangy, and the bun is just the right amount of bread. Another dish that is absolutely worth ordering is the *sopa de mani,* a soup made of ground peanuts, beef broth, vegetables, and french fries. Chunks of beef are also present.

Natural Tofu, 40-06 Queens Blvd., Sunnyside, NY 11104; (718) 706-0899; Subway: 7 to 40th Street; Korean; $. Sunnyside is lucky to have this excellent Korean restaurant, popular with the local Korean community, conveniently located steps away from the 40th Street subway station. The menu is fairly small compared to a lot of Korean restaurants, but the options on it are tasty. As the name of the restaurant implies, tofu dishes are a major part of the menu, in the form of *sundubu,* a sort of tofu casserole/stew made with uncurdled tofu. This dish ranges from a totally vegetarian version to ones with seafood or meat, including beef intestine. Bibimbap, one of the most popular and well-known Korean dishes, also graces the menu—it's full of rice, vegetables, pork, and an egg, and lots of flavor. It is served in a stone bowl, which allows the rice on the bottom to develop a wonderful crust; the bowl arrives very hot, so do not touch it, or you'll burn yourself. Be sure to turn the egg under into the hot vegetables and rice below, so that it will cook. Another home run on the menu is the crispy kimchi pancake, which really does arrive crispy! It's fairly large and arrives cut into slices like a pizza. It's everything a kimchi pancake should be—savory, salty, and spicy, and the crispness makes the pancake extra special. The BBQ chicken also gets high marks—be sure to ask for it spicy for best results.

Quaint, 46-10 Skillman Ave., Sunnyside, NY 11104; (917) 779-9220; Subway: 7 to 46th Avenue; quaintnyc.com; New American; $$. This comfortable yet elegant spot on the edge of Sunnyside Gardens is perfect for food lovers looking for a place to enjoy a seasonal meal. A big draw on the menu is the Monday night all-you-can-eat mussels and *frites* from 5 to 9 p.m. The mussels come in either a white wine broth or a coconut curry broth, and the fries come with the skin on. It really is a lovely way to enjoy a Monday evening here. The soup of the day is worth paying attention to, which is usually loaded with flavor; other specials are also worth considering. The rest of the menu consists of roasted and grilled meats, a burger, and salads, which are all very fresh. The tasty baby arugula salad comes with blue cheese, pears, and almonds; get the vinaigrette on the side for maximum control over the greens-to-dressing ratio. The salmon (not farm raised) on Israeli couscous is grilled and juicy—not one piece of it was dry and overcooked when we had it. The toothsome Israeli couscous is studded with moist bits of sun-dried tomato, which are absolutely delicious. The cocktails tend to be crisp and citrusy, which is particularly appropriate in the Farmer 75, essentially a very nice gin and tonic. Desserts change from time to time, but if you find the apple cobbler as an offering, definitely get it. It's served warm with vanilla ice cream and a toffee sauce drizzled on top.

Salt and Fat, 41-16 Queens Blvd., Sunnyside, NY 11104; (718) 433-3702; Subway: 7 to 40th Street; saltandfatny.com; New American; $$. This is the hippest restaurant in Sunnyside. The restaurant is no secret in NYC—shortly after opening in the early evening, it's not unusual to find a line with a 30- to 60-minute wait (reservations are not accepted). When you do get seated, however, be sure to savor the complimentary bacon-fat popcorn, full of salty, smoky goodness. The menu is pretty small—fewer than two dozen items on it—so you could order everything on the menu if your party is big enough (and yes, people have done this). The drink menu is also small, consisting of a few soft drinks (soda, iced tea, sparkling water), wine, and beer (the Apricot Wheat from Ithaca Beer Company is fabulous). Standouts on the menu include . . . well, pretty much everything. The BLT salad is incredible, with the addition of lobster to the mix along with bacon, heirloom tomatoes, and a house-made herb ranch dressing. The Korean BBQ wraps—marinated hanger steak, pickled daikon, and miso—are also excellent. The braised pork belly tacos also get high marks. For something both traditional and different, treat yourself to the oxtail terrine, a cube of terrine sitting atop mushrooms with a caramelized onion puree—glorious. Salt and Fat also has a small dessert menu—the panna cotta is a knockout and changes flavors from time to time (lime, lychee, etc). The Rice Krispies treat is also a lot of fun.

Souk El Shater, 43-03 Queens Blvd., Sunnyside, NY 11104; (718) 392-2702; Subway: 7 to 40th Street; Lebanese/Mediterranean; $. Back in 2011, there was a huge sigh of sadness when El Shater shut its doors. Imagine the relief felt across the city when Souk El Shater opened up, owned and run by one of the brothers behind the afore-mentioned El Shater. The focus is Lebanese food, and they do it very well. The consummate dish is falafel, and it's fantastic. The balls, made with chickpeas and fava beans, are cooked then wrapped in a lavash-type flatbread. Tahini sauce and pickled vegetables are part of the sandwich, and if you like, get their excellent hot sauce added (recommended). It's heartening to see this falafel sandwich arrive wrapped up like a tube, instead of the usual boat-like configuration with a pocket pita—it makes for a much neater/less messy experi-ence. A sweet peach nectar, Chaba, is a great way to wash it all down. Another very popular item is the chicken shawarma, which also comes with pickled vegetables, and *toom,* a pungent paste/sauce of garlic, oil, and a little yogurt. All meats are halal, so no pork is present, although beef and lamb are. Note also all the dif-ferent pies in the display case—spinach, meat, and cheese; everything is made there.

Sweets are also available, including baklava, substantial *ma'amoul* filled with dates, and the *kounafa* with cheese—a thin layer of nabulsi cheese topped with shredded phyllo. Souk El Shater mainly focuses on takeout, but there are about four stools on which to sit and enjoy your sandwich.

Thailand's Center Point, 63-19 39th Ave., Woodside, NY 11377; (718) 651-6888; Subway: 7 to 61st Street; thaifooddirect.com/ thailandscenterpoint; Thai; $. This spot located down the street from the neighborhood's dominant Thai restaurant, **Sripraphai** (p. 136), is part restaurant, part Thai market. The market is located right as you walk in, with stacks of big bags of rice to your left, sauces, vinegars, and the like a little further down from you, and there's even a refrigerated case containing Thai sausages on the right. The dining area is on the left side of the space, and inside it feels somewhat beach-like—this could have something to do with the casual look, the high ceilings, and the ample sunlight that pours into the restaurant. The menu is very accessible, with a lot of familiar items on it, as well as some more unusual ones for those looking for something a little different. Be sure to check the tall blackboard featuring the specials of the day, like Crispy Fish Basket or Thai Bibimbap. The appetizer section is probably the most conventional, with things like curry puffs (their version looks like tiny samosas), fish cakes, summer rolls, and chicken satay. But turn to the salad section, and you'll find some real gems. The pork *larb*—a warm ground-meat salad—is phenomenal, bursting with fresh flavors of mint, lime, and onion, along with a beautiful porkiness. Look to the curries and you'll find a couple that don't contain coconut milk—the more familiar Jungle Curry and the less ordinary Sour Curry, which is truly pleasantly sour, and contains perfectly cooked vegetables like carrots, cabbage, and broccoli. It's very good with duck, which is also cooked to perfection. The tamarind fried rice, served with an egg (preserved in a brine, and quite salty, especially the yolk) and shredded sweet pork, is another unusual menu item, and is absolutely delicious. Be sure to add a squirt of lime juice for extra flavor.

Tito Rad's Grill & Restaurant, 49-12 Queens Blvd., Sunnyside, NY 11377; (718) 205-7299; Subway: 7 to 46th Street or 52nd Street; titorads.com; Filipino; $. Quite a bit farther west than the rest of Queens' Little Manila, Tito Rad's serves up delicious Filipino food in modest surroundings. Walk into the restaurant and your ears might be assaulted with the sounds of Filipino television shows, but don't let that dissuade you from sticking around—the food is worth it. If you have questions about any of the menu items, the waitstaff is happy to answer your questions, too. A great way to start the meal is with the Sizzling Sisig—pork belly marinated with lemon and hot peppers, then finely chopped and served on a sizzling hot plate (it sizzles loudly). You will be asked if you want egg on it, so be sure to say yes. It arrives raw on top of the meat, and mixing it in will help balance the richness of the pork. Another tasty appetizer is *ukoy,* a bean sprout fritter that contains shrimp and vegetables. It's mixed together and fried in a batter, resulting in a 4- or 5-inch giant fritter—be sure to enjoy it with the accompanying vinegar and garlic sauce. Tito Rad's has a number of tamarind-based soups on the menu, and a particularly delicious one is the *sinigang na baboy,* which contains pork and vegetables. It's deliciously sour and the pork is so tender. A much milder option is the *manok sa gata,* which is chicken on the bone cooked in coconut milk with ginger; this coconut broth is velvety and smooth. For dessert, a good choice is the Tito's Delight, which brings together three of their most popular desserts—the purple *ube* "ice cream," which is more like a thick pudding; a dense flan with a deep caramel notes, and the cassava cake. For those desiring a Filipino breakfast, they serve *tapsilog* (thinly sliced beef, fried egg, garlic fried rice) and *longsilog* (longanisa sausage, egg, and garlic fried rice), among others in the *silog* (fried rice and egg) family.

Turkish Grill, 42-03 Queens Blvd., Sunnyside, NY 11104; (718) 392-3838; Subway: 7 to 40th Street; Turkish; $. One of the coolest parts of the decor at Turkish Grill is the display of hanging evil eyes on the back wall. The rest of the dining room is comfortable, with an attentive and professional staff. Their kebabs are very well regarded, and are made with lamb, chicken, and beef, some consisting of ground meat and whole pieces (the ground meat kebabs are very tender). The *betyi* kebab, made with ground lamb and spiced with garlic and hot peppers, is fork tender and goes great with the accompanying vegetables (grilled tomato and peppers), spiced sweet onions, and a fabulous pickled red cabbage. The kebab comes with rice, but feel free to eat it with the *pide*, a traditional Turkish bread, served warm at the table. While the Turkish pop music over the sound system continues to play, enjoy dessert. The *katandibi* is lovely—it's a slightly caramelized milk pudding, creamy and sweet with cinnamon. It tastes a little like pulverized rice pudding. A demitasse of Turkish coffee is the perfect accompaniment, too.

Woodside Cafe, 64-23 Broadway, Woodside, NY 11377; (347) 642-3445; Subway: M/R to 65th Street; Nepalese; $. This is the former site of the much beloved and much missed Spicy Mina's (which may return elsewhere in Queens one day), but the good news is the Woodside Cafe makes some seriously impressive Nepalese food. The dining room looks very much like that of a pizza parlor (they do make pizzas there), but with decorative subcontinent sculptures on the walls. A great way to start is with a banana lassi—it resembles a sweet lassi that's a little on the tart side, but with more of the tannins found in banana peels. *Achar* consists of potato tossed with ground sesame, fenugreek leaves, lemon juice, and spices—sort of a warm Nepalese potato salad. *Samay baji* is traditionally a ritual dish, and consists of multiple elements, including *chiura* (a kind of beaten rice, made in house in this case), grilled meat (beef or chicken), black-eyed peas, chickpeas, roasted soybeans, spicy potatoes, radish pickle, and finally topped with a mini *woh*, which is a patty of soft lentils. As are found in most Nepalese restaurants, steamed vegetable and beef *momos* are available, which come with a piquant orange and red sauce on the side. Their vegetable *momos* are incredible. *Chatamari,* a rice-flour crepe, is the closest thing to pizza in Nepalese cuisine, and it is topped with mashed potatoes, black-eyed peas, chicken (optional), and an egg, with a side of goat gravy. The vegetable *thali* is also very good, with the superstar *urad daal,* prepared in a very traditional way, with a thin broth flavored subtly with tomatoes, onions, and spices.

Zabb Elee, 71-28 Roosevelt Ave., Woodside, NY 11377; (718) 426-7992; Subway: 7 to 69th Street; Thai (Northern); $. Some of the most inventive and tasty Thai food in Queens is found here. It's incredibly flavorful, and there are many dishes on the menu that you just won't find anywhere else, and familiar dishes may be slightly different from what you're used to. For instance, their pork *larb* contains both ground pork and pork liver, something you really don't see a lot of. The liver isn't very "livery," which can be a good or bad thing, depending on your point of view. The flavors are strong—cilantro, onion, chili pepper, fish sauce—and they actually mask the liver flavor quite successfully. The bits of ground rice also add to an enticing texture. Overall the dish is a great success. On the opposite side of the spectrum is the omelet with pickled garlic—mild and earthy, it's really different, and a nice addition to the meal. A terrific dish is the Thai Esarn sausage, which arrives sliced with peanuts, raw onion, chilies, and ginger matchsticks on the side. Among the more classic dishes, the Thai papaya salad is amazing—spicy, tangy, with strong flavors of lime and fish sauce. It can be a real sinus cleanser. The restaurant has a menu populated with more conventional Thai dishes, and one of the tastiest is the

Sunnyside and Woodside's Irish Pubs and Bars

Under the 7 line in Sunnyside and Woodside lies a series of Irish pubs, gathering spots for the past and present Irish populations in those neighborhoods, and now popular with pretty much anyone who 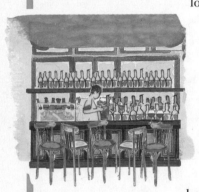 loves a good pint of beer and some quality pub grub. These pubs are very popular with the locals as well as with visitors on St. Patrick's Day—on March 17, the pubs often have extra drink specials and holiday food, like the classic black pudding, bangers and mash, as well as corned beef and cabbage. A great place to start is Donovan's Pub, which pours one of the best pints of Guinness in town, plus they have an excellent burger, which has been recognized over the years as one of the greats in New York City.

PJ Horgan's also serves food along with their beer, and they tout their burger as being one of the best; you'll find that everyone has an opinion as to the best burger in town, and theirs is a good one, as is their chicken pot pie. The fish-and-chips are also terrific. You'll no doubt be given a basket of slightly sweet Irish soda bread at the start, which really is delicious, especially with a layer of butter slathered on it. Have a pint of Guinness, or for something perhaps a bit lighter, a Smithwick's.

If you're just looking to drink without being distracted by delicious Irish pub food, head to The Gaslight, though you can bring food in with you—maybe some tacos from the El Vagabundo truck, if it's late enough. This place tends to attract a slightly younger crowd, and it gets pretty packed later into the evening; head outside to their patio to try to escape some of the people and noise if you need to. Or get there early for the happy hour (before 9 p.m.), which features three beers for $10.

Molly Blooms did a big renovation a couple of years ago and it's a really wonderful spot. It's a bit brighter than a lot of the local pubs, which adds to the welcoming feel people get from here. The front area is a bit narrow, which is taken up mostly by the bar and stools, but the back patio/garden area feels quite spacious. The food is very good and they have a great selection of beers that goes beyond the average offerings of Guinness, Smithwick's, Harp, and Bass. Their fish-and-chips are terrific and the burger is popular, too.

Donovan's Pub, 57-24 Roosevelt Ave., Woodside, NY 11377; (718) 429-9339; Subway: 7 to 61st Street.

PJ Horgan's, 42-17 Queens Blvd., Sunnyside, NY 11104; (718) 361-9680; Subway: 7 to 40th Street.

The Gaslight, 43-17 Queens Blvd., Sunnyside, NY 11104; (718) 729-9900; Subway: 7 to 40th Street.

Molly Blooms, 43-13 Queens Blvd., Sunnyside, NY 11104; (718) 433-1916; Subway: 7 to 40th Street; mollybloomsnewyork.com.

chicken basil over rice—get the chicken ground for a slightly different textural experience. Of course, Thai iced tea goes well with all of this, especially the spicy dishes (the dairy in the tea helps moderate the spiciness).

Landmarks

Donovan's Pub, 57-24 Roosevelt Ave., Woodside, NY 11377; (718) 429-9339; Subway: 7 to 61st Street; Pub; $. For many years, Donovan's was the home of the "Best Burger" in New York City. Yes, that's right—not just in Queens but in all of New York City (there's a giant sign about this attached to the outside of the restaurant in case you forget). Nowadays, there are many contenders for this crown, but Donovan's still serves up a solid, classic pub burger. It's a grilled half-pound of meat, and you can get cheese or bacon on top; thick steak fries come with it. It's a hefty sort of meal, and in an Irish pub, what better to drink with it than one of their expertly poured pints of Guinness. Of course, there are other things on the menu, but it's really the burger and a pint one comes to Donovan's for. Please note that they are cash only here.

Sripraphai, 64-13 39th Ave., Woodside, NY 11377; (718) 899-9599; Subway: 7 to 61st Street; Thai; $$. This is the heavy-hitter Thai restaurant in all of NYC—for many years, it has been considered the best Thai restaurant in the city, though there are a number of excellent Thai restaurants nearby that are vying for that crown. Still, judging from the crowds, which are overwhelmingly pan-Asian, their popularity is not anywhere near its sunset. The food is delicious and pretty authentic. The presence of a lot of customers also means a lot of turnover in their ingredient stock, so everything is very fresh. The menu is huge—seriously, it's like a book, almost—so there are a couple of approaches to take: Try something familiar or try something new. The good thing is, even the true Thai classics are excellent, like the pad thai. The Panang curry is also amazing, and while you can find this curry on almost any Thai restaurant menu, Sripraphai does it a little differently. This curry is not swimming in a thick coconut milk broth, but is simply saucy and served on a flat plate. It's beautifully red with a layer of creamy coconut milk drizzled on top. It is simply wonderful and very memorable. The papaya salad is refreshing and tangy, and spicy; it's also dotted with little dry shrimp and peanuts, adding rich flavor to the dish. The fried watercress salad is beyond delicious and a must-order dish, at least once (though if you're like many, you'll be hooked for future visits). For dessert, the black rice with taro (a kind of purple tuber) and coconut milk is a great choice—it's full of sweetness, textural interest, and great flavor.

Arsi's Pateseria, 39-39 47th Ave., Sunnyside, NY 11104; (718) 786-3276; Subway: 7 to 40th Street; Bakery. For 10 years, this little bakery has provided Sunnyside with delicious baklava, strudels, croissants, pastries, and more. And speaking of the baklava, it is really wonderful. It's sweet, buttery, stuffed with walnuts, and bathed in sugar syrup, and the nice thing about it is that it is not cloyingly sweet. Pieces are available in small and large sizes. It goes very well with a glass of their strong iced coffee. Their phyllo products also include a good spinach and cheese *burek* that is lightly seasoned but not lacking in flavor. Other *bureks* are filled with things like potatoes, mushrooms, and chicken. If you're lucky, owner Anna will have a plate of small *bureks* out for you to taste. In the display case you'll find cannoli, tiramisu, and napoleons, and in the back behind the counter are strudels and turnovers filled with cherries and apples. You can enjoy your treats at the tables inside or the chairs outside the bakery. Take home a container of homemade *zacusca* (a nod to her family's Hungarian roots), taramosalata, tabouli, or eggplant spread, too. Recommendation from Anna: Drizzle a little pomegranate molasses over your tabouli for an extra-special treat.

Baruir's Coffee, 40-07 Queens Blvd., Sunnyside, NY 11104; (718) 784-0842; Subway: 7 to 40th Street; Coffee/Tea/Grocery. Baruir's has been around since the 1960s, and continues to be a reliable source for whole coffee beans, which are not always as easy to find in Queens as you might think. Here, you can purchase beans by the pound. They'll grind them for you, or you can take them home as is. If you are a fan of dark roasts, the Colombian Dark is a great choice. Prepared coffee is also available for purchase—try the iced coffee not with milk but with cream, for an extra-special treat. They even make their iced coffee with coffee ice cubes, which you almost never see. There's one table in the back, so snag it if you can. Along with the coffee, you can buy a variety of other gourmet items here—spices, legumes, dried fruits, cheeses, and some cured meats. Take a gander at the giant coffee roaster machine displayed at the front of the shop, too. It's pretty cool.

Butcher Block, 43-46 41st St., Sunnyside, NY 11104; (718) 784-1078; Subway: 7 to 40th Street; Butcher and UK Products. **For UK** and Irish products in Queens, this is the place to be; many an Irish expat has felt soothed while perusing the aisles at Butcher Block. Not only are the usual suspects of Cadbury bars, Taytos, and PG Tips tea present, but there's also an extensive assortment of biscuits, tea brands, Irish bread products, Irish flour, Kerrygold butters and cheeses, candy bars, drinks, soup/sauce bases, and more. The staff at Butcher Block also  make their own black pudding and white pudding, Scotch eggs, and rashers; the sausage rolls get high marks. They also make gigantic sandwiches and other prepared dishes—amazing comfort food made with skill and love.

Habibi, 43-02 43rd Ave., Sunnyside, NY 11104; (718) 706-0600; Subway: 7 to 40th Street; Middle Eastern; $. Lebanese food reigns supreme at this bright, clean corner spot in the north side of Sunnyside; it is the former location of the beloved El Shater. Here, you can buy Middle Eastern specialties—olive oil, tahini, rose and *jallab* syrup, tinned vegetables, spices such as sumac and zaatar, grains, legumes, preserved lemons, dates, and olives. Arabic-language newspapers are also for sale. Additionally, expertly pre-pared Lebanese food abounds, and it is some of the best you'll find in Sunnyside. The tabouli is parsley-heavy—which is the traditional way to make this dish—and studded with raw tomato and onion, with just a little bit of small-grain bulgur. It's fresh and balanced with clean, clear flavors. The baba ghanoush is super creamy, thanks to all the tahini used. The grilled meats are served with a wonderfully lemony tahini sauce and a spicy green sauce, and the meats themselves are delicious. The chicken, lamb, and beef kofta are all great choices—the chicken is quite tender and the beef kofta tastes of the grill with a touch of cinnamon. The sweet side of things is also present, in the form of various baklava (filled with pistachio or walnut), chewy and sweet Turkish delight, crumbly *ma'amoul,* crunchy *gorayebeh,* and more. Their baklava, made by the owner's wife, are slightly and pleasantly salty, which sets them apart from many others. Particularly good in this respect is their *kanafe,* which in this case is a generous layer of toasted *kataifi* layered on top of walnuts in syrup.

Han Ah Reum, 59-18 Woodside Ave., Woodside, NY 11377; (718) 446-0759; Subway: 7 to 61st Street; hmart.com; Korean Grocery. This small Korean market is the original H-Mart, which is now a chain. It's conveniently located near the 7 train, is small, but it's full of everything you'll need to make Korean food. A big draw is the fresh tofu they make in the store, as is the plethora of prepared foods, including various pancakes (kimchi, crab, potato, fish, sweet and sour, etc.); soups and broths (beef bone soup, whiting soup, etc.); puddings (acorn is particularly striking), vegetables (stir fries, salads), Korean sushi, and rice cakes. They also stock a variety of kimchis, some in big tubs and some in plastic bags, including radish, sliced cabbage, and young cabbage. But you'll find Korean staples here—rice (including sweet rice) and other grains (Job's tears, roasted millet, glutinous millet), beans (soybeans, black beans), tubs of *gochujang,* frozen dumplings, teas (green, roasted corn, roasted barley), oils, soy sauce, packaged curries, seasoned bean pastes, dried fish, noodles (fresh and dried), snacks—as well as produce. There is a small meat counter in the back and cuts are neatly packaged and have great color to them. You can also purchase various cooking tools and implements here.

Inthira Thai Market, 64-04 39th Ave., Woodside, NY 11377; (718) 606-2523; Subway: 7 to 61st Street; inthirathaimarket.com; Thai Market. This small Thai market across the street and down from

Sripraphai stocks a decent selection of Thai products like Thai loose tea, rice, palm sugar, chili paste, chilies, frozen banana leaves, fish sauce, and prepared meats, as well as less familiar items—at least to American eyes—like pickled tamarind leaves, fermented mustard greens, *o-lieng* powder, and crab paste. The staff is very friendly, so if you have questions about anything, just ask. If you're lucky, you might even catch a glimpse of Mimi, the store cat (who apparently believes she owns the place).

Las Americas Carniceria, 45-12 Greenpoint Ave., Sunnyside, NY 11104; (718) 937-0553; Subway: 7 to 46th Street; Meat Market. **This** butcher shop/meat market/*carniceria* caters primarily to Sunnyside's Latino community, which means it's full of awesomeness. They have a great selection of non-meat items—yerba maté (*bombillos*—the vessels in which you drink maté—were not to be found, though), Latin spices, dried chilies, dried corn (purple, yellow, and white) and beans, quinoa and *kiwicha* (amaranth), rendered lard, *maca,* chicharron, arepas, and frozen fruits and vegetables, including a variety of potatoes. The meat is of excellent quality, and the butchers will cut things to your preference. If you are a fan of "variety cuts," this is the place for you. Here you will find tongue, neck bones, tripe, liver, small intestine, and cow's feet—and that's just to start. Real ox tails are also sold here, as well as goat. Prices are excellent and business is brisk, meaning lots of turnover and fresh meats.

Massis Food, 4220 43rd Ave., Sunnyside, NY 11104; (718) 729-3749; Subway: 7 to 40th Street; Mediterranean Market/Deli. If you are on the hunt for Romanian and Turkish food products in Sunnyside, Massis is the place. Their shelves are well stocked with pantry items such as *ajvar,* cucumbers in brine, cabbage leaves, jams, tinned vegetables, olive oil, grape leaves, herbs, mountain tea, and *lutenitsa;* you'll find various kinds of cheese like feta and *kashkaval;* meats, including sausages, *soujouk,* and basturma; frozen *manti;* and smoked fish. There's a meat counter where you can ask about different sausages or meats, in case you're confused or curious. *Burek* and strudel are available, and they stock a nice selection of baked goods, like *raluca* and *mascot,* from the excellent Krystal European Bakery in Ridgewood, Queens. You can even pick up an *ibrik,* the vessel used to make Turkish coffee, and pick up some coffee grounds there, too.

New Long Cheng Market, 57-13 Roosevelt Ave., Woodside, NY 11377; (718) 803-0309; Subway: 7 to 61st Street; Asian Market. This small Asian market carries Asian pantry goods, fresh fish and meats, and produce. Here, you'll find a whole variety of noodles (mostly dried but some fresh), rice, sauces, spice mixes, tofu, sausages, and more. Vegetables are inside, and include Asian greens and long beans, and fruit is outside, including mangoes and guavas. There are a few bagged Mexican spices and chilies available, and *chicharones,* too. Fish, both on ice and still swimming, can be purchased, and the butchers will gut and clean the fish for you if you like (of course, you can also take it home and do it yourself, too).

Shellfish such as shrimp and scallops are next to the fish, also on ice. Adjacent to the market is a Chinese bakery, which sells white bread (some with raisins), sponge cake, red bean buns, sugar buns, coconut macaroons, florentines, and the like. Here, you'll find a "sweetheart cake," an extremely flaky pastry filled with candied winter melon, dotted with peanuts. The red bean buns are a bit unusual in that a layer of sweet red bean paste has been swirled with the bun dough and baked like that, for a marbling effect. There are a few tables, so feel free to hang out for a while with something sweet.

Nita's European Bakery, 40-10 Greenpoint Ave., Sunnyside, NY 11104; (718) 784-4047; Subway: 7 to 40th Street; Bakery. Nita's, which has been around for 30 years, makes Romanian baked goods, from breads to pastries to cakes. Their cakes are outstanding and they make a number of them in the style of roulades and tortes. The layered cakes consist of thin layers of moist sponge cake with cream in between; the roulades also involve layers of cake and cream, with the addition of fruit to some, and are rolled up instead of stacked. A particularly delicious cake includes thin layers of vanilla sponge cake interspersed with chocolate cream, with a shiny apricot-colored hard candy top layer. These cakes can be purchased as whole entities or by the slice. Amandinas, one of the most common of Romanian cakes, also make an appearance, covered in chocolate, though some are covered in a lavender-colored coating. The apple strudel is also delicious—flaky pastry with an apple filling through and through; raisins are nowhere to be seen. If you'd like to eat your cake at the bakery, there are a few tables available. They get their coffee beans from neighboring Baruir's, so if coffee is your thing, you can be sure that theirs is of high quality.

Ottomanelli & Sons, 61-05 Woodside Ave., Woodside, NY 11377; (718) 651-5544; Subway: 7 to 61st Street; Butcher. Just a hop, skip, and a jump from the 61st Street express stop on the 7 lies Ottomanelli & Sons, an old-school butcher that's been in business in Woodside since 1960. They do their best to source their meat locally (New Jersey, for starters), and they break down the carcasses there at the shop, a refreshing change in a world that embraces prepackaged styrofoam- and plastic-wrapped meat. They also have a dry aging room for the beef, which hangs out (literally) for a few weeks; the aging helps tenderize the meat. They'll aim to sell you cuts you prefer, and there are plenty of cuts already there in the refrigerated display if you are in a hurry. Bonus: They sell D'Artagnan duck bacon. Beyond the domesticated animal products on hand, they sell a variety of game meats. If you're willing to walk on the wild side, you can take home cuts of rattlesnake, kangaroo, frog's legs, venison, and much, much more.

Parrot Coffee Grocery, 45-15 Queens Blvd., Sunnyside, NY 11104; (718) 392-4515; Subway: 7 to 46th Street; European Grocer. Parrot is a bright and shiny specialty food wonderland on Queens Boulevard, not far from the subway. From chocolates to bread, homemade phyllo delicacies to olives, they stock some of the most interesting and flavorful products around. The focus is on foodstuffs from the Balkans and Turkey. It's a great place to find bulk nuts and dried fruit; there are also some nuts already prepackaged in 1-pound bags; dried fruit is also available both in bulk and in bags. Bulk coffee is also available. The refrigerated section contains various butters, a wonderful strained goat yogurt from Greece, as well as a Bulgarian whole-milk yogurt made from the milk of grass-fed cows, and different kinds of Eastern European and Mediterranean cheeses. The freezer section contains *bureks, cevapi,* phyllo dough, various Eastern European sausages, slab bacon, hummus, and homemade dips and spreads. Parrot carries the best medjool dates around, too. They are huge.

Pecas Y Mas, 44-20 Greenpoint Ave., Sunnyside, NY 11104; (718) 389-4443; Subway: 7 to 46th Street; Colombian. This little Colombian spot is the home of a very tasty *cholado,* an icy, sweet, tangy, and fruity treat made popular in Cali, Colombia, and imported to America via the numerous Colombian immigrants in Queens. It is prepared with care and has a wonderful balance of sweet and tart. The raspberry and passion-fruit syrups have a tangy heft along with their inherent sweetness, they don't overdo it with the sweetened condensed milk, and the fruit chunks are small enough to manage comfortably with the spoon that comes with the mixture. The straw also has a spoon-like opening at the bottom, which is an additional help. A nice touch is the napkin they give you to wrap around the cup, to keep your hands from freezing up. Apart from the *cholados*, *batidos* are also very popular drinks (give the pineapple a try). Colombian comfort food is the name of the game as far as edibles, go, but the *cholados* are especially awesome here.

Phil-Am Foods, 70-02 Roosevelt Ave., Woodside, NY 11372; (718) 899-1797; Subway: 7 to 69th Street; Filipino Market. This is the main food market dedicated to Filipino food in this little area of Woodside known as Little Manila. It's right there on the corner, so it's hard to miss. Inside you'll find all sorts of prepared foods, which is one of the store's main draws—cassava cake, *ube halaya* (purple yam custard), *maja mais* (coconut corn pudding), *dinuguan* (meat stew), and chicken *afritada* (chicken stew), among others. Shelf-stable products include *agar agar* in multiple colors, jackfruit in syrup, *nata de coco,* and sauces like fish sauce,  banana sauce, soy sauce, and sweet chili sauce. You'll also find basic staples like dry noodles (rice, *pancit,* and canton), sweet rice, *pinipig* (pounded sweet rice), and shrimp crackers. In the back is a counter where you can buy pork and sweet chicken *longaniza,* pork *tocino, lumpia,* rice cakes, and fried milk fish. Cooked and salted duck eggs in their bright red shells are also for sale in the front of the store.

Queens County Market, Sunnyside, NY; queenscountymarket
.com; Artisanal Food Market. This young market is a "pop-up,"
meaning it (theoretically) shows up at different locations in Queens.
At its start, it was in residence at Sunnyside Community Services,
located at 43-31 39th St. Conceived and organized by Queens resident Katrina Schultz Richter, it happens one day a month. Local food
artisans gather to sell the food they love, including the Chocolate
Swirl (amazing cake pops), Black and Blanco (cookies), and Mel's
Melting Pot (sauces and condiments). When I spoke to Katrina,
she said there was even a vendor selling Ethiopian food, making
this the only place where you could get Ethiopian in Queens. Keep
up with what's happening with the market by subscribing to their
mailing list on their website. Attendance grows exponentially as the
months go by, so expect to see big things from this plucky market.

Red Ribbon Bake Shop, 65-02 Roosevelt Ave., Woodside, NY
11377; (718) 335-1150; redribbonbakeshop.us; Subway: 7 to 61st
Street; Filipino Bakery. It's very easy to stop in and grab an indi-
vidually packaged butter *mamon,* a light and sweet, slightly salty,
round sponge cake that is pretty much irresistible and
will have you coming back again and again. In fact it's
so light, it's easy to wolf one down in less than a
minute, despite efforts to hold back (resistance
is futile sometimes). *Mamon* also comes in
a mocha flavor, which adds just a tiny
bit of pleasant bitterness to the mix.
Red Ribbon makes whole cakes, too,

including mango, *ube,* and *macapuno,* which is a kind of coconut found in the Phillippines, and a novel kind of cake that is a mix of four different kinds they sell—Black Forest (cherries on top), chocolate mocha crunch (brown), *ube* cake (purple) and *pandan macapuno* (green); it's a very cool combination and there's really something for everyone here. For something a little different, try the *halo halo,* a mix of disparate elements where the sum is greater than its parts—it's shaved ice combined with red beans, various fruit, flan, and a few other things. It's very good and very sweet. The bakery also sells some savory dishes, including empanadas and *pancit.*

Sunnyside Greenmarket, Skillman Ave. between 42nd & 43rd Streets, Sunnyside, NY 11104; Subway: 7 to 40th Street; Farmers' Market. This seasonal market, which runs on Saturday, 8 a.m. to 3 p.m., from early June to mid/late December, takes place in front of the southeast corner of Torsney Playground. A good variety of products are available, including fruit, vegetables, herbs, eggs, cider, grass-fed meats, fresh fish, wine, and more. It draws people from all parts of Sunnyside and beyond, and the market serves as a place for neighbors to connect. If you are looking for seasonal foods of all kinds, this is the place to be. EBT/food stamps, debit/credit cards, and WIC and FMNP coupons are accepted at this market.

Sunnyside Meat Market, 43-10 43rd St., Sunnyside, NY 11104; (718) 786-2626; Subway: 7 to 40th Street; Butcher. This meat shop on a side street in Sunnyside smells amazing, like smoked and cured meats, many of which are hanging above the display cases. There are also fresh sausages in the refrigerated display, made from lamb and pork, some spicy and some not. Apart from the cured meats, they make a delightful homemade sheep's milk cheese that is very soft, sort of like a farmer's cheese, which spreads well and is excellent on eggs. Additionally, on the counter next to the wall behind the meat display is a container of fried pork rinds; they are rich and delicious, and can be purchased by weight or by the piece. Pantry items like sauces, jams, and spreads are also available for purchase.

Superior Market, 40-08 Queens Blvd., Sunnyside, NY 11104; (718) 392-3178; Subway: 7 to 40th Street; Grocery. **At first,** this appears to be your average narrow-aisled New York City grocery store, but then you come upon the extreme beer selection located on the northeast side of the store. It's epic. Many, many beers are available, enough to do a virtual world tour in beer. Adjacent to that in the refrigerated section, you'll find such treats as imported Romanian feta, house-made yogurt cheese, and Belgian butter. Near the checkout, large discs of flaky onion bread are available, which go very well with yogurt cheese or feta.

Turkiyem Market, 46-31 Skillman Ave., Sunnyside, NY 11104; (718) 937-3456; Subway: 7 to 46th Street; Turkish Market. **This** little market on Skillman is chock full of Turkish products, including legumes of all sorts, rice, mint-nettle tea (a very unusual find), halal meats, Turkish coffee supplies, and a variety of semisoft white cheeses. In the refrigerated display next to the register, you'll find small containers of smooth *muhammara,* a red pepper spread that is excellent on bread with some of that aforementioned cheese.

V & V Bakery, 61-19 Roosevelt Ave., Woodside, NY 11377; (718) 476-1669; Subway: 7 to 61st Street; Italian Bakery. This Italian-style bakery is hidden under the 7 train at 61st Street, and has been serving baked goods to the Woodside community for the past 40 years. They bake a variety of things, from breads to pastries to cakes. The mini strawberry tarts are pleasantly diminutive, starting with a crust that is somewhere between a traditional pie crust and cake, filled with pastry cream, and topped with a piece of glazed strawberry. It is not overly sweet and is the perfect little snack. Their Italian cheesecake is lightly sweet and creamy, and the semolina bread is also excellent. During the holidays they prepare traditional breads, like the braided Easter egg bread, complete with brightly colored hard-boiled eggs.

Street Food

El Rey de Oro, 52nd St. & Roosevelt Ave., Woodside, NY 11377; Subway: 7 to 52nd Street; Mexican; $. You'll find this taco truck on the north side of Roosevelt Avenue alongside Vincent Daniels Square in Woodside. They offer *tortas,* quesadillas, *huaraches,* and

tacos, filled with meats like *lengua* (tongue), *suadero* (brisket), chorizo (Mexican sausage), and chicken, along with some combo meats like *campechana* (beef and sausage) and *mixta* (pork, chicken, and sausage). They also do a vegetarian taco and *torta*. The enchilada (spicy pork) taco is fantastic, quite spicy with red-tinged pork, but with sweet overtones that are really nice. The meat has a nice char on it as well, and that goes for meats other than pork. Red and green sauce are available, and both are very good. This taco can be quite hot to the touch right when they serve it to you, so let it cool a bit before digging in. Unless, of course, you just can't help yourself, which is totally understandable when it comes to food this delicious.

Los Cuatro Vientos Truck, Roosevelt Ave. & 65th St., Woodside, NY 11377; Subway: 7 to 69th Street; Mexican; $. Tacos and *tortas* dominate the menu at this unmarked taco truck in Woodside. The usual meats are available—beef, pork, chicken, tongue, and sausage—but there are some less conventional choices, including *campechano* (beef and sausage), *pernil* (pork), and *sobrebarriga* (flank steak). Pork lovers will be fast fans of the *al pastor* and enchilada tacos as well as the *pernil* taco (filled with luscious, soft pork). It has wonderful flavor! The carnitas taco is also quite good and full of tender pork. Along with the requisite cilantro and onions, shredded lettuce is also added to the tacos. They have green and red sauce, of course, and the red sauce is blazing hot with a peppery kick.

Tacos El Vagabundo Truck, Queens Blvd. & 41st St., Sunnyside, NY 11104; (347) 276-4522; Subway: 7 to 40th Street; Mexican; $. This is a very popular truck, just outside the 40th Street subway stop on the 7 train. The menu here is very simple and takes up the space of one sign—they offer quesadillas, burritos, *tortas,* tacos, and tostadas. They offer nine meat options (from chicken to sausages to *mixtos*), including carne asada (billed as "asada beef"), which is a delicious mass of marinated slightly saucy beef. It's topped with cilantro, onions, lettuce, tomato, and green sauce; *crema* is also available, which adds a nice cool tang to the mix. You can get extra cheese for a small price, too. As is the case with most *tortas* and *cemitas,* they are pretty big and chock full of delicious ingredients like chicken, *queso blanco,* refried beans, and vegetables. Nice to see they adver-tise the best of the Jarritos out there, the Toronja, which is a grapefruit soda. They also offer Boing! brand juices in both mango and peach (the mango is sweet, tangy, and slightly creamy, if you can believe it). Tacos El Vagabundo also delivers.

Jackson Heights

Jackson Heights is home to one of the most diverse communities in Queens, which also happens to be the most diverse county in America, with a vibrant energy. There are people everywhere, and it's really exciting to see so much life in this community. People are shopping, socializing, and eating, whether its Indian snacks, Nepalese momos, Columbian tamal, or Taiwanese bubble tea. And they are open to eating in both modest and more lavish spots, as well as straight from street carts right there on the road. All along Roosevelt Avenue, and slightly north or south of it, are said street carts, food trucks, and food stands, offering up some of the best eats you'll find in NYC. Since native Spanish speakers are making the food, it helps to know some basic Spanish when ordering. I usually start by saying "hola" and go from there. Sometimes they answer back in English, but the majority continue in Spanish. You can communicate solely in English most of the time, though— smiling and pointing help a lot. It's totally worth the effort because the food is that good.

Arunee Thai, 37-68 79th St., Jackson Heights, NY 11372; (718) 205-5559; Subway: 7 to 74th Street or E/F/M/R to Roosevelt Avenue; aruneeny.com; Thai; $. In an area that is filled with Indian, Nepalese, Ecuadorian, and Colombian places, Arunee is a nice change of pace. It's also a few hundred feet off the main thoroughfare of Roosevelt Avenue, but it feels like it's much farther away; the modest dining room feels calm and quiet compared to its environs. The Thai iced tea, usually a predictable staple of any Thai restaurant's menu, is nice and strong, with a bit of a pleasant tannic edge. A nice way to start is with their moist chicken satay, which comes with their amazing peanut sauce. Their noodle dishes are excellent, especially the *pad kra praow* (a nice element of the fabulous lunch special); the *jan pad poo* is wonderfully spicy, made with crabmeat, chili, garlic, and scallions—noodles with spicy crab, it's hard to go wrong with that. The menu is really extensive, and dishes in general tend to be in large portions, so you won't go home hungry at all. For dessert, have a scoop of mango ice cream, and if you're looking for something a little more extreme, give the durian ice cream a shot. Embrace the funk.

Cevicheria El Rey, 85-16 Roosevelt Ave., Jackson Heights, NY 11372; (718) 606-9077; Subway: 7 to 82nd Street; Peruvian; $. If you are craving ceviche, look no further than Cevicheria El Rey, where there is a whole world of ceviche to choose from. For the classic fish-citrus combo (*ceviche tiradito*), go for the *ceviche de pescado*, which is white fish marinated in a spicy lemon juice. The extra heat gives it a wonderful kick. It's also topped with thin slices of raw onion that add yet another pleasant bite to the dish. Plates of ceviche are served with roasted corn kernels; a slice of *choclo*, a kind of big kernel corn on the cob that is less sweet and starchier (but quite tasty) than our American sweet corn; and chunks of yucca and sweet potato. Other seafood is also given the citrus marinade treatment—shrimp, octopus, crab, and squid. Perhaps the most elaborate dish on the ceviche menu is the impressive looking *Leche de Pantera,* or, Panther Milk. This fancifully named dish comes served in a large martini glass and is filled with shrimp, crab, and chopped seafood, some of it hanging off the side of the glass, a la shrimp cocktail. It also looks like everything is sitting in a gray soup, but that is just from the *concha negre* (black clams). Aside from the ceviche, the menu is populated with cooked fish and seafood dishes—their *causa de mariscos,* consisting of a mix of seafood in between layers of soft, luscious *aji amarillo*–flavored mashed potato, is quite nice and very filling—as well as meats, poultry, soup, spaghetti dishes, and even *salchipapas.* Be sure to order some of the house-made *chicha morada,* too—you can get it by the glass or the pitcher.

El Chivito D'Oro, 84-02 37th Ave., Jackson Heights, NY 11372; (718) 424-0600; Subway: 7 to 82nd Street; Uruguayan; $$. **Grilled**

meats done well are the main attraction at this friendly Uruguayan spot. *Parrillada Para Uno* is a great way to get a sense of what the restaurant is capable of. This is a tray of mixed grilled meats—skirt steak, veal steak, sweetbreads, sausage, and blood sausage (which is good spread on bread). They are all done very well, especially the skirt steak, which is very easy to cut and eat. The blood sausage is a bit on the soft side, but it has a wonderful flavor, spiced with a touch of what tastes like cinnamon, and the sweetbreads are soft and buttery. The deep green, garlicky chimichurri sauce goes perfectly with the grilled meats, too. Note that this dish indicates it's "para uno," but it easily feeds three adults comfortably. There are myriad options for sides to accompany the mixed grill, and a simple green salad, full of fresh vegetables, is a perfect foil to the rich meat feast in front of you. Their empanadas are also very good, especially the chicken—spread some of their delicious tomato salsa on them and you're  good to go. They do a number of *batidos* for drinks, and they really taste great. On the sweeter side is the *mora* (blackberry) and on the tangier side is the *maracuya* (passion fruit) and *lulo*. You can get the fruit blended with water or milk. For dessert, the *chaja* is a classic Uruguayan sweet, made of meringue, peaches, sponge cake, *dulce de leche*, and whipped cream. It's very sweet, very good, and can easily satisfy three or four people.

El Riconcito de Tito, 37-61 79th St., Jackson Heights, NY 11372; (718) 803-0284; Subway: 7 to 82nd Street; Colombian; $.

This little hole-in-the-wall spot, with its ramshackle Spanish tile roof, looks like it should be on the beach somewhere and not in the middle of a busy area of Queens. They have an extensive menu and their sandwich board outside indicates more delicious things inside. Their empanadas are very good—and are only $1 each. They are made with a corn-flour dough, which makes the empanadas a bit crispy. The chicken empanada is filled with chicken and potatoes, and is a perfect combination of savory, meaty, starchy, and fatty. Their homemade salsa—very reminiscent in both smell and taste of Chilean *pebre*—is a must with the empanadas. Their tamales are big and meaty and also do well with their salsa. Inside, there is a small dining room to the right, where you can enjoy big plates of Colombian comfort food for breakfast, lunch, or dinner. And while most places offer only Manzana Postobón, they offer multiple flavors, including grape, pineapple, and orange.

Espresso 77, 35-57 77th St., Jackson Heights, NY 11372; (718) 424-1077; Subway: 7 to 74th Street or E/F/M/R to Roosevelt Avenue; espresso77.com; Cafe; $. This is Jackson Heights' only West Coast–style cafe, complete with good coffee, pastries, sandwiches, and a few comfy seats. They make regular drip coffee—with a roast of the day, often—and espresso drinks. The cappuccino is tasty, with a cloud of fluffy steamed milk sitting atop the mug. The chairs up front—grab them if you see they are available—are in a great spot for people-watching out the front window, plus they are very spacious and comfortable. Espresso 77 offers pastries and sandwiches, too. The grilled cheese, served on the East Coast version of sourdough, is filled with cheddar and swiss, accompanied by fresh tomato—the tomato is placed between the slices of cheese, which is a nice touch. The breakfast wrap is also good, and is served warm, having been heated in a panini press. It's slightly sweet, and filled with bacon, cheese, tomato, and vegetables. The small salad that comes with it is very fresh and enjoyable. You can bring your laptop, iPad, or other wireless Internet device, but be aware that the staff likes to limit access to their Wi-Fi to an hour, max.

Gangjong Kitchen, 72-24 Roosevelt Ave., Jackson Heights, NY 11373; (347) 848-0349; Subway: 7 to 74th Street or E/F/M/R to Roosevelt Avenue; Tibetan/Indian/Chinese; $. Award-winning Tibetan chef Chef Tenzing Lama runs this modest spot just west of the busy 74th Street/Roosevelt intersection. The food comes primarily from Tibetan traditions, with a bit of Indian and Chinese food as well. The Tibetan *boja*—a yak butter tea—is sweet here (often you'll find it salty), and tastes like a milder version of Indian masala tea, though the tea here is much creamier. The mango lassi is fantastic, thick with a pronounced mango flavor. *Momos* are on the menu, and the vegetable ones are excellent, filled with a dark leafy green that is visually striking and quite tasty. There are a number of vegetable dishes on the menu, including shredded chayote, which is very mild, cooked with scallions and tomatoes, and served warm. The fry dhal, bright yellow and likely made with split moong dhal, is also mild, seasoned with onions and some garlic.

As you can see, most of the food is on the mild side, but it suffers no lack of flavor. Fortunately for those who like their food spicy, there is a delicious red spicy sauce available that you can add to any dish to spice it up. It's great on all these dishes, as well as the lovely chicken with fresh coriander—white meat chicken in a sauce that is strongly flavored with cilantro. You can get these saucier dishes with either rice or *tingmo,* a beautifully shaped bun that is perfect for scooping up sauce.

Kababish, 70-64 Broadway; Jackson Heights, NY 11372; (718) 565-5131; Subway: 7 to 74th Street or E/F/M/R to Roosevelt Avenue; Pakistani/Indian/Bangladeshi; $. This hole in the wall is the place for *gola kebab,* the soft, spicy ground meat kebab that is popular in north India. The meat is so soft that it must be bound with string to keep it on the skewer while cooking on the grill (so don't be surprised when you see the thin string in with the meat—this is not a mistake). The meat almost melts in your mouth, and with the mix of spices and heat, it is a super taste treat. Raw onions and a little squeeze of lemon are nice additions, and the mild yogurt *raita* is a refreshing touch, plus it helps to relieve the heat a bit. Apart from the *gola kebab,* there are other kebabs, curries, and rice dishes on the menu. On top of the steam table display, there are some other items, like samosas and the very tasty *shami kebab,* a popular snack in Pakistan. It consists of ground chicken and lentils mixed with spices, formed into a patty and fried. It also goes well with the *raita*. Kababish also makes a number of naan—the excellent onion naan is studded with scallions and red pepper flakes—gorgeous and spicy.

Lali Guras, 37-63 76th St., Jackson Heights, NY 11372; (718) 424-0017; Subway: 7 to 74th Street or E/F/M/R to Roosevelt Avenue; Tibetan/Nepalese/Bhutanese; $. The awning on this small hole-in-the-wall restaurant advertises food from Tibet, Nepal, and Bhutan, for breakfast, lunch, and dinner. The name means "rhododendron," an image of which is visible on their sign. The food is likened to what you might find at a South Asian roadside cafe, with various *momos, thalis,* and the delicious *laphing* on the menu. The chicken *momos* are popular (so much so that the staff recommends them over the other *momos* (which are also good). There's the requisite red sauce and orange sauce that goes with them, and the red sauce is lovely and spicy with a little bit of a tang at the very end. The *thalis* are also great, especially the vegetable version. It's full of all sorts of delicious vegetables in various preparations. The greens are chopped and steamed and had an almost nutty flavor; they go well with the spoonful of pickle and the spicy *achar* made with radish. The dhal is watery and tastes of cilantro and goes perfectly with the rice. Cauliflower, long beans, and potato are combined together in a light curry that also goes well with the rice. Their plain lassi, which looks watery at first glance, tastes and feels thick and creamy; it's not overly sweet either.

Lhasa Fast Food, 37-50 74th St., Jackson Heights, NY 11372; (718) 205-2339; Subway: 7 to 74th Street or E/F/M/R to Roosevelt Avenue; Tibetan; $. I'd say this is probably the most mysterious location for a restaurant in Queens (unless you're talking about underground stuff, which is a whole other animal). A friend had told me about this spot—"there's a *momo* counter hidden in the back of a cell phone store." I poked around, did some research, and I'm pleased to tell you that I have found the hidden *momos!* Head a short way north along 74th Street from the subway and look for the AT&T store on your left; from what I can gather, this is casually referred to as "Tibetan Mobile." Head in (don't go down the stairs) and keep going toward the back. You'll find cell phones and accouterments up front, videos, DVDs, and candles in the middle, with the food counter in the back. It smells like incense in there, which is very appealing. They offer up more than *momos—thantuk,* a noodle soup and the lovely *tingmo,* a kind of bun, for starters— but the *momos* are what really move. They are only offered with beef filling, but that filling is mighty tasty, and nice and juicy as well. They have a couple of hot sauces on the table, and one is basically ground-up dried chilies in oil. There is a red chili sauce that is really good—it has more of a vinegar punch than a lot of the sauces served with *momos* in Jackson Heights. It really adds a lot to the *momos*.

Los Arrieros Restaurant, 76-02 Roosevelt Ave., Jackson Heights, NY 11372; (718) 898-3359; Subway: 7 to 74th Street or E/F/M/R to Roosevelt Avenue; Colombian; $. This quaint, charming corner restaurant is a calm spot on busy Roosevelt Avenue, where delicious Colombian comfort food abounds. Breakfast, lunch, and dinner are served here, and the portions are large and substantial. One particular epic platter of food is the *Bandeja Tipica Los Arrieros* platter, which consists of carne asada (grilled steak), pork loin and sausage, rice, beans, sweet plantains, egg, avocado, an arepa, and chicharron. It's filling and delicious, and could easily be split between two people (and particularly good after a night of carousing). Less elaborate is the *lomo de cerdo* platter, a pork loin cutlet served with *maduros,* rice, beans, and salad. Even lighter are the daily soups; try Thursday's beef and vegetable, which features a rich broth, chunks of well-done flavorful beef that is firm yet breaks apart easily, various vegetables, and cilantro. You get to choose a couple of sides, and their beans are magical—creamy and porky and simply fabulous. Add some of their tangy, spicy green sauce for extra tastiness. The *maduros* (fried sweet plantain) are also great. The ends get cooked a little more and develop nice caramelization. And in a neighborhood where tamales are not hard to find, their *tamal valluno con arepa* is a whole other animal (liken it to a distant cousin of the pot pie). First, it's gigantic—a soft scallion-studded corn-flour dough filled with potatoes, carrots, chicken and/or pork (some of the meat may be on the bone, allowing the meat to stay moist and flavorful)—all wrapped up in a banana leaf. The afore-mentioned spicy green sauce goes great with it. As far as beverages go, try the *agua panela* (sugar cane drink) or Champus (a fruit drink), and the *lulo* and *mora* (blackberry) *batidos* are also good choices (I recommend getting your *batido* with milk rather than water). The staff here is very friendly, too.

Los Chipotles Restaurant, 77-04 Roosevelt Ave., Jackson Heights, NY 11372; (718) 476-3330 or (347) 336-7223; Subway: 7 to 74th Street; Mexican; $. It's hard to resist this spot, with its lively music and inviting display of fresh Mexican ingredients just inside the doorway. The menu is filled with familiar Mexican dishes—*tortas,* burritos, quesadillas, *cemitas, huaraches,* and the like. The tacos are excellent, with the *campechanos* being the most

interesting of the lot—the taco is filled with a combination of chorizo, beef, and chicken, resulting in a rich, porky, beefy, tender mix (the chicken is more subdued); have them add avocado if you like. But speaking of chicken, their chicken taco is one of the best on Roosevelt Avenue—it's very tender and savory, with simple, clean flavors. Their corn tortillas are imported from Mexico, and have a tender, toothsome bite that you don't find with most mass-produced corn tortillas here in the US. Their flour tortillas, which are used for quesadillas, are made in the store—you can watch the cook make the tortillas as you wait. The service is very friendly and they are happy to accommodate you as you wish. The *aguas frescas* are worth trying, or just grab a bottle of Mango Boing! from the refrigerator.

Los Chuzo Y Algo Mas, 79-01 Roosevelt Ave., Jackson Heights, NY 11372; Subway: 7 to 82nd Street; Fresh Juices; $. *Chuzos* are the Colombian version of *kebabs,* colloquially known as "meat on a stick." They grill them here throughout the day, with meats like chicken and sausage, and serve them with an arepa. Come here for the fresh juices which are super tasty and the perfect cure for a hot day. They do both fruit and vegetable juices—try the combination of strawberry, pineapple, celery, and orange juice. They also make a very tasty *salpicon,* a popular fruit-based dish with origins in Colombia. It's made of finely diced fruit—apples, pears, watermelon, cantaloupe, and bananas—in orange juice. That's it! It's sort of a soupy fruit  salad—eat the fruit, then drink the juice, which is very fruity by the end. I call that fun food. There are a few stools in this little luncheonette, in case you want to hang out and enjoy your food or drink there.

Los Perros de Nico, 40-09 81st St., Jackson Heights, NY 11372; (786) 337-3689; Subway: 7 to 82nd Street; Colombian Hot Dogs; $. This tiny stall around the corner from the 82nd Street subway station makes some pretty tasty dogs. They do four flavor combos— Hawaiiano (Hawaiian), Traqui (Iraqi), Romano (Roman), and Mexicano (Mexican). I must admit, it's the Mexicano that speaks to me, though the Hawaiian is intriguing with its pineapple sauce. The Mexicano combines a spicy pico de gallo and potato chips, along with the ubiquitous pink sauce, mustard, mayo, tomato sauce, and hot sauce. Everything melds into a spicy, tangy, savory mess, and boy is it good. Be sure to get a juice with your hot dog. If you get it with milk it's a *batido,* which is like a light shake, and really delicious. There is no place to sit here—this is a walk-up joint—so takeout is your only option.

Mustang Thakali Kitchen, 74-14 37th Ave., Jackson Heights, NY 11372; (718) 898-5088; Subway: 7 to 74th Street or E/F/M/R to Roosevelt Avenue; thakalikitchen.com; Nepalese; $. The photo of *momos* affixed to the restaurant's window is a true temptress, luring you into the restaurant. The dining room has a peaceful vibe with relaxing music playing over the sound system. A great way to start the meal is with a sweet lassi (and the dairy will help ameliorate some of the spiciness you may encounter later), which really is sweet with a tart tang. One of the more interesting elements on the menu is "buff," meaning buffalo, and it appears here and there throughout. A particularly vibrant use of it is in the Buff Chilly—buffalo (which tastes like lean grass-fed beef), green pepper, and onion in a peppery-sweet-spicy sauce. The meat and vegetable chunks are similar in size, and the whole thing is absolutely delicious. Their steamed vegetable *momos* come with a few sauces, one made with sesame, one with tomato, and one is full-on

spicy. The *momos* themselves are very mild and a good choice for people with varying spice tolerance levels. *Thalis* are very popular in Nepalese cuisine, and the *puri thali* is a good choice, and a great introduction to the *thali* concept. It's completely vegetarian too, with pickles, spicy potatoes, mustard greens, *urad daal,* and paratha all included.

Merit Kabab Palace, 37-67 74th St., Jackson Heights, NY 11372; (718) 396-5827; Subway: 7 to 74th Street or E/F/M/R to Roosevelt Avenue; Indian; $. You can't miss this place if you descend the stairs from the subway on the northeastern corner of Roosevelt and 74th Street—it's pretty much right at the bottom of those steps. From the outside you might think, from the display of fried shrimp and onion rings visible through the front window, "Is this even an Indian restaurant?" Then you see the samosas and that pretty much answers the question. And the samosas—chicken or vegetable—are pretty dang good. They are triangular, yes, but plump at the same time, with the vegetable ones filled with savory and spiced potatoes and peas, and the chicken ones filled with beautifully spiced chicken and vegetables. Eat in and they'll give you a squirt bottle of green sauce that is an oh-so-heavenly accompaniment. Kebabs are also a good choice, and taste spiced and smoky, made from juicy, delicious ground meat. Alongside the dining room is a steam table filled with pans of rice, biryani, chicken dishes, and curries, among other things. Order yourself a plate of their tasty chicken tikka masala, a freshly made naan, a mango lassi (they are located in the refrigerator behind the counter, difficult to resist with their intense orange color), and you'll have a great meal in front of you. There's even a TV on the back wall up toward the ceiling for

Indian Sweets

One of the biggest ethnic groups in Jackson Heights is from India, and among the many things they brought with them was their food, both savory and sweet. Most of us are familiar with curries, daal, biryani, and the like, but many people are unfamiliar with the sweet side of things beyond *kheer* and *gulab jamun*. There is way more to Indian sweets than that and spending time in some of the sweets shops will show you the incredible world of Indian desserts. As to the aforementioned sweet dishes, which are found on almost any Indian restaurant's dessert menu, *kheer* isn't that common at the sweet shops in Jackson Heights, but *gulab jamun* is. It is presented as a simple fried dough ball in cardamom or rosewater sugar syrup; sometimes it is covered in a light coating of coconut shavings. When it is made into an oblong shape, split in two, and filled with sweetened cream cheese, it goes by the name of *chum chum*.

Here is a selection of other sweets you might find in Jackson Heights:

Burfi is sort of like fudge—it is very firm and made from ingredients such as nuts, beans, fruit, and spices. It's common for it to be cut into diamond, square, or round shapes, and some are covered in edible metal leaf.

Milk cake is a very sweet crumbly cake made from milk and sugar cut with lemon juice and allowed to boil until the curds and whey split (the whey is removed) and everything reduces. A little goes a long way.

Kalakand is also prepared with milk and sugar, but uses citric acid instead of lemon juice. It creates a sweet that is more akin to Italian cheesecake—firmer in texture than milk cake, but softer than *burfis*. *Kalakand* is flavored with nuts, fruit, and sometimes includes edible metal leaf.

Ladoo is a round sweet often using *besan* (chickpea) flour and sugar. *Rasgula* is another round sweet made with cottage cheese and sugar. And *halwa* is made with semolina, ghee, sugar, and water.

Here are some places to get Indian sweets in Jackson Heights:

Al Naimat Sweets & Restaurant, 37-03 74th St., Jackson Heights, NY 11372; (718) 476-1100; Subway: 7 to 74th Street. Recommended: *halwa,* almond *kalakand, gulab jamun* with coconut.

Maharaja Sweets & Snacks, 73-10 37th Ave., Jackson Heights, NY 11372; Subway: 7 to 74th Street. Recommended: mango *kalakand, anjeer* (fig) *burfi.*

Raja Sweets, 72-31 37th Ave., Jackson Heights, NY 11372; (718) 424-1850; Subway: 7 to 74th Street. Recommended: *gajar* (carrot) *kalakand,* almond *burfi, gulab jamun, chum chum,* pistachio *kalakand, besan ladoo.*

Rajbhog Sweets, 72-27 37th Ave., Jackson Heights, NY 11372; (718) 458-8512; Subway: 7 to 74th Street; rajbhog.com. Recommended: gulab jamun, chum chum, pistachio *kalakand,* milk cake, masala tea.

entertainment (you'll discover that Indian commercials are eerily like American ones).

Namaste Tashi Delek Momo Dumpling Palace, 37-67 74th St., Jackson Heights, NY 11372; (646) 203-9938; Subway: 7 to 74th Street or E/F/M/R to Roosevelt Avenue; Nepalese; $. **This** little stand is located in the back of Merit Kabab Palace, a popular Indian restaurant at the bottom of the steps leading down from the 74th Street 7 subway station. Here, they serve Nepalese, Tibetan, and Bhutanese foods. As the name indicates, this is a place for *momos,* and the chicken ones are good, flavored with scallion and cilantro. They come with a mild yellow-orange sauce and spicy red sauce, which is the better of the two. They also make beef, vegetable, and fried *momos*. In addition to that, the menu contains Nepalese *thali* plates (vegetable, chicken, beef, and goat), chow mein, a fantastic radish *achar,* soups, and some appetizers, which are displayed on top of the counter. Especially good is the Chicken Chilly, with lightly breaded chicken (white and dark meat) in a spicy sauce with scallions and red and green bell peppers. It's wonderfully spicy and just overall extremely tasty. In fact, I might recommend that over the *momos,* but don't tell anyone.

Phayul, 74-06 37th Rd., Jackson Heights, NY 11372; Subway: 7 to 74th Street or E/F/M/R to Roosevelt Avenue; Tibetan; $. **The** enticing smell of searing umami-rich meat greets you as you enter

Phayul's dining room. The entire menu takes two pages, but the variety is great. One of the most unusual things on the menu is the "butter tea," which tastes a bit like melted salted butter without the mouthfeel of butterfat (if you let sit too long undisturbed it will develop a skin from the milk); if you are looking for something a bit more familiar, try the yogurt-rich lassi. If blood sausage is your thing, try the *gyuma ngoe ma,* which comes fried with onions and green chilies. Also spicy is the *shogo khatsa*—spicy, starchy potatoes (imagine a classic Idaho potato) that carry the crunch of black mustard seeds. Continuing on the potato track, the steamed *tsel momo,* representative of the famous dumplings from Tibet/Nepal, are filled with potatoes and a bit of green herb, and are quite mild. There are a couple of chili sauces available to spice it up if you like—one is like a paste and one is almost pure chili seed. A very nourishing soup option is the *tsak sha la kor hot,* which contains slices of beef, radish, and Tibetan mountain herbs, along with some excellent noodles, which appear to be hand shaved. It easily serves two as part of a meal, and for four if only a small bowl of soup is desired. The broth is savory but not overpowering and deeply nourishing, thanks to the bones and marrow used to make it. The menu includes a selection of side dishes, and the *phaksha gotsel ngoema* (pork with garlic and green pepper) is a delight. Hefty matchsticks of salty, smoky pork are mixed with additional matchsticks of sturdy scallion and garlic, and although green pepper was listed, I didn't find any—but don't let that dissuade you from ordering it, as it's a wonderful savory dish.

Taqueria Coatzingo, 76-05 Roosevelt Ave., Jackson Heights, NY 11372; (718) 424-1977; Subway: 7 to 74th Street or E/F/M/R to Roosevelt Avenue; Mexican; $. Here, the tacos are king, and definitely worth your time and space in your belly. Meats like *al pastor,* chorizo, *carne enchilada,* and tripe are excellent, and arrive slathered with guacamole. Apart from that, the menu is pretty extensive—*huaraches,* quesadillas, tostadas, *cemitas, tortas, sopes,* enchiladas, chalupas, salads, soup, seafood cocktails, and platters of meats and fish. If you want a bit of a deviation from tacos, but still need your masa fix, give the *sopes* a try. Three come to an order and the fried gorditas are piled high with meat (the *al pastor*—meat cooked on a spit in the front of the room—is excellent), a schmear of beans, shredded lettuce, powdery cotija cheese, and a slice of fresh tomato. It's worth it to request them spicy as the rust red–colored hot sauce they use adds extra earthy flavor to the whole thing. Sour cream/*crema* can be ordered on the side, too. Their enchiladas are very good, and come either three or five to a plate. Green, red, or mole sauce are options with beef, chicken, and

cheese as fillings. You can also get *combinadas,* meaning a mixture of fillings; beef and cheese is a terrific combo. They are served with beans and rice—the beans are so creamy, making them totally irresistible. Drinks come in the form of beer, sodas, *aguas frescas,* and *licuados* (shakes). The beer is a tad pricey, to be honest, but the *licuados* are a great way to go. You can get them with milk or water, using a variety of tropical fruits like mamey, mango, and guanabana; try the lulo, otherwise known as *naranjilla*. This fruit is a member of the nightshade family (tomatoes and eggplant are, too), and its juice is green, making your *licuado* green as well.

Tawa Food, 37-38 72nd St., Jackson Heights, NY 11372; Subway: 7 to 74th Street or E/F/M/R to Roosevelt Avenue; Nepalese; $. Outstanding Nepalese food—cuisine from the Newar people, an ethnic group of Nepal that is indigenous to the Kathmandu Valley— is found at Tawa Food, a tiny hole-in-the-wall spot on a side street off busy Broadway. There are only a few tables, and they sort of feel in the way, but you are more than welcome to sit there; takeout is a popular option, naturally. Their chicken *momos* are amazing and come highly recommended by the staff. They come with a red (spicy) and an orange (sweet and tart) sauce, which are also very flavorful. Their *dosas* are fantastic—the *masala dosa* is a vegetarian option and is filled with a mix of potatoes, red onions, and chilies with an irresistible mix of spices. The *dosa* arrives conveniently cut into pieces, which makes it easy to handle. Alongside it is a thick and bright-tasting coconut chutney, spicy tomato chutney, and a cup of sambal that is watery and almost buttery. These condiments are provided as something for you to dip your *dosa* into. The *dosa* wrap itself has a slight tang to it, as it is a fermented bread made from rice and lentils, and is light and delicious. Don't forget to try the chicken *kathi* roll, either! In the way back of the space, you'll see people making *parathas,* which are also for sale, prepackaged in plastic bags. These are round, thin, substantial discs that resemble tortillas, and are flavored with things like corn, potato, and "spices."

Terazza 7, 40-19 Gleane St., Jackson Heights, NY 11373; (718) 803-9602; Subway: 7 to 82nd Street; terrazacafe.org; Cocktails. Chill and cool is an apt description of Terazza 7, a hip Latin cafe a short walk from the 82nd Street 7 stop, in the heart of Jackson Heights. Both the staff and your fellow patrons are really friendly, and are obviously proud of their establishment, now 11 years old at the time of this writing. Food is sparse—a few sweet snacks are available, made by local pastry chef Isabel Sanchez, including miniature red velvet cupcakes, chocolate bites, and coconut macaroons. The drinks, on the other hand,  are inventive and creative. Give the Cumbia Amazonica a try, which consists of a mix of pisco, kiwi, rosemary, and passion fruit. The Tierra Prometica is also a delicious mix of flavors—tequila, pomegranate, and mint. Coffee is also available, both by itself or spiked with liquor. The Cafe Chonta, a mix of coffee, rum, cinnamon, and cloves, is a great combination. The coffee itself can be ordered as a single-origin bean—try the rich Sumatra, with or without hazelnut syrup. A big part of Terazza 7's contribution to the community is the regular schedule of live music, mostly Latin in flavor. Great musicians come to perform here, which is an extra-special treat—there's seating upstairs, but since the stage is made of a perforated metal slab hanging from the ceiling, the music flows downstairs as well, so it's easy to enjoy amazing sounds right at the bar.

Urubamba, 86-20 37th Ave., Jackson Heights, NY 11372; (718) 672-2224; Subway: 7 to 82nd Street; Peruvian; $$. Urubamba, home to seriously delicious Peruvian food, has an extensive menu consisting of *bocaditos* to soups, ceviche to *pollos a la brasa*. Best way to start out your meal is with a *chicha morada*—juice from purple corn mixed with pineapple and lemon juice. It's seasoned with a little cinnamon and tiny bits of tart apple. It's bright, fresh, and apparently helps lower blood pressure (or so said the Peruvian woman at the table next to me during one visit). Their soups are excellent, and particularly lovely is a bowl of *aguadito de pescado,* a thick fish soup made with rice and cilantro, served with a black pepper and a spicy, creamy jalapeño sauce. The serving sizes are huge—the "small" could easily feed two to three people. Their tamales are wonderful, too, filled with pork or chicken, and wrapped in a banana leaf. The tender tamale dough is made from corn and contains a distinct flavor of olives. It is served with a small bowl of thinly sliced red onions soaked in fresh lime juice and cilantro, and it goes perfectly with the tamal. French fries are on the menu, but a nice alternative is yucca fries, served with a creamy and mild sauce called *huancaína*—made from *aji amarillo,* a very important chili in Peruvian cooking. The yucca fries, as with potato dishes, can also be accompanied by an *ocopa* sauce, made from *huacatay,* the Peruvian black mint. Various configurations of the famous Peruvian chicken, *pollos a la brasa,* are available, in whole, half, and quarter chicken servings. There's a combination plate that includes chicken, salad, and french fries (ask to try the Peruvian sauces mentioned above on your fries). A delightful *alfajor* is a great way to end your meal. Theirs are very traditional, with two crumbly shortbread cookies sandwiching a layer of sweet *dulce de leche* and dusted in powdered sugar.

Landmarks

Jackson Diner, 37-47 74th St., Jackson Heights, NY 11372; (718) 672-1232; Subway: 7 to 74th Street or E/F/M/R to Roosevelt Avenue; jacksondiner.com; Indian; $$. **Not to be confused with Jackson Hole Diner in Astoria, home of the steamed burger, Jackson Diner is the best-known Indian restaurant to those outside the borough, and is popular with Manhattanites in general. It really is a mainstay of the neighborhood. Portions are large and the lunch buffet is very popular. The food spans all regions of India, so both North and South Indian specialties are on the menu. Reliable versions of favorites like lamb vindaloo, *masala dosa, saag paneer,* and *navrattan korma***

are all done well. For dessert, the familiar *gulab jamun* and *kheer* are available. They make a number of "Indian cocktails," including the mango margarita, made from tequila, mango nectar, and lime juice—simple and straightforward, and pretty darn tasty.

Jahn's, 81-04 37th Ave., Jackson Heights, NY 11372; (718) 651-0700; Subway: 7 to 82nd Street; Indian; $. The original Jahn's opened in 1897 on Alexander Avenue in the Bronx, with three additional locations opening up later around New York City. One of them is this Jackson Heights spot, now the only Jahn's left. Walk in, and the place oozes nostalgia. There are swivel stools at the luncheonette bar; oversized booths across from that, and tables and chairs along the way and into the back dining room. The food is pure diner fare, and as at most New York City diners, the offerings are extensive. This is a great place for a New York City–style diner brunch, and both the fluffy pancakes and crispy waffles get high marks; note that you can also get deep-fried french toast here, too. Beyond that there are omelets, sandwiches hot and cold, burgers, pasta, meats, seafood, and more. What I come here for, though, is the ice cream. A hot fudge or hot caramel sundae is the simplest of choices, and sundaes can be made with even a single scoop of ice cream; of course, a two-scoop sundae is totally possible. You have 12 different flavors of ice cream to choose from, including chocolate, vanilla, mint chip, and cookies and cream.

Ice cream desserts have an entire page of the menu devoted to them, and many have mysterious, creative names, like Screwball's Delight and A Shissel. Jahn's is also home to The Kitchen Sink, which involves about 30 scoops of ice cream, suitable for eight people. You can even get an old fashioned New York egg cream (chocolate or vanilla), a milk shake, float, or malted, not to mention the classic banana split.

La Pequeña Colombia, 83-27 Roosevelt Ave., Jackson Heights, NY 11372; (718) 478-8700; Subway: 7 to 82nd Street; pequena colombia.com; Colombian; $$. Terrific classic Colombian food is served at this long-standing restaurant; once you taste the quality of the food they prepare, you'll understand why they've had such staying power. There's plenty of meat, chicken, and seafood on the menu, but they've also put together a vegetarian plate for those who eschew meat. It's pretty much a standard Colombian plate of rice, beans, plantains, potato, or yucca, with the addition of vegetables. For omnivores, though, the Plato Montañero is a great way to enjoy Colombian comfort food—rice, beans, an egg, *chicharones, maduros,* and carne asada (beef). The accompanying *aji picante*—a sharp, spicy green sauce—is a perfect match to this and most meats offered. To start, though, don't miss out on the empanadas. Three come to an order, and they are filled with soft, spicy shredded beef, surrounded by a crisp, thin outer shell. The *aji* also goes well with this. The large tamal is also delicious, with a filling of extremely tender chicken and beef still on the bone, accompanied by carrots and potatoes and surrounded by delicate, soft, golden masa, all wrapped up in a banana leaf. Daily specials include meaty rib soups and casseroles—Sunday is a great day because they make the classic *sancocho de gallina*, a hearty hen stew. If you'd like to stray from traditional Colombian food here, you can also order up a grilled chicken sandwich, a variety of wraps, and a burger.

Specialty Stores, Markets & Producers

Apna Bazar Cash & Carry, 72-20 37th Ave., Jackson Heights, NY 11372; Subway: 7 to 74th Street or E/F/M/R to Roosevelt Avenue; Indian Market. One of the most striking aspects of Apna Bazar is how everything in bags is piled so neatly throughout the store—rice, legumes, dhal, and spices. It makes it very easy to find things and sort through them. The whole store is very clean. They sell a huge variety of dhal, plenty of basmati rice, lots and lots of spices, some boxed meals, ghee, and a selection of grain and legume flours. The produce section is very good, and they sell things like fresh banana flowers, fresh *methi* (fenugreek), *tindora*, fresh turmeric root, bitter melon, jackfruit, and the sweet and juicy Alphonso mangoes. A good selection of frozen vegetables, like *methi, palak,* and *bindi* are also available in the frozen food section. You can even find stainless steel food containers for sale here.

Buenos Aires Bakery, 90-09 Roosevelt Ave., Jackson Heights, NY 11372; (718) 672-4046; Subway: 7 to 90th Street; Bakery. The clear blue awning on the corner of 91st Street and Roosevelt Avenue reads "B'Aires Bakery," which can be confusing. Never fear, this is the Buenos Aires Bakery, specializing in Argentinian and Uruguayan pastries and baked goods. They make a good *alfajor de maizena* with a nice balance of *dulce de leche* in between two crumbly yellow cookies. They also make a number of other things filled with *dulce de leche* (as at any good Argentinian bakery), including pastry horns, and mini pastries (located in the window). Particularly popular are the sweets made with a buttery pastry reminiscent of Danish dough that are filled with fruit or more caramel. They are soft yet flaky and just fantastic. The *sanguche de miga* aka *sandwiches de miga* and the empanadas are also very popular.

Cannelle Patisserie, 75-59 31st Ave., Jackson Heights, NY 11370; (718) 565-6200; Subway: 7 to 74th Street or E/F/M/R to Roosevelt Avenue; cannellepatisserie.com; French Bakery; $. Cannelle, located in a nondescript strip mall in the north end of Jackson Heights, is not close to any subway stop, but it is worth finding a way to get there, because their baked goods are some of the best in Queens. They bake high quality French pastries, like *pain au chocolat,* croissants, *gâteau breton,* and almond croissants—in

fact, the last time I was there, the almond croissants were flying off the shelves, they were
so popular. They also make the pastry that
is their namesake, the *canelé,* which are
delicious—caramelized outside and creamy
inside with a hint of vanilla. They are really,
really good. They also bake a lot of bread, and their baguettes
are very popular. You can also get the traditional French sandwich
croque monsieur, as well as a selection of quiches.

Chong Hat Market, 72-11 Roosevelt, Jackson Heights, NY 11372;
(718) 476-8743; Subway: 7 to 74th Street or E/F/M/R to Roosevelt
Avenue; Korean Market. This medium-size, bright and clean Korean
market stocks an amazing array of Korean and Asian food products,
both fresh and prepared. Their fish market is clean and well stocked,
with some fish pieces already wrapped up, including sashimi-grade
salmon and whole fish heads (good for fish stock). You'll also find
live crabs for sale. The meat is also fresh. Basics like noodles (fresh
and dried), rice, vinegar, soy souce, tofu, tea (including boxthorn,
roasted corn, and green), dried seaweed and mushrooms are all
stocked. Frozen foods like dumplings and fish cakes are also available. And we can't forget the snacks. They also carry a large amount
of fermented hot red pepper paste. There's even a kimchi bar where
you can serve yourself from a half-dozen different kinds of store-
prepared kimchi; the kirby kimchi looks particularly tasty. Bonus: If
you're driving, there's a parking lot in front of the store.

Despaña Brand Foods, 86-17 Northern Blvd., Jackson Heights, NY 11372; (888) 779-8617; Subway: 7 to 90th Street; Spanish. This is the retail outlet attached to their factory in Queens. Despaña was originally started by a Cuban family, then sold to the present owners in the 1970s. All food with their brand displayed on it is actually made right here in Queens. They make a variety of sausages, including the famous Spanish chorizo. The space is stocked to the gills with Spanish cheeses (both raw and pasteurized), chocolate, cookies, jams, sauces, olive oils, vinegars, crackers, tinned fish and seafood, cazuelas, and pitchers. You can even buy Chufi here, a *horchata*-type beverage made from tiger nut milk (it's in the refrigerator behind the counter). On Saturday they are open from 9 a.m. to 4 p.m. and open a wide variety of products for tastings. The owner even provides wine to go with the cheese, meats, and more; people come from miles away (like Maryland) to participate in the tastings, they are that popular. Come by any day of the week, except Sunday, and check out their delectable Spanish products—you won't be disappointed.

Haat Bazar, 37-11 73rd St., Jackson Heights, NY 11372; (718) 205-8588; Subway: 7 to 74th Street or E/F/M/R to Roosevelt Avenue; Bangladeshi. Here, you'll find both a small grocery and a

Bengali steam-table restaurant side by side. The grocery has good-quality produce, both fruit and vegetables. They sell greens like fresh *methi* and a variety of South Asian greens, some wrapped in plastic. Spices, mustard oil, rice and pounded rice, *rooh afza* syrup, Bengali snacks, frozen fish, and halal meats can all be found here; cooking implements are located in the back, too. Homemade *pitha* and other traditional breads are also for sale. Next door is a sort of diner with a steam table, though some of the dishes are heated up in a microwave. A favorite here is the thick slices of roasted eggplant. They are served at room temperature with a bit of cilantro, and they are wonderfully soft—a bit custardy—but without being mushy. To spice it up, get the warm cooked papaya, prepared with black sesame seeds, onions, and chilies. There's a variety of dishes displayed (chicken biryani seems to be quite popular), so just point and ask for a serving of the things you want.

Jackson Heights Greenmarket, 34th Ave. at 77th St. alongside Travers Park, Jackson Heights, NY 11372; Subway: 7 to 74th Street or E/F/M/R to Roosevelt Avenue; grownyc.org/jacksonheights greenmarket; Greenmarket. This is the only greenmarket in Queens that is open year-round, each Sunday from 8 a.m. to 3 p.m. It's a very popular market and is one of the few spots in the neighborhood where one can consistently buy local and organic produce and meats. It's also the largest of the Queens greenmarkets. In addition to selling food, they have a textile recycling program and a composting program in place. The foodstuffs one can buy range from vegetables and fruits, to wild-caught seafood and grass-fed/grain-finished meats, to honey and cheese, dairy, eggs, and more. The Friends of Travers Park have also managed to get 78th Street designated as a "playstreet"—family-friendly events happen each Sunday next to the market. On your way out of the market, look east across 78th Street and you might spy the tamale woman selling her plump corn husk–wrapped treasures.

Kung Fu Tea, 82-02 Roosevelt Ave., Jackson Heights, NY 11373; (718) 755-7900; Subway: 7 to 82nd Street; Bubble Tea. This location is part of the same chain as the Kung Fu Tea shops in Flushing, though their drink options here in Jackson Heights are less extensive. Bubble tea is king here, and by far the most popular is the taro flavor, and rightly so—it is fantastic. It's got a lovely, clean flavor—it's a bit nutty, sweet, and quite milky. The bubbles are just right—not too firm and not too soft. The passion fruit is also an extremely popular flavor, and the jasmine gets high marks, too. To mix up the tea, they put the contents in a glass, then insert it into a machine that shakes it up—it's kind of reminiscent of a paint shaker at the hardware store. They also put a flat plastic seal over the top, which you then break with the pointy tip of the black bubble tea straws in the container on the counter. Available sizes are medium and large, which is nice if you are not craving such a huge glass of bubble tea. You can also get your tea hot.

La Delicia en Pandebono, 40-23 82nd St., Elmhurst, NY 11373; (347) 448-8020; Subway: 7 to 82nd Street; Colombian Bakery. This is located so close to Jackson Heights, it deserves to be in this chapter. Wonderful smells waft out of this Colombian bakery, well placed to entice morning commuters on their way to the train into Manhattan. Traditional Colombian baked goods, from pastries to bread, are produced here. As the name suggests, the *pandebono* is delicious. If you don't see them out, don't fret—they live in a warm oven behind the counter, so you will always get that "fresh out of the oven" experience when you bite into one. It has a strong yet pleasant cheese flavor, and matched with the sweetness within it's just about a perfect marriage of sweet and savory. Their *buñuelos* are also very good, as is the bread. They also make *cholados,* full of sweet, milky, fruity, icy glory.

La Gran Uruguaya Bakery, 85-06 37th Ave., Jackson Heights, NY 11372; (718) 505-0474; Subway: 7 to 82nd Street; Uruguayan Bakery. Located on commercial 37th Avenue, La Gran Uruguaya Bakery is a calm oasis in a very busy and active area of Jackson Heights. It's both a bakery and cafe, and the dining room has plenty of seats for you to take a load off. They serve both American-style cakes and Latin pastries, and it's these pastries that really shine. The *pasta frola,* filled with guava paste and sweet cream cheese, is heavenly, and neither too moist nor too dry. They also make a version with *membrillo,* a quince paste. Their *bizcocho,* a buttery flaky pastry, is simple and straightforward, using just sugar as a sweetener. Their *alfajores de maizena,* made with cornstarch, are wonderfully crumbly, lightly sweet and sandwiched in the middle is a quarter-inch layer of *dulce de leche. Dulce de leche* makes an appearance in other pastries, including the more traditional *alfajores,* covered in chocolate. Their empanadas are excellent too, with savory fillings (the chicken is particularly good) in a lovely flaky pastry. Everything goes great with their *cafe con leche,* which is made by steaming milk first, then adding the coffee.

Las Americas Bakery, 40-30 82nd St., Elmhurst, NY, 11372; (718) 457-6437; Subway: 7 to 82nd Street; Bakery. A Jackson Heights institution for decades, this is a great Colombian bakery. Flaky croissant-type pastries, *pandebono,* cheesecakes, *dulce de leche*–filled pastry horns, *palmiers,* and whipped cream–filled cakes are all here. Their *dulce de leche* cake is fantastic. They also make great *raspados,* a kind of Mexican snow cone, as well as a heavenly *cholado.* Theirs is very fruity (strawberry, mango, pineapple, and honeydew) and it feels like eating a fruit salad most

of the time. They shave the ice fresh for you, with a very industrial, mechanical-looking contraption. The spoon they give you doesn't fit through the hole in the lid, so the best thing to do is to suck down as much of the delicious liquid as possible, until the overall level decreases so that it won't spill over when you take off the lid; then you can eat the fruit and ice inside. These are the best *cholados* in Jackson Heights. There are a few seats, and you are welcome to hang out and enjoy your food and drink there.

Lety Bakery, 77-07 37th Ave., Jackson Heights, NY 11372; (718) 507-6539; Subway: 7 to 74th Street or E/F/M/R to Roosevelt Avenue; Bakery. Tucked into a small storefront on 37th Avenue is Lety Bakery, providing various excellent sweet treats to the neighborhood. It's also a nice place to take a load off, sit for a while, and enjoy a cup of coffee (the iced coffee is medium strength and very nice). Their raisin roll is outstanding—buttery and flaky, with a soft interior and perfectly sweet. Their rugelach, both raspberry and apricot, are just the right size for a few bites, and covered in crunchy slivered almonds. Their little round New York–style cheesecakes are smooth, taste great, and are just the right size. Mexican wedding cookies take the form of a small flat disc as opposed to the more traditional nugget shape, but they are a delight—crispy, flaky, and buttery, dotted with pecans. Consider their black and white cookie, as well as the flan. Whole cakes like strawberry shortcake, carrot cake, and chocolate sit in the short display case, tempting you with their sweet, sweet beauty. They'll also make birthday cakes for your loved ones. During the warmer weather, the gelato comes out of hiding, and it's made in house. I'm partial to their chocolate gelato, which is rich and chocolaty, but their coffee gelato is very good, too. Ask them to put a couple scoops of gelato in a cup with ice, then add cold coffee to it—instant *affogato,* of sorts! This is not a menu item, but definitely something they can do if you just ask.

Manann Halal Meat & Grocery, 37-08 73rd St., Jackson Heights, NY 11372; Subway: 7 to 74th Street or E/F/M/R to Roosevelt Avenue; Bangladeshi/Halal Grocery. This clean, brightly lit market lies on 74th Street's Bangladeshi-oriented strip in Jackson Heights. It might seem surprising at first to see so much fish for sale, but fish plays an important role in the national diet, due to the presence of hundreds of rivers and ponds, not to mention an extensive coastline that is part of the Ganges Delta in Bangladesh. At Manann Halal you'll find big and small fish, as well as eel, frozen and fresh—*kalibaus* (orange fin labeo) and *baim* (eel) are only a couple of the varieties for sale. Various vegetables are also for sale, from green, leafy varieties to legumes. Whole-wheat *chappatis,* whole-spice *garam masala,* whole tamarind, as well as the infamous durian can all be found there as well. For a sweet treat, pick up a bottle of honey sweetened basil-seed drink.

Mi Tierra Supermarket, 85-15 Roosevelt Ave., Jackson Heights, NY 11377; (347) 642-3235; Subway: 7 to 82nd Street; Latin Market. By far the best part of this supermarket is the produce section, stocked with all sorts of products common in Latin American cuisine. Particularly impressive is the display of chilies and peppers, spilling out from baskets and available for you to pick and choose instead of buying them prepackaged in bags (or wrapped in plastic on styrofoam trays). There are dried and fresh chilies, from really spicy to quite mild, and it's just the most beautiful sight if you are a chili-head. They also have inexpensive avocados, *tomatillo de milpa* (tomatillos about a quarter the size of conventional ones), and a nice variety of starchy vegetables, like yucca, *rulo, batata,* and *eddoes*. You'll also find plenty of Latin coffees— Cafe Bustelo, El Pico, Pilon, etc.—and big bags of yerba mate. La Costeña, Goya, Incas, and Doña Isabel products line the shelves. Corn tortillas and arepas are also available aplenty. American products are stocked in full force as well, but the draw to this place is the extensive variety of Latin American products.

Mira Cali II, 76-04 Roosevelt Ave., Jackson Heights, NY 11372; (718) 779-7175; Subway: 7 to 74th Street or E/F/M/R to Roosevelt Avenue; Colombian Bakery. Everything at this bakery is always really fresh. The *pandebono* is nicely balanced in the sweet, salty, and cheesy areas. The various sweet breads and buns are soft and lightly sweet, and always fresh. The *arroz con leche* as well as the empanadas (try the sweet *empanada de choclo* or chicken empanada) are also very good. Since there's no place to sit down, takeout is best here. But enjoy the salsa music as you stand in line!

Pacific Supermarket, 75-01 Broadway, Jackson Heights, NY 11373; (718) 507-8181; Subway: 7 to 74th Street or E/F/M/R to Roosevelt Avenue; Asian Supermarket. This is truly a supermarket, with many aisles, a full-service meat and fish department, fresh vegetables, and fruit (located outside). There's even a sushi stall on the right as you enter. Take a left as you enter the store and you'll see a huge selection of bowls and other serving pieces, perfect for rice or noodles. Basics like rice, vinegars, sauces, oils, and tea are present in great abundance. They also have an inordinate amount of candy and snacks, too (like yuzu-flavored Kasugai gummy candy). The selection of pickled vegetables and fruit—*mayom,* lotus root, and peach, just to name a few)—is extensive. Beans and peanuts are available in bulk. The meat and fish department stocks fish and seafood, both alive and on ice, fish that have been cleaned and filleted, as well as fish paste, offal, and even frozen blood and bile from pigs and cows. The vegetable department carries a number of Asian greens, as well as things like winter melon and burdock. Overall, prices are excellent, and business is brisk.

Patel Brothers, 37-27 74th St., Jackson Heights, NY 11372; (718) 898-3445; Subway: 7 to 74th Street or E/F/M/R to Roosevelt Avenue; Indian Supermarket. This is Jackson Heights' best-known and most popular Indian market. You can find all your Indian food needs here, and then some. They excel particularly in their large array of spices, legumes, tea, rice, ghee, snacks, sauces/chutneys, and frozen foods. The quality of the produce is very good. It does get very crowded despite the good number of registers, but the prices are so reasonable, it is worth the wait and the crowds.

Subzi Mandi, 72-30 37th Ave. (73rd Street), Jackson Heights, NY 11372; Subway: 7 to 74th Street or E/F/M/R to Roosevelt Avenue; Indian Grocery. A slightly more rumpled-looking store than neighboring Apna Bazar, the standout here is the produce—there's some outside and some inside. It's a joy to gaze upon the fresh bunches of *saag* (spinach—nice with *paneer,* a fresh Indian cheese), fresh *methi* (fenugreek leaves—good in curries) and handle the giant *toori* (Chinese okra). Fresh jackfruit is also for sale up by the register. Indian snacks abound. Big bags of spices are also for sale at prices that are simply a steal. A nice variety of tea is also available—from the UK brand PG Tips, to Pakistani Tapal, to American Lipton. Toward the back of the store is a large area full of big bags of basmati rice. All sorts of ghee are also packed in large and small tins. Subzi Mandi resembles the groceries in India quite authentically, and there's a generous amount of chaos that ensues after work and before dinner (frankly, you'll find that same chaos in an American Safeway or Key Food around 6 p.m., too). If you are not really into crowds, the later morning/early afternoon is a calmer and less frenetic time to shop.

Table Wine, 79-14 37th Ave., Jackson Heights, NY 11372; Subway: 7 to 82nd Street; Wine Shop. This little independent shop near Jackson Heights Gardens is the best place to buy wine in the neighborhood. The staff is very knowledgeable and will no doubt help you find exactly what you're looking for. Wines are arranged not by country, but by the kind of wine it is, from lighter (nearest the door) to heavier (nearest the back wall). Speaking of the back wall, it is lined with beautiful bottles of liqueurs and spirits. Local wines also have a place of their own, up in the front. Come by on Friday (and sometimes Thursday) for their weekly tastings, which are both delicious and informative. And the majority of their wines are under $20, which makes them pretty affordable; according to the owner, the most expensive wine is about $50.

Street Food

Antojitos Mexicanos Cart, 82nd St. and Baxter Ave., Jackson Heights, NY 11378; (347) 307-0465; Subway: 7 to 82nd Street; Mexican; $. Typical Mexican fare is offered at this cart—*huaraches, tortas, tlacoyos,* and quesadillas—as well as some things you don't find that often at your average Mexican food cart—*picaditas,* chalupas, and the even less common *taco placero,* topped with either egg or sausage (*longaniza*). Even more unusual is that the quesa-dillas are made fresh, right after you place your order. The fillings offered are wonderfully varied—things like cheese, *tinga* (shredded chicken), huitlacoche, and the awesome mix of *calabaza* (summer squash) and *chicharron*. The mild vegetable flavor mixes with the porky and crunchy goodness of the *chicharron* in a fresh, homemade tortilla (crisped up and browned a bit while on the grill), topped with shredded lettuce and *crema,* and the effect is outstanding. Have them add some of the spicy green sauce to

finish it all off. The *taco placero* is topped with rice, jalepeños, and either eggs or sausage, making for a hearty meal. Probably the most unusual thing about this cart is that your typical taco—your choice of meat on griddled tortillas, topped with onions and cilantro—is not on the menu.

Arepa Lady, Roosevelt Ave. and 79th St., Jackson Heights, NY 11378; Subway: 7 to 82nd Street; twitter.com/arepalady; Colombian; $. The most heavenly arepas come from this food cart, and the Arepa Lady's reputation for making such a delicious thing is what makes her cart the best-known of the late-night Roosevelt Avenue street carts. If you haven't had one before, go for the *arepa de queso.* She also makes the *arepa de choclo,* which is sweeter, a bit bigger, and is folded over onto grated cheese. She makes a non-cheese arepa, too, which is also very good. Seriously, it's hard to find anything bad at this cart; no matter what you order, it's very

MOMOS IN HIMALAYA HEIGHTS

In recent years, Jackson Heights has seen an influx of people from Nepal, Tibet, and to a certain extent Bhutan, which means restaurants catering to their likes and needs have popped up. This is a very good thing, as this food is delicious. And while it all might look similar, there is a difference between Nepalese and Tibetan food. For one, Nepalese food tends to be a bit spicier than Tibetan food.

Momos are a favorite element of Nepalese and Tibetan cuisine. They are little round dumplings, with a wheat-based dumpling skin filled with meat or vegetables and served steamed, though panfried or deep-fried *momos* are sometimes an option. Sometimes you'll come across crescent shaped *momos*—they look a bit like Chinese potstickers—but those are usually commercially made. Dipping sauces usually come with the *momos*, and they can be relatively mild, quite spicy, or somewhere in between.

Here are some places in Jackson Heights were you can get delicious *momos:*

---

good. Note that the weather plays a part in her setting up shop on the street, so if she's not there, don't be alarmed; she'll be back, as long as it's warm. Keep an eye on her Twitter account for information as to when/where she'll be on any given night.

El Coyote Dormilon, Bentham St. and Roosevelt Ave., Jackson Heights, NY 11378; Subway: 7 to 90th Street; Mexican; $. Aside from the usual suspects—tacos, quesadillas, burritos, *tortas,* and

Gangjong Kitchen, 72-24 Roosevelt Ave. Recommended: steamed vegetable *momos*.

Lali Guras, 37-63 76th St. Recommended: steamed chicken *momos*.

Lhasa Fast Food, 37-50 74th St. Recommended: steamed beef *momos* (this is the only kind they serve).

Mustang Thakali Kitchen, 74-14 37th Ave. Recommended: steamed vegetable *momos*.

Namaste Tashi Delek Momo Dumpling Palace, 37-67 74th St. Recommended: steamed chicken *momos*.

Potala Fresh Food, Broadway and 37th Rd. Recommended: steamed beef *momos* (this is the only kind they serve).

Phayul, 74-06 37th Rd. Recommended: steamed tsel *momos*.

Tawa Food, 37-38 72nd St. Recommended: steamed chicken *momos*.

 *tlacoyos*—this three-person cart offers a selection of more unusual taste treats. This includes gorditas (a thick tortilla filled with cheese, lettuce, and *chicharron*), *tacos dorados, sopesitos* (small *sopes* topped with beans and salsa, with origins in Acapulco), *pambazos* (white bread roll dipped in red sauce and filled with potatoes and chorizo), *picaditas*, and *chicharron preparado*. The gordita is especially delicious.

El Gallo Giro, Roosevelt Ave. and 74th St., Jackson Heights, NY 11372; Subway 7 to 74th Street or E/F/M/R to Roosevelt Avenue; Mexican; $. This very popular cart serves up *tortas,* burritos, *sopes, huaraches,* tostadas, and the ever-popular taco, which is really the runaway hit of the menu. It's hard to go wrong here, what with beautifully grilled asada (beef) or chicken, and luscious carnitas (pork). The braised *lengua* (tongue) is also fantastic. They are liberal with the avocado sauce, but if you want more, just ask.

Hornado Ecuatoriano/Pique y Pase "Pepin," Warren St. and Roosevelt Ave., Jackson Heights, NY 11372; Subway: 7 to Junction Boulevard; Ecuadorian; $. Often on the sidewalk across from this food truck sits a man calling out "venga, venga!" encouraging people to come try the food. The truck puts out a nice variety of Ecuadorian specialties, like *carne guisada, hornado, fritada,* and *enceobollado de pescado.* The *ceviche de camaron* is truly awesome—a good many medium-size shrimp bathe in a cool broth/sauce containing thinly sliced red onion, cilantro, with a bit of spice. Be sure to add the roasted corn kernels that come with it, as they add a wonderful nuttiness to the dish. An eye-catching dish is the bright yellow *guatita,* a tripe and potato stew. They also offer drinks, like a sweet, iced coconut drink (reminiscent of watered-down coconut milk), which is full of delicious coconut flavor; it's great on a warm day. But when it's cold out there, get a cup of *morocho,* a warm beverage that tastes a little like rice pudding (it's the cinnamon)—drink the milk, then eat the *morocho*—big corn kernels—that sit at the bottom of the glass. There are usually raisins in there, too!

La Quesadilla Sabrosa Taqueria, 75th St. and Roosevelt Ave., Jackson Heights, NY 11372; (646) 732-0204; Subway: 7 to 74th Street or E/F/M/R to Roosevelt Avenue; Mexican; $. Currently located right in front of the Chase bank on Roosevelt Avenue, this food cart offers delicious quesadillas. Although they offer a whole host of Mexican dishes, like *tortas,* tacos, and *huaraches,* quesadillas are their specialty. The quesadillas can be filled with either meat or vegetarian options, which is kind of a big deal in a street-food world that is primarily meat-oriented. Try interesting vegetarian fillings like *flor de calabaza* (squash flower), *calabaza* (zucchini), *hongos* (mushrooms), huitlacoche (corn smut/fungus), and simple cheese. The cheese quesadilla is actually a great way to experience their quesadillas in their most basic form, and they are really delicious this way—the corn tortilla is griddled until it's a bit crispy, and it's filled with a melted white cheese, some pulverized cotija cheese, and shredded lettuce. Add the green and/or red sauce to spice it up, with a squeeze of lime. That green sauce is also fantastic with chicken.

Mi Pequeña Terruño, Roosevelt Ave. between 80th and 81st Streets, Jackson Heights, NY 11372; Subway: 7 to 82nd Street; Colombian; $. Once, while looking for the Arepa Lady, I came across this tiny cart, operated by two middle-aged men. FYI, "mi pequeña terruño" means "my little homeland." Their handwritten sign says

"Chuzos, Chorizos & Arepas con Queso." Lo and behold, that is exactly what they had on the grill—nicely charred *chuzos* (a kind of kebab), plump red chorizo sausages, and small, thick arepas that were a sight for sore eyes. Of course, I chose this. The man next to the grill tops the arepa with cheese, which melts easily. The arepa is soft, a bit sweet, and with the salty white cheese, it is a perfect combination. Next to the grill is a plastic jug containing a bright green "guacamole," which is a mix of cilantro, bits of avocado, onion, and jalepeño, which has a bright, tangy, spicy flavor. It adds extra depth to the arepa, and makes a good thing even better.

Oblea Lady, 82nd St., half a block south of Roosevelt Ave., Jackson Heights, NY 11372; Subway: 7 to 82nd Street; Colombian; $. She can be somewhat elusive, so count yourself lucky if you find her. She sells *obleas*—large, flat, paper-thin wafers slathered with *arequipe,* otherwise known as caramel or *dulce de leche*. They are both light and sweet at the same time, and they go down fast. There really isn't anything else like it in the Roosevelt Avenue street-food scene, so I consider her product to be rather special.

Potala Fresh Food, Broadway and 37th Rd., Jackson Heights, NY 11372; (917) 767-1777; Subway: 7 to 74th Street or E/F/M/R to Roosevelt Avenue; Tibetan; $. The nice Tibetan man running this cart sells one thing and one thing only—beef *momos*. They are excellent—eight little dumplings, round with a twist at the top, steaming hot in their styrofoam container. They are tasty by themselves, but taste even better with the fiery hot red sauce that comes with them. This sauce is such a wonderful accompaniment to the *momos,* with its heat and slight tang. Water and other drinks can be purchased at this cart as well. The cart is around the corner from an outdoor seating area, so you can head over there to eat your *momos* on a nice day.

Raspado Carts, along Roosevelt Ave. in Jackson Heights; Subway: 7 to 82nd Street; Colombian; $. I have seen these carts in various places, their presence expanding when the weather warms up. *Raspados* are a kind of shave ice treat that are made right there on the spot. I think of them as *"cholado* lite," since they have some of the elements of *cholados,* but are a much pared down production. The person manning the cart will shave off the ice from a big ice block, then put it into a plastic water cup where it resembles a snow cone, complete with a round pyramid top. Choose three flavors of syrup—*naranja* (orange), *mora* (blackberry), *fresa* (strawberry), coconut, mango, and that's just the start—and they get poured over the ice. Be sure to have them add a bit of sweetened condensed milk. A straw is plunged into the ice, and then you start drinking and eating it. The hotter the day, the faster everything melts and melds. Very refreshing.

Quesadilla Lady, Roosevelt Ave. between 85th and 86th Streets, Jackson Heights, NY 11372; Subway: 7 to 82nd Street; Mexican; $.

When you arrive at this cart and decide what you want, a man standing near the order window will offer to take your order. It's a very unorthodox way of placing an order at a food cart but just go with it, as it really does seem to make it easier on the woman making the quesadillas. Numerous fillings are available—potato and chorizo, mushroom, cheese, and *tinga,* to start. The *tinga* is terrific. The quesadilla is a bit delicate, with a thin tortilla stuffed with your filling of choice, and some lettuce. There's cotija cheese in there, too. It comes with a fabulous green sauce, and some *crema* (you can get that on the side if you like). These quesadillas are very easy to eat.

Sabor Mexicana, Roosevelt Ave. and 75th St., Jackson Heights, NY 11372; Subway: 7 to 74th Street or E/F/M/R to Roosevelt Avenue; Mexican; $. This very popular cart is located right outside the 7 train station on the south side of Roosevelt Avenue. They seem to have quite the fan club, with people lining up for their food—understandably so, because it is so very tasty. The tacos are good but the quesadillas are excellent, and they are huge. They are reminiscent of the quesadillas I grew up eating—a large tortilla filled with cheese and anything else I wanted, folded over and fried up. The chicken quesadilla is very good, a large tortilla filled with chicken, Oaxacan cheese and lettuce. The green sauce is fantastic and adds a lot to the quesadilla. You can nosh on it right there at the cart or take it with you.

Sammy's Halal Cart, 73rd St. and Broadway, Jackson Heights, NY 11372; (646) 321-9961; Subway: 7 to 74th Street or E/F/M/R to Roosevelt Avenue; sammyhalalfood.com; Halal; $. As you walk toward the intersection of 73rd Street and Broadway looking for street meat, you may find it confusing because there is more than one cart with the "Sammy's Halal" name. Best choose the one that has the marketing signs on the side of the cart, proclaiming his victory in the Vendy Awards. He deserved to win because his food is very good, especially in a town where this kind of food is found pretty much everywhere. Best thing to get is the chicken over rice—and get the green sauce! The red is quite spicy and the white yogurt sauce adds a nice tang. There is a little side salad, but the main star really is that glorious chicken and rice.

Tamale Ladies, outside the southwest entrance to the 82nd Street 7 train, Jackson Heights, NY, 11372. Subway: 7 to 82nd Street; Mexican; $. Often surrounded by a crowd, the ladies at 82nd Street sell their delicious tamales out of what looks like a metal stockpot. There are a few varieties available at any one time—chicken, pork, mole, and *rajas* with cheese. If you want yours spicy, ask for it "picante." In addition to the traditional tamale wrapped in a corn husk, she also sells a tamale "sandwich," which is simply a tamale on a roll. Prices are cheap, with the traditional tamale going for about $1, the sandwich possibly a little more. If you can order in Spanish, all the better.

Tia Julia, Roosevelt Ave. and Benham St., Jackson Heights, NY 11373; (917) 757-1633; Subway: 7 to 90th Street; Mexican; $. Some really excellent food—regardless of the culture—comes out of this Mexican food truck. Patrons of Tia Julia will gladly tell you that everything is good. Their menu is full of classic Mexican snacking specialties: tacos, *tortas/cemitas, sopes,* quesadillas, *tlacoyos,* and *flautas.* The *tlacoyos* are simply beautiful, filled with varying combinations of beans, meat, and potatoes, draped with *crema,* green and red sauces, and cotija cheese—it resembles a torpedo a bit . . . a delicious, delicious torpedo. Their tacos are wonderful—the carnitas taco is chock-full of amazing, soft, and yumtastic meat, not to mention a big slice of avocado on top. Their *cemitas* are epic, gorgeous things. They use a fluffy sandwich roll, slather one side with mayo, the other with refried beans, and insert thin chicken cutlets (or beef), a heaping mound of grated white cheese, slice after slice of avocado, plus pickled jalepeños and onions on top if you want it to have a little bit of a kick going on (highly recommended). They often run specials, so look for them on a handwritten sign on the front of the truck by the ordering window.

Corona & Elmhurst

Just past Jackson Heights lies Corona, home to a very large Latin American population. For a long time, though, Corona was very Italian, and vestiges of that time lie in a few remaining restaurants—Leo's Latticini, the Lemon Ice King of Corona, and the Park Side restaurant. There is still an Italian population in Corona, though it is dwindling as time goes by. African Americans made their mark on the neighborhood, too, and a lot of famous people from the black community lived in Corona—musicians like Cannonball Adderly, Dizzy Gillespie, Clark Terry, Lena Horne, Ella Fitzgerald, and Louis Armstrong (you can visit his house, which is now a museum—highly recommended). That's quite the lineup, if you ask me. Excellent food can be found in this neighborhood, much of it Latin American. Places like Tortilleria Nixtamal (Mexican), El Gauchito (Argentinian), Empanadas Cafe, and Rincon Criollo (Cuban) to start. Somewhat elusive street vendors can be found around Flushing Meadows–Corona Park, which borders the eastern edge of the neighborhood, but they come and go; keep an eye out for them, though. And speaking of this park, it is quite a gem. It's the location of the 1964 World's Fair, whose Unisphere still graces the park. Both the US Tennis Center, where the US Open is held, and Citi Field, home to the New York Mets, are located at the park.

To the west of Corona lies Elmhurst. Established by the Dutch and once home to Italians and Jews, it now has a sizable Asian population. In fact, it's become the unofficial second Chinatown in Queens (and the fourth in New York City overall), sporting restaurants and shops that cater to the Chinese, Thai, Vietnamese, Indonesian, and Malaysian populations in the neighborhood. Here, you'll find some of the best dumplings (**Lao Bei Fang Dumpling House,** p. 214), delicious regional Chinese cuisine (Henanese at **Uncle Zhou's,** p. 222), and one of the best *banh mi* sandwiches in the city (**Joju,** p. 211). Much of this Chinatown lies along Broadway from Queens Boulevard until it hits Roosevelt and meets up with Jackson Heights' Little India; you'll also find Asian food along Woodside Avenue just off Broadway.

Foodie Faves

Ayada, 77-08 Woodside Ave., Elmhurst, NY 11373; (718) 424-0844; Subway: R/M to Elmhurst Avenue; ayadathaiwoodside.com;

Thai; $. Overwhelmingly excellent Thai food can be had here at this small restaurant on a quiet stretch of Woodside Avenue. It's cheery inside, with comfortable hardwood floors, green paint on the wall, plus piles of mangoes on the counter near the register. A number of publications have visited and reviewed Ayada, and the restaurant has call-outs on the menu to indicate what they have recommended. While a lot of places make *tom yum* soup, theirs is particularly flavorful, with a slow comfortable burn from the chilies and chili oil in the soup; the broth is addictive. Their drunken noodles—again, a Thai restaurant staple—are excellent and flavorful. The *larb* is also a real taste treat, made with ground chicken enrobed in the flavors of mint and cilantro with that wonderful texture of the roasted rice powder in it. This restaurant happens to be near Elmhurst's Thai Buddhist Temple, too. Ayada is vying for the designation of best Thai restaurant in Queens, and the food is so good here, it just might make it.

Chao Thai, 85-03 Whitney Ave., Elmhurst, NY 11373; (718) 424-4999; Subway: E/M to Elmhurst Avenue; Thai; $. This Thai restaurant in Elmhurst is excellent by all standards. The space is quite small, seating only around 25 people total, and is not the most atmospheric place, but the food more than makes up for that. It is spicy and flavorful, and portions are substantial. There are a lot of familiar dishes on the menu, like the ever-present pad thai, and then some less well-known ones, like *tua han* soup, which contains pork liver, heart, and intestines, in a broth flavored with sour mustard. A great way to start off the meal is with the papaya salad, which comes with plenty of mung bean sprouts and peanuts in a spicy tangy dressing. It is a nice dish to eat more mildly spiced, but if you want the pepper burn, they'll turn it up for you. The pork  *prik king*—pork belly fried till it's crispy, and mixed with green beans—is savory, spicy, and a little sweet, and the pork takes on a wonderful sturdy texture. The green beans are pleasantly crunchy but not raw, and the flavor of kaffir lime leaf is pervasive, leaving behind its exotic taste and aroma. As for noodles, the *pad kee mao* and the *gai kua* are great choices. These flat noodles have a wonderful texture. For something a little different, try the *pad frog garlic,* which is basically a dish of spicy garlic frog's legs. The *jungle curry,* known for its intense spiciness, has quite the kick, with a nice light broth, with no coconut milk to be found. Because the food can be so spicy, it's nice to accompany it with a glass of coconut juice, which helps cool the inferno that may be raging on your tongue.

Costa Verde, 94-59 Corona Ave., Corona, NY 11368; (718) 271-0900; Subway: 7 to Junction Boulevard; Peruvian; $. Ceviche and more is on the menu at this terrific little Peruvian spot near the intersection of Junction Boulevard and Corona Avenue; this is a fabulous food intersection, full of excellent restaurants showcasing the food from multiple South American countries. And speaking of ceviche, it's really good here. If you'd like your *ceviche de pescado* a little spicy, let them know. The fish comes on a platter, soaked in a delicious mixture of lemon juice and cilantro (with extra juice on the side) and covered with thinly sliced raw red onions. The combination is wonderful, and full of fresh flavors. Perfectly cooked sweet potato and white potato accompany it, along with toasted corn kernels. The *chaufa de pollo* is incredibly light, even though it's fried rice. It's seasoned simply with egg and scallions, and is not the least bit greasy; be sure to add some of their crazy-good green hot sauce to the rice, too. As is the case with most Peruvian restaurants, *pollos a la brasa* are on the menu in various combinations—whole or half chickens with salads, rice, and plantains. Bigger combos with avocado salad, hot dogs, and yucca are available. Enjoy soups, lo mein, and platters of meats as well. Their *chicha morado* is very good, too, and goes with pretty much everything.

El Gauchito, 94-60 Corona Ave., Elmhurst, NY 11373; (718) 271-8198; Subway: 7 to Junction Boulevard; elgauchitony.com; Argentinian; $$. A wide range of Argentinian foods are on the menu at this very comfortable spot near the excellent Latin American food corner of Corona Avenue and Junction Boulevard. Start your meal off with a bottle of Quilmes, a very popular beer in Argentina (a lot of Germans moved to Argentina in the late 19th century and brought their beer-making skills with them), or a glass of excellent Argentinian wine. You'll see on the menu that the foods range from salads to appetizers (many of which contain potatoes), then pastas (a lot of Italians emigrated to Argentina, too), and of course, meats. You can order the meats a la carte—chorizo, steaks, sweetbreads, pork chops, short ribs, etc.—or as part of a mix of meats. The big meat fest is the Churrasco El Gauchito, which includes a heck of a lot of different meats. These all come with sides, like french fries and salad; the classic Argentinian sauce, chimichurri, goes perfectly with the meat, too. Seafood is also a fine choice, with both shellfish and grilled fish of the day as options. Desserts are light, with flan and churros with caramel being excellent options; an even lighter dish of cheese and *membrillo* is also a great way to end the meal. For those of you who want to take the meat home with you, there's a butcher shop in the back of the restaurant, with various cuts of beef for purchase. They also sell a variety of Argentinian products, from yerba mate to fresh pasta, *dulce de leche* to cookies.

El Globo/La Nueva Espiga, 42-13 102 St.; Corona, NY 11368; (718) 779-7898; Subway: 7 to 103rd Street; Mexican; $. This is one of the few Mexican restaurants in all of New York City that make their own tortillas (**Tortilleria Nixtamal,** p. 221, is another one). Simple food is the name of the game here, but flavors are elevated to exciting heights. A variety of Mexican staples are served, including tacos, *huaraches,* and quesadillas, but it's the tacos that are a particularly great deal here. They are bursting with flavor and relatively large compared to a lot of tacos you'll find around town. The *bistec* (steak) taco is particularly good. The juicy bits of steak arrive sitting on two of El Globo's homemade corn tortillas and the whole thing is covered in chopped cilantro and raw white onion, accompanied by thin slices of radish and lime quarters. (Fresh lime juice really adds a nice brightness to the taco.) You can also squirt some spicy red or green sauce onto the taco, bottles of which are

on the tables. The *al pastor* (pork) taco is also delicious, slightly tinged red, with some wonderful caramelized bits of meat, and topped by more of that chopped cilantro and raw onion. Fresh lime juice is excellent on it as well. The *verde enchiladas* can house a number of different meats of your choice, and arrive at your table on an enormous plate. Refried beans and rice come with them, and their green sauce is quite spicy. Good thing there's a little bit of *crema* and avocado to counter that. It goes perfectly with a glass of their sweet *horchata*, too.

Empanadas Cafe, 56-27 Van Doren St., Corona, NY 11368; (718) 592-7288; Subway: 7 to 103 Street; empanadascafe.com; Latin American; $. Delicious empanadas abound at this tiny spot in an unassuming corner of Corona. And although the space is about the size of half a carport, there are a couple of tables available, and a few stools up at the counter. The empanadas come in three different kinds of dough—white flour, organic wheat flour, and corn flour. You'll recognize familiar fillings like shredded chicken, chopped pork, and cheese, but there are also fillings that are less orthodox, but no less of a delight, like the combination of fresh mozzarella, tomato, and pesto, a nod to the neighborhood's Italian heritage. It comes in a corn-flour dough, so this really is a multicultural eating experience. A more conventional filling is the chicken and cheese, which comes wrapped in a hearty whole-wheat dough. It is delicious, with a wonderful earthiness from the whole wheat.

It goes very well with the superb green sauce that comes with your empanadas. Also quite good is the turkey and cheese empanada, which comes in a regular white-flour dough. And perhaps the most fun empanada of all is the sweet plantain and cheese empanada. It really is like dessert—the small chunks of sweet plantain have a light banana flavor, and the cheese is hot and melty and a tiny bit salty, so you have both the sweet and salty flavor combination going on—heavenly! If you are craving something cold for dessert, South American ices are available in flavors like coconut, tamarind, and vanilla.

Java Village, 86-10 Justice Ave., Elmhurst, NY 11373; (718) 205-2166; Subway: M/R to Grand Avenue/Newtown; jvvillage.word press.com; Indonesian; $. Java Village is mainly about the steam table. The flavorful dishes here are excellent, and additional food can be made to order. The rice combination is the main event, where you pick one dish or a combination of meat and vegetable dishes with beautifully made rice. If you want that rice fried, it costs an extra dollar. The food is absolutely delicious, and there is something for both omnivores and vegetarians alike. The kale in coconut milk is sweet and a little salty, and the tofu, tempeh, and green bean stew is also delicious. Try the chicken curry, which is on the sweet side of savory, as well as a little spicy. The ginger beef is also excellent. If you want things a little spicier, have them give you a little scoop of sambal on the side. Made to order dishes include soup containing little *shumai,* stuffed tofu, and meatballs (*baso malang*); congee; fried whole tilapia; and various meats over rice. Be sure to take a look at the prepackaged food sitting up on the raised counter above the steam-table area, including *pisang goreng* (fried bananas), *lemper ayam* (sticky rice and chicken) and the *kue ongol,* which is a sort of soft, chewy mix of coconut milk, tapioca flour, bits of jackfruit, and palm sugar. It's a great mix of textures and just sweet enough. Drinks are in the refrigerator, and range from American sodas to water to a canned Thai tea drink that is quite nice. Fresh Indonesian-style drinks are also on the menu, including iced *cendol,* made of green tapioca in coconut milk.

Joju, 83-25 Broadway, Elmhurst, NY 11373; (347) 808-0887; Subway: M/R to Elmhurst Avenue; jojuny.com; Vietnamese; $. Fantastic *banh mi* sandwiches can be found at Joju, a bright, modern little spot in the middle of a mini mall on Elmhurst's Broadway shopping strip. Somehow, they've figured out how to toast the baguette perfectly, and it comes out crispy and very easy to eat. The #3 with roast pork is a well-balanced *banh mi*—get the egg option with it (you can determine how hard the yolk is cooked, too). It comes with fresh cucumber, pickled shredded daikon radish and carrot, and big leaves of cilantro, and you can get it spicy with the addition of thin slices of jalepeño and spicy mayo (highly recommended). Other tasty choices are the Classic (#1) made with Vietnamese ham, head cheese, and pâté spread, and the Lemongrass Chicken (#2),

Corona's Italian Heritage

While today's Corona is primarily a Latin American neighborhood, another group of immigrants called Corona home starting in the late 19th century—Italians. Centrally located Corona Avenue became the center of Italian settlement after 1890; magnificent St. Leo's Roman Catholic Church, which is still standing today, was the spiritual center for Corona's Italians and the congregation grew to 2,000 by 1913. Italian social clubs sprang up, as did social support services for new arrivals.

Many of these immigrants came from southern Italy and possessed manual labor skills that suited the burgeoning construction industry at the time (houses and transportation) and in agriculture. Small-scale agriculture in the form of gardens (for vegetables and fruit), grapevines (for winemaking), and chickens took place on small plots of lands and in backyards, serving as a way to keep a connection with the old country.

Corona's Italian presence is shrinking and is close to becoming extinct. It's alive through a few food-oriented places—the Lemon Ice King of Corona (p. 223), the Park Side Restaurant (p. 224), and Leo's Latticini (aka Mama's, p. 224). There's a bocce court in the triangular William F. Moore Park, known to the locals as Spaghetti Park, located near both the Lemon Ice King and the Park Side Restaurant; this really is the lingering Italian center of Corona. So, if you are curious at all about this special place in Queens, head on over and pick up some fresh mozzarella at Mama's, have a fabulous Italian feast at Park Side, and enjoy a lemon ice while watching a wicked game of bocce (in the summer).

consisting of lemongrass-marinated grilled dark meat chicken. The sandwiches go really well with a Vietnamese coffee, served either hot or cold. This coffee, using Cafe du Monde grounds and made strong and sugared up with sweetened condensed milk, holds up extremely well to being iced and doesn't seem to lose much of its punch as the ice cubes melt. Another delicious drink option is the mango- and lychee-infused iced green tea; bubbles (tapioca balls) and mango stars—pieces of mango flesh cut into star shapes—are a great addition. For dessert, either the ginger or vanilla flan is a nice, light way to end the meal.

La Esquina Criolla, 94-67 Corona Ave., Elmhurst, NY 11373; (718) 699-5579; Subway: 7 to Junction Boulevard; Argentinian; $$. One of the cool things about this place is that you can buy meat to take home with you at their small meat counter along the left wall of the restaurant. Cuts like *bola de lomo* (sirloin tip), *vacio* (flank), *bife ancho* (rib eye), as well as house made *morcilla* (blood sausage) and chorizo are all displayed and for sale. *Jamón de Parma* is also available, as is *dulce de batata,* which is a kind of sweet, sliceable potato jam, traditionally eaten with cheese. Apart from the meat counter is the comfortable restaurant with a menu that includes plenty of meat dishes. These range from the empanadas filled with either beef or chicken; the beef empanadas can be fried (recommended). Both are beautiful examples of Argentinian comfort-food snacks, and are especially good with their own house-made garlicky chimichurri sauce—this stuff is good on pretty much everything on the menu. It goes particularly well with their grilled meats, which can be ordered as part of a mix of meats or on their own. Get the Parillada Completa for the most extensive example of the restaurant's meat-grilling prowess—with it, you'll get skirt steak, short rib, sweetbread, tripe, kidney, black sausage and Argentinian sausage. It can be ordered for one or two people, and it is simply fantastic. Don't forget the chimichurri!

Lao Bei Fang Dumpling House, 83-05 Broadway, Elmhurst, NY 11373; (718) 639-3996; Subway: M/R to Elmhurst Avenue; Chinese; $. Dumplings are the name of the game here, whether you're ready to eat them at the restaurant or take them home. Dumplings come steamed or panfried, and while the majority of dumplings contain meat, there is a vegetable dumpling (fried or steamed) appropriate for vegetarians. If you eat meat, give the pork and leek dumplings a try—they are delicious steamed but even better fried, as they develop a beautiful crust along the fried side. The dumpling skin is on the thicker side, and the filling is savory, giving the whole thing a kind of rich, smooth, and almost buttery flavor. If you eat in, there are a few sauces on the table—a spicy chili oil, seeds included; soy sauce in a sriracha bottle; and a thin sriracha sauce, which has a spicy/tangy flavor that melds well with the dumplings. If you are interested in just a dumpling snack, they'll prepare four fried dumplings for $1.50.

Mie Jakarta, 86-20 Whitney Ave., Elmhurst, NY 11373; (718) 606-8025; Subway: M/R to Elmhurst Avenue; Indonesian; $. This small Indonesian restaurant serves up consistently delicious food in modest digs, and by the crowds that stream in especially on the weekend, you know they are doing something good. A great way to start the meal is with their *sate ayam,* their delectable chicken satay. Five to six skewers of tender grilled chicken—tasting of the grill and possessing grill marks—are slathered with peanut sauce that tastes sweet, savory, and a little spicy all at once. Main dishes are made from beef, chicken, fish, and oxtails; there are also noodle dishes, including their excellent *mie komplit,* made with shredded chicken, meatballs, wonton, and of course, noodles. The *nasi campur rendang* is a great beef dish, made with beef cooked with spices—as well as a whole hard-boiled egg—and covered in a peanut sauce, accompanied by rice and curried vegetables, including some nice hearty kale. For vegetarian tastes, the *solo betawi* is a great option—vegetables are cooked with coconut milk, accompanied by potatoes, tomatoes, tofu, and rice. On the drink menu there are a couple of shaved ice dishes that are really good. The *es campur*—made with shaved ice, coconut milk, green and red beans, jackfruit, jelly, and brown sugar—is sweet, creamy, icy, and a little salty all at once.

Patacon Pisao #2, 85-22 Grand Ave., Elmhurst, NY 11373; (718) 899-8922; Subway: M/R to Grand Avenue/Newtown; pataconpisao nyc.com; Venezuelan; $. Just a few blocks from the subway station lies Patacon Pisao, which serves, as the name indicates, *patacons*. This is a sandwich that uses slices of thin, flattened plantain, twice fried till crisp, in place of bread. It's a favorite treat in Venezuela. At Patacon Pisao, a variety of fillings are available, including chicken, cheese, and pork (try the *pernil*). It comes with lettuce, tomatoes, ketchup, cheese, and *wasakaka* sauce (reminiscent of the Chilean *pebre*), as well as a white and pink mayo-type sauce.

The sandwich comes wrapped in foil, which you can use to your advantage—it encases the sandwich, helping your hands to stay clean from any sauce or ingredients that might fall out and onto your fingers. Wet naps are given to you to help with any digit cleanup as well. Apart from the *patacon,* the *cachapa* is also delicious. It's softer than the *patacon,* and sweeter, and shaped like a half moon quesadilla. The sweet exterior and the savory interior—the cheese is wonderful—is an awesome combination. Venezuelan arepas, *tacuchos,* and *pepitos* are also on the menu, available with different fillings. Get a glass of their sweet and tangy brown sugarcane limeade to wash it all down—it is fabulous and not overly sweet.

Ploy Thai, 8140 Broadway, Elmhurst, NY 11373; (718) 205-2128; Subway: M/R to Elmurst Avenue; Thai; $$. *Ploy* means "gem" in Thai, and boy is this place a real gem in the neighborhood. The curry puffs are very, very good, made with a buttery, flaky pastry, and a delicious curried chicken, onion, and potato filling. The cucumber salad that comes with it is very fresh, too. The fried chive pancake is also smashing—triangles of deep-fried, savory chive dumplings with a wonderful crunchy crust. They come with soy sauce that tastes slightly sweet. Now, beyond the appetizers is quite a lengthy menu. When you are deciding on your main dishes, check the specials. Some may only be written in Thai, so ask about them if you are curious. Another "problem" is that so much of the menu is full of delicious and well-executed food, it can be hard to decide what to order. Old standards like *pad keemao, larb,* and *pad prik khing* are done really well here. The *pad kra prao* with chicken is wonderfully spicy, not only from chili flakes but also the amount of fresh green chilies in the mix. It comes with rice to help with the heat if you need it. The *som tum*—papaya salad—is particularly awesome, just bursting with flavor, with a little bit of a funk from the fish sauce. This salad can also be ordered with salted crab, too. The curry menu includes a few non-coconut milk curries; give the spicy jungle curry or roasted duck curry (duck in curry is fantastic, by the way) a try for something a little different. Wash it all down with a Thai iced tea or coffee, palm sugar juice, or a bottle of soy milk.

Shake Shack (Citi Field), 123-01 Roosevelt Ave., Citi Field, Corona, NY 11368; (718) 507-6387; Subway: 7 to Willets Point; shakeshack.com; Burgers; $. When Citi Field (home of the New York Mets baseball team) opened up, replacing the old Shea Stadium, the people behind food services at this new stadium really upped

ELMHURST, NEW YORK CITY'S FOURTH CHINATOWN

When most people think of Chinatown in NYC, they think of the one in Manhattan. However, there are multiple Chinatowns in New York, which makes sense for a city as big as this one. The "official" Chinatowns in New York City are threefold: Manhattan's Chinatown near Canal and Bowery; Flushing's Chinatown at Main Street and Roosevelt Avenue; and Brooklyn's Chinatown in the Sunset Park neighborhood along 8th Avenue between 42nd and 68th Streets. But Elmhurst could really be considered the fourth Chinatown, thanks to a plethora of East Asian and Southeast Asian businesses and restaurants in the area, with a healthy leaning toward SEA businesses.

Here in this neighborhood, you'll find a delicious array of Asian food cultures—Indonesian, Thai, Vietnamese, Malaysian, Chinese, and Taiwanese; Indian even makes an appearance with sweets and the unique Indian Chinese cuisine. In the early days, the strip of Broadway between Elmhurst Avenue and Whitney held the main concentration of Asian businesses, but that has expanded, and most of the length of Broadway between Queens Boulevard and Woodside

their game. There is plenty of quality food available, but the most celebrated new tenant was Shake Shack, an outpost of great fast food–style hamburgers in Queens. As with all the Shake Shack locations, the meat is grass-fed beef from Pat LaFrieda, and you can patronize the Shack Shack stall starting two hours before the first pitch until the ninth inning. A slightly pared down menu of the

Avenue, as well as their side streets, is lined with Asian restaurants and shops. Elmhurst is technically just south of Roosevelt Avenue, and if you follow Broadway north to Roosevelt Avenue you'll run into Jackson Heights. It's a beautiful connection, and an embarrassment of riches, food-wise.

There are a couple of ways to experience the neighborhood. You can walk the length of Broadway in the neighborhood between Queens Boulevard and Roosevelt Avenue. The M/R subway to Grand Avenue/Newtown is on the Queens Boulevard end and the E/F/M/R/7 to 74th Street and Broadway is on the other. The distance between these two stops is about a mile. Or, take the M/R to Elmhurst Avenue and focus your visit on the blocks along Broadway between Elmhurst and 51st Avenues. Along the length of Broadway, you'll encounter a plethora of delicious food, including Indonesian steam-table dishes, Vietnamese *banh mi* sandwiches, Chinese dumplings, whole fried fish Thai style, Indian *gulab jamun,* durian and mango ice cream, fresh juices, Indian Chinese fried chicken, and Hong Kong–style rice rolls. And that's just the beginning. Elmhurst is an incredible food neighborhood, and well worth a visit.

food people have grown to love at the original Shake Shack is available at the Citi Field location—thin, fast food-style burgers on squishy potato rolls; the Shack-cago dog; salty crinkle fries with or without cheese; shakes, frozen custard, and concretes. Beer

and soda are also available. New Yorkers love their Shake Shack, so be prepared for long lines. The wait is worth it.

Tangra Masala, 87-09 Grand Ave., Elmhurst, NY 11373; (718) 803-2298; Subway: M/R to Newtown/Grand; Indian Chinese; $. The cuisine here is Indian Chinese, which means it's Chinese food that's been adjusted to work with Indian ingredients and adapted for Indian-Bengali tastes. Tangra is the name of the Hakka-dominated Chinatown in Kolkata, India, the capital of West Bengal, a state in India. The menu itself is extensive, and it's notable to point out that there are beef dishes available, which is a kind of meat that is normally not offered on Indian menus but is prevalent on Chinese menus (for instance, classic beef and broccoli is on the menu). Beef also shows up in a rice dish called Tangra Masala Beef—the beef is perfectly tender and almost melts in your mouth. The rice, studded with diced vegetables, takes on a beautiful red hue and a flavor that is spicy and savory. As for the appetizers, Lolly Pop Chicken is one of their most popular appetizers, but the chicken *pakoras,* which come with a slightly spicy-vinegary-sweet green sauce, are also fantastic. Throughout the menu you'll see some patterns—meats are cooked in styles like Manchurian, Tangra Masala (like the beef dish above), and, yum, Chilli. Meats— goat, beef, seafood, and chicken— prepared in the Chilli style are flavor bombs and fantastically delicious. They can be prepared either "dry" or with "gravy," which is a thick, savory brown sauce with onions. When it comes to the Chicken Chilli, the brown sauce is the way to go. You can order anything mild to spicy, but if you want to control the heat level of your food, consider ordering it mild and spiking it with the excellent, thick, roasted chili sauce that is present at each table. For even more spiciness, add the thinly sliced small green chilies that are immersed in vinegar in the jar next to the chili sauce; just the spicy vinegar can be a nice condiment, too. Aside from the meat-focused dishes, there are soups, noodles, and chop suey. There's even an entire page of vegetarian dishes, so this is an excellent option for those eschewing meat. Stick around for dessert, though—the malai ice cream, flavored with almond, is beyond delicious.

Tortilleria Nixtamal, 104-05 47th Ave., Corona, NY 11368; (718) 699-2434; Subway: 7 to 103rd Street; tortillerianixtamal.com; Mexican; $. This is about the only place in the city that makes masa truly from scratch, starting with the corn itself, soaking it in water and lye, draining and grinding the corn into masa dough. This is the way it's been done for thousands of years, and the resulting masa and tortillas have a taste far superior to any others in Queens. Their tacos are excellent, but the cigar-shape chicken tacos are particularly wonderful, as are the pork tacos. If you see carnitas are available that day, definitely go for that. One of their most popular tamales contains sausage and peppers, which is definitely a nod to Corona's Italian past. The *verde tamale,* made with pork, is also outstanding. Both the guacamole and chips—made from their own tortillas—and the nachos are also good. Larger platters are also available, including tostadas, *sincronizadas,* enchiladas and *chilaquiles* (adding an egg and/or meat is a good idea). Here, you can also get a nice tall glass of *horchata* and a Mexican Coke; the Sidral is also a nice apple soda, popular in Mexico. They also bring in a locally baked *tres leches* cake, which is definitely worth saving room for.

Uncle Zhou Restaurant, 83-29 Broadway, Elmhurst, NY 11373; (718) 393-0888; Subway: M/R to Elmhurst Avenue; Chinese; $. The name of the restaurant is pronounced like "Uncle Joe," in case you are wondering. Here, they serve Henanese food; the Henan province is in central China and is considered to be the "breadbasket" of that country, as their output of wheat is the nation's highest. That would explain the prevalence of wheat-based noodles in the region's cuisine, and Uncle Zhou does them well. Here, you can get either hand-drawn noodles or knife-shaved noodles, wheaty and pleasantly doughy in consistency. A good way to try these noodles is in the restaurant's various soups. The lamb knife-shaved noodle soup is lamby and mild and the scads of cilantro leaves on top add a nice additional element to the mix. On the spicy end of things is the spicy beef hand-drawn noodle soup, which is true to its name and beautifully spicy. It contains what can only be considered braising-quality meat, so truth be told it's a bit chewy in parts. But what these cuts of meat really excel in is flavor, so the slices of beef taste quite beefy. Delicious. On the vegetarian side, the tomato and egg *lao main* noodle has an ever so slightly fatty, umami-rich broth in which noodles (hand-drawn or knife-shaved) coexist with raw cucumber, mushrooms, and of course tomato and a scrambled egg. Aside from the noodles, the dumplings on the menu are fantastic. The lamb dumplings are rich with lamb meat inside, and the pork and chive dumplings are also excellent. Both come with a dipping sauce, which is simply perfect with these dumplings. No doubt it's some alchemy of vinegar, soy sauce, and sesame oil.

Landmarks

Lemon Ice King of Corona, 52-02 108th St., Corona, NY 11368; (718) 699-5133; Subway: 7 to 110th Street; thelemonicekingof corona.com; $. The Lemon Ice King is a delicious part of Queens history. It's also a favorite way among locals to beat the heat on a hot summer's night. The Lemon Ice King has been serving up Italian ices for over 60 years and in that time they have developed a loyal following both in and out of the borough. Walk up to the window and get ready to be blown away by the extensive number flavors, from the classic lemon, to the earthy peanut butter, to the fun and whimsical rainbow flavor. Other mainstay flavors are cherry, straw-berry, watermelon, pistachio, creamsicle, and grape. And this is only the tip of the "ice" berg (pun intended). The texture is smooth and luscious, and satisfies kids both big and small.

Leo's Latticini's/Mamas, 46-02 104th St., Corona, NY 11368; (718) 898-6069; Subway: 7 to 103rd Street; Italian Deli and Bakery; $. Like the Lemon Ice King, Leo's Latticini, aka Mama's, is a remnant of old Corona. It's been around for over 80 years, and although Mama herself is no longer with us, her legacy lives on in the form

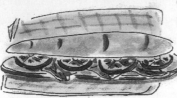

of excellent fresh mozzarella, fresh pasta, and ginormous sandwiches. The Mama's Special sandwich, complete with marinated mushrooms, red peppers, and their homemade mozzarella, is absolutely delicious and gets plenty of praise all around. When you're there, take a gander at the humongous cheeses hanging from the ceiling, too. Next door is a bakery with cafe seating out in the big back patio, and their Italian-style baked goods are some of the best in Queens. Cannolis, cream puffs (try the ones filled with hazelnut), light and airy pignoli and amaretto cookies, tiny tarts topped with a single strawberry and filled with luxurious custard. Around the middle of the Lenten season, tiny zeppoli and *sfingi* will also be available, and they are a joyful few bites. If you plan to stay, be sure to get a cappuccino to accompany your delicious pastry.

Park Side Restaurant, 107-01 Corona Ave., Corona, NY 11368; (718) 271-9871; Subway: 7 to 103rd Street; parksiderestaurantny .com; Italian; $$$. Representing the last vestiges of the longtime Italian presence in Corona, Park Side is an institution. They have a loyal following, and rightly so—their menu is full of familiar, tasty, and satisfying Italian food. Their appetizers include classic clams oreganata, garlicky *frutti di mare,* and their fabulous seasonal stuffed artichoke. It's hard to go wrong with their lovely caprese salad, made with buffalo mozzarella; prosciutto can be added, too. Rich pastas like pasta Bolognese (made with any pasta they offer) and truffle and mushroom fettuccine and the lighter *ravioli di ricotta* are all well done. Note that their chickens come from Murray's and are free range/organic. Veal, fish, lamb, and beef dishes are also available—give the veal Milanese a try. Everything tastes great with the house wine, too. For dessert, the tiramisu is fantastic.

Rincon Criollo, 40-09 Junction Blvd., Corona, NY 11368; (718) 639-8158; Subway: 7 to Junction Boulevard; rincon-criollo.com; Cuban; $$. If you're looking for well-made, classic Cuban food, look no further than Rincon Criollo. They offer a variety of dishes on the regular menu—chicken, beef, pork, and seafood—and a set of specials as well, including traditional tastes like *arroz con pollo, lechon asado,* and *ropa vieja.* And speaking of the *ropa vieja,* it is ridiculously good. The texture is incredibly tender, the shreds of beef delicate, and the sauce is flavorful, slightly acidic, and smooth. It comes with a plate of white rice and white beans stewed with potatoes and bits of ham; if white beans aren't your style, traditional Cuban black beans are an available option. They are saucy, porky, and flavored with bay leaves, and go perfectly drizzled over white rice. Their sweet plantains are magical, wonderfully sweet, soft, and caramelized. Other sides include fried yucca, fried plantain, and cassava with garlic sauce. The oxtails are also a huge hit here, and incredibly flavorful. As far as drinks go, there's beer and wine, and a homemade lemonade that is not overly sweet. They have a nice selection of desserts, including both *flan de leche* and *coco, buñuelos,* and *arroz con leche* (rice pudding) that is spectacular. The restaurant dining room is very comfortable and homey and the staff is friendly, as well as happy to give recommendations if you ask. It's also located just steps from the Junction Boulevard 7 train, which also happens to be an express stop, so it is a breeze to get there, even from Manhattan.

Specialty Stores, Markets & Producers

Bappy Sweet, 85-07 Whitney Ave., Elmhurst, NY 11373; (718) 458-0626; Subway: M/R to Elmhurst Avenue; South Asian Sweets. I must admit, it took me a little while to venture into this tiny shop, but I'm glad I finally did. Here, they sell packages of Indian and Bangladeshi sweets, like *burfi, kalakand,* and *gulab jamun*. And it's the *gulab jamun* that is a real draw here. First, the individual balls are huge and they are quite dark—usually, they are a sort of golden color, but these are more molasses colored and have a deep, smoother sweetness. They also have a wonderful texture— the dough is soft without falling apart and they are sweet all the way through. The syrup is lovely, sweet with notes of citrus and cardamom. They come six to a package. Aside from the sweets, ice cream is also for sale.

Community Beverage, 80-04 Grand Ave., Elmhurst, NY 11373; (718) 458-5254; Subway: M/R to Grand Avenue/Newtown, then Q58 or Q59 west; Beer Store. Throughout NYC there are large beer stores that fill a small warehouse, showcasing all sorts of fantastic brews from around the world. In the middle of Grand Avenue lies Community Beverage, which has the best choice in beer in the neighborhood. There's a great selection of craft beers and micro-brews, as well as the major brands, and hard cider. They fill growlers as well (ask them what's current). You can also get your fill of Mexican Coke, too.

Corona Greenmarket, Roosevelt Ave. at 103rd St., Corona, NY 11368; Subway: 7 to 103rd Street; grownyc.org/coronagreenmarket; Farmers' Market. This bustling greenmarket operates seasonally, from the beginning of July to mid November, from 8 a.m. to 5 p.m. on Friday. It's located right below the 103rd Street stop on the 7, so it's extremely convenient for people in the neighborhood and those visiting from a distance. This is the best place to get local, seasonal, organic produce in Corona. Cooking demonstrations and recipe exchanges happen each week at the market; food stamps are also accepted (pre-screening required, on the second Friday of every month). The primary product at this particular greenmarket is produce—fruits and vegetables—with the bonus of Mexican specialty products being offered. Juice and cider are also for sale.

Double Rainbow Bakery, 8251 Broadway, Elmhurst, NY 11373; (718) 639-0567; Subway: M/R to Elmhurst Avenue; Chinese Bakery. This bakery is convenient to the subway entrance, so it's a very popular place with commuters heading into the city in the morning. They sell both sweet and savory baked goods—their egg custard tarts are pleasantly sweet, the smooth yellow custard sitting in a very neat and tasty shortbread crust. The red bean buns are really unusual, but in a good way. They look like Mexican pastry, with a kind of sandy sugar topping but inside there are bits of red beans. This is one delicious pastry. On the savory side of things are steamed buns filled with things like roast pork or chicken. You'll also find styrofoam containers up on top of the display case that contain thick, savory noodles.

Du Bois Pastry, 8408 Broadway #A, Elmhurst, NY 11373; (718) 426-8586; Subway: M/R to Elmhurst Avenue; Bakery. They've been open since the 1960s and are one of the few non-Chinese and non-Latin bakeries left in the area. A tiny little place without seating, they sell unabashedly American/European baked goods—red velvet cake, napoleons, cheesecake, pecan pie, Danishes, Black Forest cake, baklava, and the much-praised strawberry shortcake.

Their baklava is made in the more syrupy style, and is rich, sticky, and sweet. The Danish pastry is light and a little sweet, and nicely flaky; they make regular-size Danish as well as tiny ones, in case you just want a touch of something sweet. They are particularly proud of their napoleons—thin layers of pastry sandwiched with a very light pastry cream—and rightly so. They are terrific.

Elmhurst Greenmarket, 41st Ave. at 80th St., Elmhurst, NY 11373; Subway: M/R to Elmhurst Avenue; Greenmarket. This greenmarket operates seasonally, from the beginning of July to mid November, from 8 a.m. to 5 p.m. The number of vendors is small but they make a big impact, as this is one of the main sources for locally grown, seasonal, and organic produce in the neighborhood. In addition to fruits and vegetables, fresh bread, granola, pastries, and fresh flowers are available for purchase. Cooking demonstrations happen at this greenmarket, as do recipe exchanges, to further assist local residents in becoming more adept at working with seasonal produce.

Elmhurst Mex Grocery Juice Stand, 80-03 Broadway, Elmhurst, NY 11373; (718) 424-0107; Subway: M/R to Elmhurst Avenue; Fresh Juice. In front of the Elmhurst Mex Grocery, which carries a selection of Mexican products, is a juice stand. Freshly made fruit and vegetable juices, fruit smoothies, *aguas frescas,* and milkshakes/ *batidas* can all be purchased here, and they are very tasty. They've put together a dozen fruit juice combinations on their menu, as well as simply fresh orange or grapefruit juice. Enjoy combinations like papaya-orange-mango; watermelon-pineapple; orange-strawberry-banana; and even orange-pineapple-nopal. Vegetables for juicing are carrot, cucumber, beet, celery, parsley, ginger, broccoli, spinach, alfalfa, and aloe vera, in varying combinations. Try the carrot-apple-ginger for a real wake up; that ginger can be a real kick in the pants. Smoothies are made with water, milk, or even soy milk. You can even add Muscle Milk (a kind of protein supplement) to your smoothie.

Fay Da Bakery, 86-12 Justice Ave., Elmhurst, NY 11373; (718) 205-5835; Subway: M/R to Grand Avenue/Newtown; fayda.com; Chinese Bakery. Part of a popular chain of Chinese bakeries, this Fay Da is quite large. The entrance is marked by a big open space, enough to hold quite a crowd. Up front is a case of Western-style pastries—cheesecakes, red velvet cake, tiramisu, and the like. The back case is filled with Chinese pastries, and is self-serve—take a tray and a set of tongs and go to town. There are sweet pastries—lemon puffs, milk cream buns filled with pastry cream, coconut buns, egg tarts, pound cake, etc.; and there are savory pastries—long cheese danishes filled with gruyère (it's both salty and sweet at the same time), tuna fish buns, roast pork buns, etc. In a heated cabinet are savory chicken, beef, and pork puffs. One of the more unusual items is the Japanese cheesecake—it tastes like a combination of Asian sponge cake and American cheesecake. It's very light and has that nice tang that cheesecake tends to have, while being lightly sweet with a cake-like texture. Aside from these individual items, bags of bread—white and wheat—are for sale. You can also get coffee and tea, bubble tea, as well as jelly fruit tea (give the passion fruit a try). In the back is a spacious seating area, which is a nice place to enjoy your treats.

Hong Kong Supermarket, 82-02 45th Ave., Elmhurst, NY 11373; (718) 651-3838; Subway: M/R to Elmhurst Avenue; Asian Supermarket. This store is part of the same chain as the others in Queens, though this location is smaller and slightly less tidy. Still, it is one of the best options in the area for pan-Asian groceries. A couple of distinctive differences between this one and the Flushing location are the presence of plenty of fruit (located outside) and a small but nice selection of Latin products—sauces, chilies, spices, tortillas, some produce like jicama and yucca—obviously a nod to the Latin American community in the neighborhood. There is one whole aisle dedicated to noodles of all kinds from different Asian cultures—ramen, soba, rice noodles, glass noodles, bean noodles, and more. Fish are both alive and on ice, and cured Chinese sausages are available for you to pick and choose from and package up yourself. One nice thing here is the big selection of rice cookers; there's also a selection of bowls and such, too. Both joss paper and joss candles are available, along with a good selection of incense. Sweets and snacks from all over East and Southeast Asia can be purchased here as well. Be sure to stop by Maengun Thai Dessert stall, located on the left as you enter the store from the 45th Avenue entrance. All sorts of Thai snacks are there, both sweet and savory. The fish balls are worth a try, as is the coconut milk tea with pandan and the sticky rice (stuffed with taro) wrapped in banana leaves. When it gets warmer, ice cream appears, including Thai iced tea, coconut, and the ultimate in funky flavors, durian.

Indo Java Market, 85-12 Queens Blvd., Ste. 1, Elmhurst, NY 11373; (718) 779-2241; Subway: M/R to Grand Avenue/Newtown; Indonesian Market. Occupying a narrow storefront, this small shop is well stocked with Indonesian ingredients and treats. Prepared foods—both snacks and full meals—from nearby Java Village and Mie Jakarta are for sale; they do sell out quickly, so get there early if you want to snag some. If you're looking for pantry items like curries, sambals, shrimp chips, palm sugar, tempeh, and *kecap manis,* you'll find them all here. The staff—often consisting of one person at the register—is very friendly and happy to dispense information and/or advice for cooking up your favorite Indonesian dishes.

Rio de la Plata Bakery Shop, 94-65 Corona Ave., Elmhurst, NY 11373; (718) 271-5422; Subway: 7 to Junction Boulevard; paradero .com/riodelaplata; Argentinian Bakery. The mini pastries are serious eye catchers here—not only are they are adorable, but they are delicious, too, helped by the presence of copious amounts of *dulce de leche* used throughout. There are full-sized pastries, too, but these mini versions allow you to try a whole variety of things, which is a lot of fun—give the *alfajores de maizena* and any of the little layered cakes a try. They also take two coconut macaroons and glue them together with *dulce de leche*—if you are a coconut lover, this one is for you. Normal-size cake slices are also available, as are whole cakes. On the savory side of things, *sandwiches de miga* are for sale, as are empanadas. The chicken empanadas are excellent, with a flaky dough and filling consisting of chicken, onions, bits of olives, and red peppers. Give their *empanadas de choclo* a try, too. In the freezer, pick up empanada discs and frozen Cassinelli pasta (all the way from Astoria!). You can even buy yerba mate and the *bombilla,* the traditional vessel in which to drink yerba mate. They sell both the gourd style (which needs a few days of curing) and the glass style, which is ready to use almost immediately. The bakery has a few tables and chairs, so you can enjoy your goodies there if you like.

Sugar Club, 81-20 Broadway, Elmhurst, NY 11373; (718) 565-9018; Subway: M/R to Elmhurst Avenue; Thai Market. In between a computer shop and a wireless store is Sugar Club, home to a smart selection of Thai groceries, a remarkable number of prepared foods, and a small selection of beautiful, fresh produce. The back of the shop is where the groceries are—coconut milk, noodles, ground chili, palm sugar, curry pastes, durian chips, preserved mango, tamarind candies, and more. Starting in the front of the store are

the prepared goods and drinks. Soy milk, chrysan-
themum drink, tamarind juice, canned coffee drinks,
fruit juices, and aloe vera juice are liquid options.
Snacks—sweet and savory—are for sale, sourced from
local Thai restaurants around the city, including SEA Thai
in Brooklyn and Arharn Thai in Astoria. The aforementioned produce includes bags of red thai chilies, lemon basil, and acacia leaf.

Thai Grocery Store, 76-13 Woodside Ave., Elmhurst, NY 11373;
(718) 426-5006; Subway: M/R to Elmhurst Avenue; Thai Grocery.
Walk into this small Thai grocery store and it immediately feels
cramped, but there are many delicious gems to be found here. You'll
find staples like rice, sweet rice, rice noodles, coconut milk, fish
sauce, palm sugar, shrimp and crab paste, pickled vegetables, curry
pastes, frozen fish and shellfish, Thai-style sausage and meatballs,
Thai tea powder, frozen banana leaves, and shrimp chips. There are
sweet and savory snacks, both prepackaged and those from neighboring Thai restaurants. Packages of sour bamboo, fresh *kamangi*
(Thai basil) and *daun jeruk* (kaffir lime leaves), sticky rice, and
sticky rice with taro in banana leaves are also for sale inside the
shop. In the back of the shop are cooking and food-prep implements, like baskets, pots, and some serious mortars and pestles.
There are a number of signs in Thai, but if you have trouble reading
them, the staff inside will help you out. Often there is Thai pro-
gramming blaring from the TV set in the front, but it just adds to
the ambience. There are also some chairs outside for you to sit on
while you enjoy the snacks you've just bought here.

Ten Ren Tea, 83-28 Broadway, Elmhurst, NY 11373; (718) 205-0861; Subway: M/R to Elmhurst Avenue; tenrenusa.com; Tea House. Here, you can get a glass of bubble tea and pick up some tea to take home; of course, it's really a whole lot more than that. You'll find black, green, passion fruit, and taro-milk teas, as well as green apple, watermelon, Thai, almond, and even chocolate. Real tea is used instead of tea powder, too. The tapioca balls are just the right texture, too—not too soft and certainly not anywhere near being hard. As for the tea leaves, both loose and tea bags are for sale—oolong, varieties of black, green, white, and King's Tea, which is oolong blended with a bit of ginseng.

Street Food

Chicharron Preparado Cart, Roosevelt Ave. (north side) near Junction Blvd., Corona, NY 11368; Subway: 7 to Junction Boulevard; Mexican; $. This unnamed cart features *chicharron preparado,* a street snack from Mexico. It consists of a light as air and quite large *chicharron* topped with chopped cabbage, slices of avocado and tomatoes, *crema*/sour cream, cotija cheese, *cueritas* (picked pork rind slices), and hot sauce (they used Salsa Valentina, *muy auténtico*). The whole thing is fabulous, and should be eaten soon after it's prepared, as the *chicharron* will get soggy if even an hour passes, and soggy *chicharron* is a food tragedy (and generally unappealing). Fresh fruit is also for sale there, on which they sprinkle chili powder, as are churros (three for a dollar).

Chinese Food Cart, 51st Ave. and Broadway, Elmhurst, NY 11373; Subway: M/R Grand Avenue/Newtown; Chinese; $. This cart, located on the corner of Broadway and 51st Avenue (across the

street from the old Elmhurst Library), is very popular, often having a line of people waiting to order the incredibly inexpensive (as in, nothing over $2) fish balls, noodles, and pork-leek dumplings, which are big and plump, by the way. The fish balls come in a broth with daikon radish, can be ordered with or without fun (rice noodles the vendor cuts apart with a pair of scissors), and topped with soy sauce, peanut sauce, barbecue sauce, and hot sauce—it's delicious; the congee with pork is also quite nice.

Hong Kong Style Rice Roll Cart, Broadway between 45th Ave. and Whitney Ave., Elmhurst, NY 11373; Subway: M/R to Elmhurst Avenue; Chinese; $. On the sidewalk in front of the strip mall is a tidy cart selling Hong Kong–style rice rolls, a fascinating and tasty Asian street snack. Each rice roll is made fresh to order. One can get a plain steamed rice roll, or one with pork, chicken, beef, or baby shrimp. The woman making the rice roll takes a large spoonful of meat and places it in a thin metal drawer and adds a watery-milky liquid to that. She inserts the drawer and in a couple of minutes, she removes what has become a soft, jelly-like flat noodle the size of the surface of the pan (perhaps the size of a piece of copy paper). It's scraped into a styrofoam cup, topped with soy sauce, peanut sauce, and chili sauce (make sure you get all three). You eat it with a fork. It has a delightful flavor, a firm yet jiggly texture, with an almost creamy consistency. It really takes on the flavor of the sauces and the meat lends delicious flavor.

Los Amigos Chimichurri, 110th St. and Roosevelt Ave., Corona, NY 11368; Subway: 7 to 111th Street; Colombian; $. The first thing your see when you approach this cart is the crowd of people standing around waiting for the food. Look to the truck to see what you'd like to order . . . and you realize there isn't anything posted. That's ok, as everything is very good. Platters of meats or seafood, rice and beans, and tostones are placed in styrofoam containers, ready for you to take away and enjoy. Thin, brothy soups and thick seafood stews are also available. This cart is open late at night, and is a great one to stop at when you crave home-style Colombian food late, or are coming home from dancing the night away.

Tortas Neza, 111th St. and Roosevelt Ave., Corona, NY 11368; Subway: 7 to 111th Street; Mexican; $. This truck is known primarily for its amazing *tortas,* full of meat, cheese, mayo, avocado, and then some, all melding together to make an amazing sandwich. Or, should I say, sandwiches. Over a dozen (closer to a dozen and a half) *tortas* are on the menu. You'll notice when you look at the menu that the Tortas Pumas is substantially more expensive than any of the others. That's because it's made with an extensive array of ingredients, including head cheese and hot dogs. This *torta* is serious business. The various *tortas* are named after different Mexican soccer clubs, too. If you are looking for something a bit smaller than the Pumas, go for anything containing their amazing carnitas, which are great on the *torta* and also as part of a taco. This cart is a gem among food carts and highly recommended.

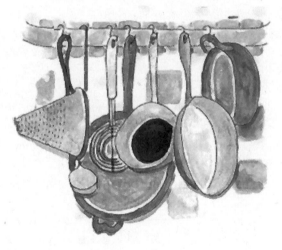

Flushing

Flushing, located at the eastern terminus of the 7 subway line, is Queens' Chinatown, and what a fantastic food destination this neighborhood is. It's full of Asian food of all kinds—Chinese, Korean, Taiwanese, Thai, Malaysian, Vietnamese, and Indian. This Chinatown is probably one of the best known places in all of Queens, and is held in high regard by food lovers throughout the NYC metro area. Although Flushing is considered demographically diverse, the central business district is primarily Chinese. This also means a great variety of Chinese food options, including restaurants, cafes, and bakeries. Some of the best Chinese food in the US is found here, eaten in fancy banquet rooms to modest restaurants to cramped underground food courts. What's especially exciting is that the restaurants overall represent extensive regional Chinese cuisine—not only will you find Cantonese restaurants, but Henanese, Dongbei, Sichuan, and beyond. Taiwanese food is also becoming more prominent, and there is a solid Korean presence. Other Asian cuisines—Southeast Asian, and South Asian—are also present, but they are in the minority (though no less delicious).

Flushing is an exciting place to be for those who appreciate flavorful and ridiculously good food, often at bargain prices.

Once you move out of the Roosevelt-Main area, you'll find less Chinese food and more food from other Asian food cultures. In particular, Northern Boulevard between Flushing and Bayside is chock-full of Korean restaurants, with no dearth of bakeries, restaurants, and Korean barbecue (some of it is all you can eat). A short walk along Bowne Street to the intersection with Holly Avenue finds you at the Ganesh Hindu Temple, which is not to be missed. In their basement is a very clean canteen serving up delicious South Indian food—the temple itself is simply gorgeous.

One thing that sets Flushing apart from the food scene in a lot of other neighborhoods is the presence of various food courts. They are located in the basements of shopping malls (which are all over Flushing) and offer foods way beyond pretzels and hot dogs on a stick—the offerings at a select few of these food courts are spectacular. They are extremely popular and a great place where one can sample foods from different regions of China all in one place.

The best way for most people to get to this neighborhood is by subway; it's easy to find where the station is located on the 7 line, as it is at the end of it. There is an LIRR station in Flushing, too, which can be convenient for those coming from the east along the Port Washington Line, or even those based in Manhattan (it's about a 20-minute ride from Penn Station). Flushing also has a bunch of parking lots and structures, so driving can be a practical option as well.

Flushing is truly a delight for the senses, especially taste, though visually it's pretty amazing. Head here for some truly fantastic and possibly life-altering eats.

Foodie Faves

Biang!, 41-10 Main St., Flushing, NY 11355; Subway: 7 to Main Street; biang-nyc.com; Chinese (Xi'an); $. Hip and happening is the name of the game at this stylish, upscale eatery that opened in spring 2012 by the people behind the well-loved Xi'an Famous Foods (located in the basement of Flushing's Golden Mall food court just up the street). The dining room is quite nice, with wooden tables and stools (aim for a seat against the wall if you want any semblance of back support), exposed brick walls, and contemporary American pop music on the sound system. The story behind the name "Biang" is twofold: first, the word—the most complicated character in the Chinese language—is part of the local dialect in Xi'an, located in the Shaanxi province, with Xi'an being the eastern end of the Silk Road; and second, it is the sound the hand-pulled noodles make when they hit the counter (it's a loud, sharp sound). Noodles are definitely on the menu, including their famous *liáng pí*—chewy and toothsome, spicy ribbon-like noodles, mixed with spongy seitan slices, blanched mung-bean sprouts, cucumber, and cilantro, dressed with chili oil, soy sauce, and vinegar. The menu is divided into five sections—*chuàn*, meaning kebab; *xiǎo* *cài*, meaning side dishes; *miàn shí*, meaning bread and noodles; *tián diǎn*, meaning dessert; and *yǐn liào,* meaning beverages. The star of the first section is the cumin lamb skewer. Along with the aforementioned *liáng pí* (noodles) is the rather unusual buckwheat pudding—it arrives as a sort of puffball of sticky bread dough with a bit of a glutinous texture, like a very thick ball of moist cotton candy. Take your chopsticks and pluck off a chunk, then dip it in the dipping sauce made of spicy mustard oil and soy sauce. For something a little more conventional, try the pork belly sandwich made of minced, stewed pork belly and served on a homemade flatbread bun. As far as drinks go, there's American soda and sparkling water, and also iced tea (ask them for hot tea, though, and they'll accommodate you). I really enjoy the sour hawberry iced tea that they make there at the restaurant. It's tangy and sweet, with flavors reminiscent of a super-mellow cranberry, and goes well with the food. Iced jasmine and chrysanthemum teas are also available.

Bangane, 165-19 Northern Blvd., Flushing, NY 11358; (718) 762-2799; LIRR: Broadway (Port Washington Line); Korean; $$. If you like goat (especially the belly and ribs), this is the place for you. Their claim to fame is a fabulous goat feast that comes in a few formats. You can order the 3-course *Soo Yook* for two or more people. This consists of steamed, shredded goat meat for *ssam* (lettuce wrap); then a spicy goat stew (*jungol*) made with the remaining goat; then rice is

Dumplings in Flushing

One of the things I get the most questions about when it comes to Flushing is where to find dumplings. The idea of a "dumpling tour" is also something people dream about doing in Flushing, and some actually put them together and stuff themselves silly. Believe me, this is easy to do, since the dumplings in Flushing are so good. Overindulging is the official Flushing pastime.

Here is a list of dumpling spots in Flushing, all of which have been written up in this chapter. You can fashion your own dumpling tour out of it, absolutely, but know that especially with Nan Xiang Dumpling House (home of excellent soup dumplings), the wait can be a while on certain mornings (read: weekends).

Henan Feng Wei Restaurant, 136-31 41st Ave. Recommended: pork and leek dumplings, sour dumpling soup.

Korean-Chinese Noodle & Dumpling/Joong Han Boon Sik, 133-33 39th Ave., Flushing Mall. Recommended: pork and chive.

My Sweet Home Dumpling House, 136-76 Roosevelt Ave. Recommended: fish, seafood, and corn dumplings.

Nan Xiang Dumpling House, 38-12 Prince St. Recommended: pork soup dumplings.

Peking Duck Sandwich Stall, Main Street and 40th Road. Recommended: the duck buns, of course!

Sifu Chio, 40-09 Prince St. Recommended: thin skin wontons with lo mein.

White Bear, 135-02 Roosevelt Ave., #5. Recommended: Number 6, wontons in chili oil.

Zhu Ji Dumpling Stall, 40-52 Main St. Recommended: pork and leek fried dumplings.

fried with some *jungol,* with seaweed and sesame oil added. This is a gut busting meal, but furiously delicious. You can opt for just the 2-course *Jun-Gol* (which is slightly more expensive), which consists of the goat stew (*jungol*) and the fried rice. Then there's the *Moo-Chim* (for two) made of goat meat and spicy sauce. Other proteins like chicken, beef, pork, and fish are available, including *galbi* (short ribs), but there really aren't many places in NYC where one can get what's called a "large format" goat meal. So come here and have a unique experience. And don't forget the soju.

Best North Dumpling Shop, 41-42A Main St., Flushing, NY 11355; Subway: 7 to Main Street; Dumplings (Northern Style); $. Located in the Friendship Shopping Mall, this stall is about halfway back along the narrow corridor and on the right. They offer a variety of dumplings with interesting fillings like pickled vegetable and pork, steamed turnip and beef, and mutton, just to name a few. The pork and fennel dumplings are a huge favorite and highly recommended. Dumplings can also be purchased frozen, mostly in 50-count packages, but the steamed turnip and beef dumplings come in a 36-count package. And while the dumplings get plenty of love here, I encourage you to try the steamed beef bun, which is spectacular. Encased in light, cloud-like dough, the filling is a serious umami bomb, so full of savory flavor with a touch of sweetness. This is one fantastic meat bun that may haunt your dreams after you've tasted it.

Curry Leaves, 135-31 40th Rd., Flushing, NY 11354; (718) 762-9313; Subway: 7 to Main Street; Malaysian; $. Located on a side street off bustling Main Street, this little hole-in-the-wall spot is really two restaurants in one. During regular daytime hours, it's a sit-down restaurant with table service. Starting at around 4 a.m., though, it's a pared-down setup, with a steam table, desserts, and soup, available until 11 a.m. A lot of people like to stop by on the way to work to grab something for the subway ride into the city. It's also a very popular destination in the middle of the night, post-drinking. During normal hours, an extensive menu is in place, with lots of Malaysian classic dishes available like chili chicken, *mee goring* noodles (spicy if you like), *roti canai,* and *rojak*. Their *roti canai* with egg is particularly nice, very light and not greasy at all. It comes with a small bowl of very tasty chicken curry, which is a traditional paring. Their *rajak,* a sticky kind of fruit salad (theirs includes jicama), dusted with chopped peanuts and sesame seeds, is oddly addictive (the crispy pappadums that come with it are delicate and tasty vehicles with which to scoop up some of the dark, sticky sauce). There's also a Malaysian-style tofu curry dish that contains fish cakes (vegetarians beware), in a wonderful savory broth. Malaysia's national dish, *nasi lemak,* is also on the menu. The chicken version boasts the requisite rice, a saucy serving of curry chicken (on the bone), a couple of pickles, a hard-boiled egg, and peanuts.

Dosa Hutt, 45-63 Bowne St., Flushing, NY 11355; (718) 961-5897; Subway: 7 to Main Street; Indian (Vegetarian); $. Located right next to the Ganesh Hindu Temple, this is a prime place to catch some delicious *dosas* for lunch or dinner. Be prepared to pay very little for something so expertly made—this is Queens at its best. *Dosas* are a popular south Indian snack, consisting of a thin, fermented crepe surrounding various fillings. The *masala dosa* is a great way to enjoy this dish, the crepe filled with beautifully spiced potatoes, and served with coconut chutney and *sambar*. You really do get a lot of bang for your buck here—*dosas* are under $5 and the food is quite filling, despite the look of the thin crepe (the ends of the crepe get nice and crispy, which is texturally appealing). Accompany your *dosa* with one of their tasty mango lassis, which also helps mute the sting of anything overly spicy you may have eaten. Everything here is vegetarian, but most omnivores will be happy with the food despite the absence of meat.

Fu Run, 40-09 Prince St., Flushing, NY 11354; (718) 321-1363; Subway: 7 to Main Street; Chinese (Dongbei); $$. Three words: Muslim Lamb Chop. By far, this is the most celebrated dish at the restaurant, and it deserves any and all accolades it receives; this is one spectacular dish. Despite the word "chop" in the name, the meat is really lamb ribs, which have a nice balance of soft, unctuous fat and rich, savory meat. When the dish arrives at your table, it really is a stunning sight—an entire plate full of lamb encased in a blanket of toasted cumin seeds, black and white sesame seeds, and chili seeds. The waitstaff takes a knife and fork and starts cutting the lamb apart and what you hear is a beautiful crunching sound— not of bones, but of crispy, deep-fried goodness. Yes, this lamb has been braised then deep fried and covered in spices. The lamb is so well cooked, so soft and lovely, it just falls off the bone and is easy to eat with chopsticks. It is a truly wonderful dish. It's hard to say that anything else on the menu can compare, but there are some additional beloved dishes, including the candied taro. This consists of cubes of deep-fried taro, covered in hot liquid sugar. In order to enjoy this dish without burning the inside of your mouth, you dip the cubes in ice water, which then causes the sugar to seize and harden.

Ganesh Temple Canteen, 45-57 Bowne St., Flushing, NY 11355; (718) 460-8484; Subway: 7 to Main Street; nyganeshtemple.org; Indian Vegetarian; $. The Canteen is located below ground underneath the Ganesh Hindu Temple in residential Flushing. As you face the entrance to the temple, go as far to the right as you can, and head down that walkway to the sign that indicates the Canteen; subsequent signs should help you find your way. When you arrive, head to the counter and order off the menu what you'd like to eat. There's a selection of *dosas*—masala, Mysore, and Pondicherry, just to name a few. The Mysore *dosa* is nice and spicy, and is accompanied by a wonderful coconut chutney and *sambar*. Apart from the *dosas,* there are *uttappam, idli,* and *vada.* The highly spiced and fantastically delicious *besi bela bath* is also on the menu, accompanied by a lovely *raita* and some Indian snacks. Mango lassi is the perfect drink with this food, but masala tea and Madras coffee are also available. Please note that you are not required to take off your shoes to enter the Canteen, but you are required to do so if you enter the Temple.

Golden Mall, 41-28 Main St., Flushing, NY 11355; Subway: 7 to Main Street; Chinese; $. The Golden Mall's dilapidated food court is in the basement, accessed by stairs on both Main Street and 41st Road around the corner. Try the wonton in chili oil and the cold cooked noodles at **Chengdu Heavenly Snacks,** located to the right of the entrance to the food court. **Xi'an Famous Foods** is famous for their hand pulled noodles, as well as the Liang Pi Cold Noodles, and the spicy cumin lamb burger, with a wonderful earthiness to that spice. The lamb burger is stuffed with scallions, jalapeños and onions, then sandwiched between two thin halves of a bun. Another place for noodles is the **Lan Zhou Pulled Noodle** stall, which prepares enormous bowls of noodle soup made with things like roast duck, scallions, and cilantro. If you want it a little spicier, add a bit of the chili oil spicy sauce on the table. Lan Zhou has a menu section called "B.B.Q." They offer various "sticks," including squid, mushroom, vegetable, and fish balls. The mushroom stick is divine, having been barbecued with a slightly sweet sauce. The vegetable stick is just a half dozen or so pieces of long bean skewered. It looks very cool and is extremely tasty. There are lots of other delicious things in the Golden Mall—dumplings, hot pot, extremely spicy Sichuan food. It is worth heading downstairs and trying things. Most people understand rudimentary English, and if they don't just point to what you want and smile. A smile and politeness will take you a long way.

Golden Palace, 140-09 Cherry Ave., Flushing, NY 11355; (718) 886-4383; Subway: 7 to Main Street; Chinese (Dongbei); $$. This is probably one of the most authentic food spots in Flushing, serving the less prominent food from northern China. In English, this region has been referred to as Manchuria, because it was the territory of the Manchu, an ethnic minority in China. The food is a bit different from what one is used to from more southerly areas, but it is delicious and intriguing. Those of you who like pickled things are in luck—pickled foods are commonplace in Manchu cuisine. Noodles, dumplings, and pancakes are also common edibles in the north. And speaking of noodles, the *green bean sheet jelly* is an excellent vegetarian dish, which omnivores will enjoy, too. The noodles are made from mung bean starch and are mixed with very small, thin matchsticks of cucumber. Another delicious meatless dish is sliced potato, eggplant, and pepper. The potatoes are cooked until they are slightly caramelized on the exterior, and then mixed with perfectly cooked eggplant and hot green chili peppers. For the meat eaters, try ordering a whole fish—either the braised yellow fish with brown sauce (recommended by the staff) or the crispy flounder with chili pepper. The flounder is a flat fish, so it's not the meatiest one out there, but certainly tasty. They treat the fish in a way similar to another northern dish of lamb and cumin (like the

Muslim Lamb Chops at **Fu Run,** p. 246)—they coat it in a very light batter, deep fry it and top it with a mixture of toasted cumin seeds and chili flakes. If you turn the fish over, too, there's more meat to pick at with a more pronounced batter-fried crust (it's also less spicy). The shredded beef in spicy sauce is totally loaded with cilantro—especially the stems—and with the spicy sauce the flavors are very bold and harmonize perfectly. As I mentioned earlier, dumplings are popular in the north, and the lamb dumplings here are terrific. The dumpling skin, which is a little bit shiny, is somewhere between thick and thin, and the filling is juicy and lamby. They come with a dipping sauce of soy and garlic.

Henan Feng Wei Restaurant, 136-31 41st Ave., Flushing, NY 11355; (718) 762-1818; Subway: 7 to Main Street; Chinese (Henanese); $. Located downstairs in a basement storefront, the restaurant is simple, modest, and feels miles away from the hustle and bustle of Main Street. Walk through to the far end of the room and take a look at the dishes in the display case—there are peanuts, shredded vegetable dishes, tripe, lamb chops, and thick slabs of marinated tofu. Across the way on another counter are the thick tasty pancakes filled with pork. Pork-leek dumplings are on the menu, which are very good. The dumpling skin itself does not have much flavor, but that's a good thing because it doesn't get in the way of the wonderful flavor of the pork and leek filling. Dumplings also make a star appearance in the sour dumpling soup, which isn't really all that sour, honestly. It is liberally flavored with fresh cilantro. Down at the bottom of the bowl are tiny little shrimp, which is where some of the tang comes from. Casseroles and soups, as well as a few hearty chopped meat dishes populate the rest of the menu. The food here isn't terribly spicy per se (as is the case with a lot of Henan cuisine), so you can add some heat with the chilies in oil sitting in a container on each table; black vinegar is also a condiment that is particularly great on the dumplings. Mix the two condiments together and that's also a real taste treat.

Imperial Palace, 136-13 37th Ave., Flushing, NY 11354; (718) 939-3501; Subway: 7 to Main Street; Chinese; $$. If Cantonese food is what you're looking for, this is the place to go. Their menu reads, in part, much like your local Chinese-American takeout spot—General Tso's chicken, beef with broccoli, *ma po* tofu, sweet and sour pork, and the like. That being said, the quality and taste of the food vastly obliterates the typical Queens Chinese takeout joint. Other parts of the menu reflect more sophisticated dishes, like steamed chicken with ginger and scallion, which comes in a lightly salty sauce, with pieces of beautifully steamed chicken on the bone. It is mild and friendly. The fried noodle with pork is also tasty—pieces of saucy pork atop a bed of crispy ramen noodles (let the pork sit there for a while—the sauce will soften the noodles enough for you to spoon out servings). But by far, the star of the menu is the Dungeness crab with steamed glutinous rice. It arrives in a steam basket and everything is perfumed with crabby goodness. The briny crab pairs with the buttery-smooth sticky rice, and this combination is a real treat. It's easy to have sticky hands after handling the crab, but it's worth it, plus they give you towelettes with which to clean your hands at the end. The dining room is quite large and filled with white tablecloth–clad tables—big groups can enjoy occupying one of the big round tables.

Joo Mak Gol, 35-26 Farrington St., Flushing, NY 11354; (718) 460-0042; Subway: 7 to Main Street; Korean; $. On a quiet side street north of Northern Boulevard is this small Korean restaurant located in the basement of a fairly nondescript building. When you walk into the restaurant, you'll notice many signs on the wall in Korean only, but don't let that deter you at all if you don't speak or read the language—the staff is really friendly, welcoming, and happy to answer any questions you have, whether it's about what the specials are on the wall or what's on the menu. Another thing to know is that portions are quite large, and it's very easy to eat well here for relatively cheap. The menu itself is small—only two pages of dishes. There are a lot of other things listed on the walls, including some seasonal dishes. Prepared food and barbecue are options here, so if you want barbecue be sure to let them know, so that you'll be seated at a table with a grill. One of the most popular and well-loved things to eat here is the *ssam bap,* which consists of meats and vegetables that you wrap in lettuce leaves—on the menu it's indicated as either bulgogi or roasted pork with spicy sauce. Bowls of noodle dishes are also popular, and are mentioned on the wall (in Korean). Soups and stews are on the menu, and include mixed vegetable soup, the tofu- and vegetable-oriented bean paste stew, and the nourishing and comforting spicy fermented kimchi stew. It arrives at your table, hot and bubbling, containing the spicy tangy kimchi, small pieces of beef, delicate slabs of tofu, and chewy rice cakes. *Ojokbap,* a five-grain rice consisting of rice, barley, and millet, is served with it. Of course, *banchan* is delivered to your table at the start, and it's wonderful—tiny sweet and salty shrimp (with the heads on), kimchi, sweet chewy black beans, bok choi, mung bean sprouts, and a whole variety of other things (it's rare to get the same set of dishes each time). Soju, the popular Korean rice spirit, is also on the menu, and goes extremely well with your meal; otherwise, your choices include the average macrobeer (Coors Light, Bud, and Heineken) or water.

King 5 Noodle House/Nan Bei Ho Corp., 39-07 Prince St., 1G, Flushing, NY 11354; (718) 888-1268; Subway: 7 to Main Street; Taiwanese; $. First, know that this restaurant does not display its name in English. Look for the "1G" in the address, because this whole building—the Prince Center Condo building—has the address of 39-07 Prince Street. Another way to identify the restaurant is that the storefront has a block of yellow Chinese characters affixed to the front window, accompanied the words "noodle house," and a red band above the doorway with three black Chinese characters. Now, on to the food—this is a great place to get a Taiwanese breakfast in Flushing, which is served all week starting at 8 a.m. Start your meal with a long, slightly oily deep fried cruller (*youtiao*), and either sweet or salty soy milk. The sweet soy milk is recognizable as your typical soy milk, with a light, sweet taste, but the salty soy milk is much more substantial. Unsweetened soy milk is made to curdle, thanks to the addition of vinegar, resulting in a soft, delicate sort of tofu. Chunks of the aforementioned cruller are added and they eventually take on the flavor of the whole mix. There are also tiny dried shrimp, bits of dried pork, and the whole thing is topped with chopped scallions. There are a number of scallion pancakes on the menu, including a simple scallion pancake by itself, one with egg, and the most delicious of the options, the scallion pancake rolled with beef. This is a real standout and combines sweet and savory beautifully; there's hoisin sauce in there to make it a little sweet and the scallion pancake has a solid yet flaky consistency. If you are looking for soup dumplings, they are on the menu as "steamed meat buns" and come eight to an order. They are tasty, especially with the the traditional soy sauce/ginger accompaniment. Tea is on the table so you can serve yourself.

Korean-Chinese Noodle & Dumpling/Joong Han Boon Sik, 133-33 39th Ave., Flushing Mall, Flushing, NY 11354; (718) 358-1478; Subway: 7 to Main Street; Chinese (Northern); $. There's a relatively short border between China and Korea, with the province of Jilin occupying most of the Chinese side—that's where the ladies at the Korean-Chinese dumpling spot on the first floor of the Flushing Mall are from. They make dumplings with a variety of fillings, made up of two to five options. If you're someone who likes things rather simple, the pork and leek is sure to make your day. Others prefer pork, shrimp, and chive, and you can even get a little sea cucumber in yours if you like. Dumplings are served with a spicy dipping sauce and a little kimchi. These dumplings are the real deal, made by hand and well worth a visit. When you get your order, either sit at the little bar or head over to one of the nearby tables or benches. This is a great place to enjoy some dumplings while you recharge your phone—there are outlets nearby!

Ku-Shiang Taiwanese Restaurant, 135-38 39th Ave., Flushing, NY 11355; (718) 939-5468; Subway: 7 to Main Street; Taiwanese; $. Some of the best Taiwanese food in Flushing can be found in this hole-in-the-wall spot on a quiet side street (actually a couple doors down from **Apollo Bakery,** p. 266), and the menu is full of tantalizing dishes, including some old standards that are done very well here, like three-cup chicken or stinky tofu. Portions are quite large, too. Well-known soups like hot and sour and wonton grace the menu, but there are also soups like light clam soup, simple bean curd vegetable soup, and an excellent shredded pork soup with Chinese pickle. This is a brothy soup containing slices of shiitake mushrooms, thin pieces of pork, pickled vegetables, julienned tender bamboo, scallion, and cilantro. Light yet satisfying, and could easily feed three to four people. The oyster pancake with egg and vegetable is also a light delight, arriving in the form of a thin omelet mixed with oysters (or shrimp if they run out of oysters), a layer of glutinous rice below the egg, and the whole thing is topped with a sweet and tangy brown sauce and fresh spinach leaves. Meat dishes—pork, beef, seafood, chicken, and duck—populate the menu, but there are both vegetable dishes and dishes for vegetarians using imitation meats, which are very well done. Noodle and rice dishes are also available, including wonton Szechuan style and diced chicken with hot pepper sauce over rice (this is *kung pao* Chicken), accompanied by a small amount of very tasty, lightly pickled vegetables, which is a real treat. Be sure to peruse the boxes of prepared takeout food near the door to see if there's anything you want to take home with you.

Little Pepper, 18-24 College Point Blvd., Flushing, NY 11356; (718) 939-7788; Subway: 7 to Main Street, then catch the Q65 bus; Chinese (Sichuan); $. It was a sad day for many when Little Pepper moved from its convenient Roosevelt Avenue digs all the way out to College Point, but the food is so good it is worth hopping a bus to get there. This is Sichuan food, which means it is spicy, but the beauty of this food is that along with the heat lies amazing, vibrant flavor. The *dan dan* noodles are spectacular, as is the shredded tea-smoked duck with ginger—the wonderful smoky flavor married with the richness of the duck is just fantastic. Even their *kung pao* chicken, easily found in Chinese-American restaurants, is kicked up a notch and wonderfully spicy and flavorful. The lamb with cumin (spicy sauce) is spicy, earthy, and fragrant—and the shower of chopped cilantro pleasantly disrupts the richness of the cumin/lamb combo. Little Pepper cooks a good number of offal dishes—try the intestines or beef tendon dishes.

My Sweet Home Dumpling House, 136-76 Roosevelt Ave., Flushing, NY 11354; (718) 461-0201; Subway: 7 to Main Street; Chinese (Dumplings); $. Located in the back of the Maxim Bakery, this clean, small stall makes a wide variety of dumplings, some boiled and some fried. The menu lists about a dozen different kinds of fillings—fish, vegetable, pork and leek, chicken and cabbage, seafood and corn. And that's just half of the offerings! Both the pork and leek and vegetable dumplings are panfried. Prices are ridiculously cheap, especially for the 10-piece serving ($3.50 to $4.75). A few other things grace the menu, like wonton soup (yet another kind of dumpling) and beef noodle soup, in case dumplings aren't your thing. Enjoy watching them make the dumplings right there, thanks to the open kitchen; you can also take frozen dumplings home with you.

Nan Xiang Dumpling House, 38-12 Prince St., Flushing, NY 11354; (718) 321-3838; Subway: 7 to Main Street; Chinese (Shanghai); $. This is the best place in Queens to get *xiao long bao*—soup dumplings. They are called "steamed pork buns" on the menu, come six to an order, and arrive in a bamboo steam basket (multiple orders arrive in stacked bamboo baskets). Both the pork and the pork and crab are great choices and quite delicious. Both the pepper sauce/paste on the table and the little bowl of black vinegar with ginger go very well with these dumplings, filled with broth and meat. Apart from the soup dumplings, there are a number of cold dishes on the menu (be aware, sometimes they may run out of some things during certain times of the day). The spicy beef and tripe is full of contrasting textures—the beef is very tender while the tripe is chewy. The tripe lends a bit of sweetness to the dish overall, and with the spicy element it is a real taste sensation. The scallion puff, a small disk of flaky pastry containing a pleasantly salty scallion filling, is complementary to spicy dishes, and its buttery pastry is irresistible. The sesame seeds on top add a nice nuttiness as well. The scallion pancake is also very good and not greasy. Some people really like the warm soy milk with their meal, too.

New World Mall Food Court, 40-21 Main St., Flushing, NY 11354; Subway: 7 to Main Street; Chinese, Taiwanese, Korean, and Thai; $. This food court is relatively new, having opened in 2011. At the lowest level of the mall are communal tables in the middle of the room, with the stalls lining the outside. There's plenty of regional Chinese food here, as well as some Thai and Korean food, and fresh juices. Head over to **Jiao Jiao Inc.,** which serves noodle soups—Number 5, the Spicy Diced Chicken with Sliced Noodles is fantastic. These toothsome noodles come in a dark broth that is a bit spicy, along with strips of seaweed and fungus—wood ear, most likely—as well as bok choi and cilantro stems and tips. The chicken is dark meat for the most part and very tender. You can add pickled green vegetables to it if you like, which are located at the counter; chili oil is there to spice it up some more to your liking. **"Casserole. Big bowl of noodle"** serves a variety of dumplings, and, of course, casseroles! The fish casserole is very popular, with the bowl full of battered white fish, cabbage, enoki mushrooms, cilantro, and glass noodles (FYI, if you eat in there is a deposit for the casserole dish). The Dumpling with Spicy Sauce (Number 16 on the menu) is pork wontons in chili oil, topped with cilantro and diced pickled vegetables. If you want something sweet to end your meal, there are juices over at **Ponji**—the watermelon mint is worth a try, and the mango juice/mango/banana whipped with ice is a great frozen treat. But the serious frozen treat is Snopo, a wondrous shaved ice dessert. It arrives like a cloud—piles of light and airy shaved ice topped with myriad ingredients, some more whimsical than others. Some of the shaved ice is infused with flavors, (strawberry, green tea, and lychee for example), but you can also order plain shaved ice and choose your own toppings, like red beans, sweet cereals, various jellies (mango, coffee, etc.), tapioca balls, and fresh fruit. A tasty combination is simple shaved ice drizzled with sweetened condensed milk, and topped with mango jelly and tapioca balls. Or, you can go all out and get the Strawberry Princess Snowy, made of strawberry flavored shaved ice, sweetened condensed milk, jellies, red beans, and sugary cereal.

153 Fusion Pochu, 40-11 149th Pl., Flushing, NY 11354; (718) 353-3292; LIRR: Murray Hill (Port Washington Line); Korean; $$. Come here for a soju nightcap, enjoy a few rounds of drinks with friends, or simply to get hammered on the aforementioned soju. If you're going to do that anywhere in Flushing, 153 Pocha is the place to do it. But if you want to enjoy the soju but keep your head on straight, order some small dishes, like the quirky Korean modern classic *budae jjigae,* made with myriad and disparate elements like hot dogs, tofu, Spam, noodles, kimchi, and vegetables. The *buldak* (translates as "fire chicken") is a super-spicy chicken favorite and is a perfect match with beer. There are a variety of small, meaty dishes, which are a help while drinking copious amounts of alcohol.

Picnic Garden, 147-42 Northern Blvd., Flushing, NY 11354; (718) 358-5959; LIRR: Port Washington Line to Murray Hill, or Subway: 7 to Main Street; Korean; $. The main attraction here is the meat—it is a Korean meat heaven. The highly sought after *galbi* (beef short ribs) is plentiful, and by all means you can get your fill here. Other meats, including chicken, pork belly, Italian sausages (yes, it's true), and various kinds of offal like intestines and liver are also some of the options for your barbecuing pleasure. The meats are all you can eat, so this is the right place for a grand meat fest. Prices are about $10 cheaper at lunch compared to dinner, too.

Savor Fusion Mall, 42-01 Main St., Flushing, NY 11355; (718) 886-6966; Chinese; $. There are eight stalls total in this mall, and the food is from various regions in China—Sichuan, Tianjin, and Henan, just to name a few. When you walk in off of Main Street, there's a stall on the left that sells buns—the round ones look alike except for one that is slightly darker, which contains peanut. It's

very good—definitely peanutty but not overly sweet. Way in the back of the mall is the dumpling stall. The steamed vegetable dumplings are very good, as are the steamed pork and leek dumplings. Fried lamb dumplings are spectacular, and they develop a lovely, light crust on the bottom. Spicy chili oil is at the counter in case you want to spice them up a little bit. Next to the dumplings is a Fujianese stall that makes hand pulled noodles and hand shaved noodles. In between, in stall Number 5, are these warm, narrow vegetable wraps containing shredded carrot, cabbage, bean sprouts, and glass noodles. They are a little spicy. The cumin lamb wrap is spectacular, filled with earthy cumin infused lamb that is spicy and savory all in one. In stall Number 3 there is a vegetable roll of a different kind, resembling a kind of burrito, which is also delicious. Drinks in general are either soda or water.

Sifu Chio, 40-09 Prince St., Flushing, NY 11354; (718) 888-9295; Subway: 7 to Main Street; Chinese (Hong Kong); $. This is a perfect spot to get your dumpling on, as they offer a variety of them—thin skin wontons with noodles (Hong Kong–style), wonton and dumpling brothy soups, crispy fried wontons and potstickers, savory beef balls and pungent fish balls. They are all delicious and delightful, cheap and filling. There are other menu items, like congee, braised brisket and pig's feet, and yummy fried fish cake, but the thing to get, really, is an order of the dumplings in whichever form you prefer. Note: the awning doesn't spell it out—at least in English— as "Sifu Chio," but reads as "CHML HK, Inc."

How to Eat a Soup Dumpling

If you've never had a soup dumpling, it's imperative that you know what you're getting into so you won't hurt yourself. And when I say "hurt yourself" I mean burn the inside of your mouth within an inch of its life. The dumplings are indeed filled with scalding hot soup and this filling can be extreme. And if you've ever wondered how they get the soup into these dumplings, the secret is that the broth is very gelatinous and is spooned into the dumpling skin while cold, then it melts as the dumplings heat up—brilliant!

Of course, you can just pop the whole thing in your mouth if you are a daredevil or have a high tolerance for pain. Anyway, here's one way to eat a soup dumpling, with the goal of not burning your mouth:

Ready your chopsticks in one hand and the big soup spoon in the other.

Lift the dumpling from its tip out of the steamer with the chopsticks and place it on the spoon.

Supporting the dumpling with your spoon, pinch the tip of the dumpling (it's on the top of the dumpling) with the chopsticks and bite it off. This allows the steam to escape and the soup to cool down.

Slurp the soup out of the dumpling (be careful, it's still a bit hot!).

Pick up the remaining meatball (it takes up a lot of the dumpling interior) and dumpling skin with your chopsticks and eat that. The pepper sauce/paste on the table and the little bowl of black vinegar with ginger are a perfect match with your dumpling.

Enjoy the flavors and the awesomeness of this unique food treasure.

Move on to the next soup dumpling!

Sik Gaek, 40-01 149th Pl., Flushing, NY 11354; (718) 460-4564; LIRR: Port Washington Line to Murray Hill; Korean; $. Just a couple of blocks from the LIRR station is the doorway to another world. This is a world where you are served live food—not the yogurt or kombucha kind of alive, but live octopus! Yes, Sik Gaek has a mondo reputation for serving live octopus (in season, of course). The octopus is still moving, and it's up to you to finish off the job that started in the kitchen. (Note: For most people, when presented with a live octopus, the instinct is to cut off the tentacles and let them settle down, but some people enjoy the sensation of the moving appendage and down the gullet it goes.) The other famous (or infamous, depending on your POV) dish is the giant hot pot of live seafood called *sannakji chulpan*. It comes with all sorts of sea creatures inside a hot broth, which eventually cooks them to their death. As I mentioned, it's a huge pot, and contains really enough food for four to six, so don't let the $100 price give you a heart attack. Aside from these two things, there's great *galbi* and kimchi fried rice, so both the adventurous and those less inclined to plunge into the live food world can enjoy a great Korean meal together.

SN New Restaurant Inc., 44-09 Kissena Blvd., Flushing, NY 11355; (718) 539-4100; Subway: 7 to Main Street; Chinese (Qingdao); $. New Yorkers who know the neighborhood will remember this location as the former home of M&T. The food here comes from Qingdao, a major city in the Shandong province, located in eastern China. In the West, Qingdao is known also as Tsingtao, which is the same name as the famed beer that comes from that part of the world (the Germans helped found the brewery in the early 20th century). The menu at the current restaurant is virtually unchanged from the M&T menu, and features a number of Qingdao specialties. One of them is the leek with sea intestines, made with tubes of the *Urechis unicinctus,* the marine spoon worm. It comes highly recommended by the staff and it's likely you won't

find anything else like it nearby. The sea cucumber with elbow (which is really pork) also comes recommended. On a more conventional level, the simple dish of clams with Chinese cabbage on rice is just lovely. The cabbage gets a little char on the ends, the clams are nice and plump, and then there are the slices of garlic here and there. And it's hard to go wrong with their lamb with cumin seed in hot chili oil. Tender slices of lamb are cooked until they are almost caramelized, taking on a pleasantly chewy consistency, made spicy with toasted cumin seeds and chili oil, then mixed with fresh cilantro. This dish is a real winner. And while it's expected to have tea at the table in a Chinese restaurant, the green tea that is served here is very good, and a definite step up from your average pot of tea. The tea comes straight from Qingdao.

Spicy and Tasty, 39-07 Prince St., Flushing, NY 11354; (718) 359-1601; Subway: 7 to Main Street; spicyandtasty.com; Chinese (Sichuan); $. Lovers of regional Chinese food—Sichuan, in this case—have flocked to Spicy and Tasty for years. As you can tell from the name of the restaurant, the food is indeed spicy and it is very tasty. One of the most memorable dishes is the bamboo in hot spicy sauce—these are not the tough, fibrous bamboo shoots of the canned La Choy variety, but they are oh so tender and absolutely delicious. Other great appetizers are the eggplant with garlic sauce and the chicken in wine sauce. The wonton in red chili sauce is also fantastic. And though it sounds simple on paper, the diced chicken and peanuts with hot pepper possesses a complex spice mix, and is not just spicy to be spicy; the flavor is amazing. The lamb homestyle is also very good, a mix of sour and spicy. The smoked tea duck has an exuberant smoky flavor that goes well with the rich duck meat. I could go on and on about the menu items—it is really hard to go wrong. Best thing is to find a meat or vegetable you like and go to town with that.

White Bear, 135-02 Roosevelt Ave., #5, Flushing, NY 11354; (718) 961-2322; Subway: 7 to Main Street; Chinese (Wontons); $. This tiny spot is mostly a counter and a couple of tables, but they serve up some of the best-known dumplings and wontons in all of Flushing. And rightly so—they are delicious. Shockingly white in appearance, the wontons with chili oil (#6) are spectacular. They are filled with pork and topped with a sort of sandy red pepper paste and chili oil, along with bits of caramelized onions and freshly chopped scallions. They are truly spectacular and highly addicting. You can also purchase frozen dumplings and wontons here, in quantities from 50 to 200. Apart from the dumplings, the *dan dan noodles* are also a big hit.

Landmarks

Lucia Pizza, 136-55 Roosevelt Ave., Flushing, NY 11354; (718) 445-1313; Subway: 7 to Main Street; Pizza; $. This is a remnant of old-school Flushing, when there were more Italians living in the neighborhood. It opened in 1958 and has been serving pies and slices since then, not to mention garlic knots, heroes, a few pasta dishes, calzones, and Jamaican beef patties. Best way to try their excellent NY–style pizza is a plain slice. This is a somewhat saucier slice than you find at your average pizza joint, but the balance of cheese and sauce is fantastic. The crust is light and toothsome and serves as great support for the cheese and sauce. There's often a line to order and the space can get crowded, but that's because the pizza is so good. Order up at the front—where to do this can be a little confusing at first. They also sell Italian ices, which are very popular, especially on a warm day or evening. By the way, next door is Chatime, a bubble tea spot that has a buy-one-get-one-free special ongoing. How about that for old-meets-new Flushing? Nice.

Specialty Stores, Markets & Producers

Apollo Bakery, 135-36 39th Ave., Flushing, NY 11354; (718) 961-0596; Subway: 7 to Main Street. This tiny slip of a bakery has such a narrow storefront, you just might miss it if you don't keep an eye out for it. They have some delicious items, including pork buns, moon cakes—some with colorful Chinese characters stamped on them—and in particular, little cakes made of a short-crust pastry filled with a sweet pineapple paste. The buns and bread are obviously fresh, and you can see condensation from the warm bread against the plastic wrapping. Turnover is fast at this little bakery, so best thing to do if you don't find your favorite is to try something new! Everything is good here.

Durso's Pasta and Ravioli Company, 189-01 Crocheron Ave., Flushing, NY 11358; (718) 358-1311; LIRR: Auburndale (Port Washington Line); dursos.com. What a delight this place is! They've been around for over 40 years, but their space is bright, clean, and modern—not to mention filled with delicious food and awesome aromas. They make a variety of pastas there—the more conventional penne and ziti, but also radiatore, cavatelli, rope, and *mafalda;* they also make a jalapeño linguini. They are pushed through brass dies in a pasta machine from Italy. They also make pastas  that are stored in the freezer, like tortellini, ravioli, and gnocchi. On one side of the room are high-quality pantry items—olive oils, vinegars, dry imported pastas, tomatoes, jams, and the like, as well as a nice selection of cheeses. On the other side of the room is their magnificent deli counter, filled with delicious items made in house. There's vegetable dishes, salads, arancini, fresh mozzarella (bocconcini and larger balls), fresh sausages—the list goes on. There are even a few desserts, some of which are provided by the excellent Joe's Sicilian Bakery in Bayside. And everything is presented in extremely clean surroundings. Truly, every town should have a place like this—it's fantastic.

Fa Guo San Candy Shop USA, 38-03 Main St., Flushing, NY 11354; (718) 886-8866; Subway: 7 to Main Street; Asian Candy. Although it's not the cheapest place to buy candy, it has some of the most interesting items in the neighborhood, especially to Western eyes. Not only will you find the more common varieties of Pocky, an almost complete selection of the wonderful Japanese Kasugai-brand gummies (you'll find mangosteen but not yuzu), and Hello Panda cookies, but there are also more esoteric sweets, like preserved rose, salted plum, preserved olive, and sweet/salty/spicy bits of dried fish candies made of sea creatures like cuttlefish and shrimp. Big gold coins, sour gummy worms, and simple dried mango are also available. This is just a tiny fraction of what is stocked and displayed, too. The bulk items require purchasing a quarter-pound minimum, and don't be surprised if the staff shadows you a little, as they are just keeping an eye on things.

Fang Gourmet Tea, 135-25 Roosevelt Ave., Flushing, NY 11354; (888) 888-0216; Subway: 7 to Main Street; fangtea.com; Tea House. This calm tea house (though most of it is a shop), removed from the hustle and bustle of downtown Flushing, is serious about tea and is revered by tea connoisseurs everywhere. Here, you can buy tea-making equipment, or "teaware"— teapots, teacups, and tea scoops, in materials like clay and porcelain. Very expensive tea is also for sale, from pu-erh to oolong, pomelo to herbal, some of which can cost in the hundreds of dollars. The staff is helpful and eager to share their knowledge of tea with you. One way they'll do that is via a tea tasting, which is similar in concept to coffee cupping or wine tasting—a little bit of each item at a time, enough for you to get a good impression of each tea and the differences among them. It's inexpensive, too—each tea you try costs $5, unless you join their free tea club, and then it's $3 a taste. For deals/discounts on tea, follow them on twitter at @fangtea—they'll have 10 percent off specials from time to time.

H Mart, 141-40 Northern Blvd., Flushing, NY 11354; (718) 888-0005; Subway: 7 to Main Street; Korean Market. What sets this H Mart apart from the many others in Queens is the fact that it is open 24 hours, which means you can hit it up whenever you want. It's a little bit of a walk from the Main Street 7 train station but it's manageable for sure, plus there is a parking lot if you choose to drive. Along Northern Boulevard is a separate area for some of their produce, with the entrance to the rest of the store set in from the street a bit. When you enter, two things strike you—all the housewares for sale on the right and on the left the plethora of plastic containers containing a huge variety of side dishes, all packed up for you to grab and go. It's really impressive. Here, you'll find things like seasoned sesame leaves, pickled garlic in vinegar, seasoned squid, salted calamari, fried anchovy and bean, salted cod roe, stir-fried peanuts, sweet-and-sour tofu, fried croaker (a kind of fish), Korean omelet—you get the picture. Meats like marinated black pork belly, pork butt, and marinated chicken thigh are also stocked in this area. In the store is a nice little fish department. Here you can buy whole fish or fillets and steaks, fish roe, and nice packages of fish heads and other extra parts of the fish, perfect for making fish stock. The produce is fresh, there's plenty of kimchi, *gochujang*, and red pepper. You'll find all sorts of Korean staples, like oils, sauces, rice, noodles, tofu, tea, frozen dumplings, seaweed, pickled vegetables, miso, rice cakes, snacks, and more.

Hong Kong Supermarket, 3711 Main St., Flushing, NY 11354; (718) 539-6868; Subway: 7 to Main Street; Asian Supermarket. If you are in the market for pan-Asian groceries, you'll be happy to find one-stop shopping in this large, clean supermarket. From frozen foods to fresh fish, Chinese sausages to tea, seaweed snacks to *daifuku*, it's all here. In the refrigerated/frozen section, there are numerous kinds of tofu/soybean curd, packaged meats like short ribs, silky chicken (head and feet attached), gigantic frozen beef tongue, jars of fermented rice sauce (red and white), and many, many kinds of fresh noodles. Much of the fish and seafood is alive before you take it home. Strands of Chinese sausages, as well as spatchcocked cured ducks hang across from the meat department.

The interior of the store is stocked with myriad pantry items, including curries, Chinese herbs, tea, seaweed, snacks, sauces, sweets, dried noodles, rice, and pretty much anything else you'd  need to cook food from both East and Southeast Asian traditions. Produce is on the far end of the supermarket, and consists mostly of vegetables; the minor selection of fruit is a common criticism. But you'll find a few things, like apples and dragon fruit. The vegetables all look happy and fresh—you'll find giant oyster mushrooms, cheap avocados, lots and lots of greens, fresh lotus root, and more.

Jmart, 136-20 Roosevelt Ave., Flushing, NY 11354; (718) 353-0551; Subway: 7 to Main Street; Asian Supermarket. It's really hard to find anything wrong with this place—it's shiny and new, well stocked, has great prices, and it's in the New World Mall, which is also the home to an amazing food court in the basement. Asian staples like rice, noodles, sauces, and greens are all present in excess, and the fresh fish department is extremely clean. There is an entire aisle dedicated to Asian snacks, too. This supermarket is always busy, which means there is a lot of turnover of product—always good for the consumer.

Maxin Bakery, 37-01 Main St., Flushing, NY 11354; (718) 886-8558; Subway: 7 to Flushing Main Street; Taiwanese Bakery. This Maxin Bakery (it's part of a chain) is not far from the 7 station on Main Street and displays a variety of buns, cakes, and rolls. For those who like glutinous rice pancakes, the red bean flavor is really good, with a nice, smooth, sweetened red bean paste inside. Up at the counter under the register are some cool cases containing more Western-style cakes. The cheesecake square is light and slightly tangy, with a quarter-inch crust of sponge cake. If you want something on the savory side of things, beef, chicken, and pork buns are available. You can satisfy your bubble tea craving here, too.

New Flushing Bakery, 135-45 Roosevelt Ave., Flushing, NY 11354; (718) 539-6363; Subway: 7 to Main Street; Bakery. Egg tarts are the name of the game here, with a seemingly perpetual special of buy three egg tarts get one free. There are a number of flavors—Portuguese, traditional egg custard, green tea, coconut, red bean, and more. With that in mind, it is easy for me to say that this is the home of the best Portuguese egg tart—the custard itself is very creamy with a nicely caramelized top, sitting inside a beautifully flaky pastry. It's also flavored with a touch of cinnamon. They are really remarkable. They are good both in the morning and after a day in the fridge. The coconut tart is much thicker and sturdier, with a clean toasted-coconut taste. The bakery is conveniently located right next to the stairs leading down to the subway, so it's easy to grab and go on your way to the train.

Paris Baguette, 38-16 138th St., Flushing, NY 11354; (718) 713-0404; Subway: 7 to Main Street; parisbaguetteusa.com; Bakery. Part of a Korean-owned chain, Paris Baguette puts out sweet treats based in French classical technique, but with touches of Asian dessert flavor profiles like sweet potato, red bean, and green tea, not to mention the presence of a dim sum favorite, the egg custard tart. Apart from that, there are things like cakes, cheesecakes, *and croissants*. Particularly adorable is the Royal Pudding, available in the refrigerated case by the register. It comes in a miniature glass milk bottle and consists of a creamy top layer, caramel on the bottom, and custard in the middle. They even give you a skinny spoon with which to eat it, perfectly sized for this little bottle.  Their croissant-based pastries are beautifully flaky; the *pain au chocolat* is really nice and not gigantic. Also check out the large cream puff filled with pastry cream and studded with slices of strawberries, topped with a little streusel which isn't overly sweet. As far as how you gather up your pastries of choice, it works like a lot of Asian bakeries in Flushing— there are trays (be sure to put a piece of the provided tissue paper on the tray) and tongs for your use. Use the tongs to place each item on the tray, and then take it up to the register.

Share Tea, 37-27 Main St., Flushing, NY 11354; (718) 321-9866; Subway: 7 to Main Street; Tea House. **Having opened in Taiwan in 1992, this bubble tea shop is the first Share Tea that calls New York City home, as well as the very first location in the US. This particular shop in Flushing is located in the front of a shoe store; it reminds one of the famous *banh mi* shop located in a jewelry store in Manhattan. The taro milk tea is very good—it has a clean,**

milky flavor and a nice nuttiness to it. Also, it contains a couple of different sizes of tapioca balls—regular size and mini size, which makes for a nice contrast in texture. Plus, more balls can be consumed through the straw at one time. When you order tea, they'll ask you how sweet you want it (30, 50, or 80 percent? I chose 50 percent), and how much ice you'd like. It's nice to have such options presented to you. Share Tea also makes drinks with *yakult*, a probiotic dairy beverage popular in Japan, so you can amp up your tea drink and increase your good gut flora all at the same time. As far as the shoe shop goes, head toward the back to see the majority of what they sell. It smells a little like ginseng back there, too.

Siruyeon, 150-36 Northern Blvd., Flushing, NY 11354; (718) 461-6677; LIRR: Murray Hill stop (Port Washington Line); Korean Sweets. This little independent Korean sweet shop sells a variety of homemade items like strawberry and green tea rice-flour cakes and even rice-flour brownies, which are pleasantly chewy. They also make rice waffles, incorporating them into a fantastic dessert involving ice cream and  fresh fruit. Everything sits on or around the waffle, and is drizzled with a little chocolate sauce, accompanied by small mounds of a unique mixture of heavy cream and corn flour (it tastes a bit like peanut butter). The waffle is served warm, which causes the scoop of ice cream to start melting, and by the end, everything is kind of a big delicious mess. Hot tea, coffee, and bubble tea are also available—try the mango milk tea with bubbles! It's kind of like eating liquid mango cheesecake. Very tasty.

Taipan Bakery, 37-25 Main St., Flushing, NY 11354; (718) 888-1111; Subway: 7 to Main Street; taipanbakeryonline.com; Asian Bakery. If you try one thing at Taipan Bakery, make it the egg tarts. Not only do they carry the classic egg tart with the flaky crust (you are one lucky person if you get one that's warm out of the oven—and the Portuguese style has a crème brûlée torched top), but they also carry the ones with the cookie-style crust, those filled with only egg whites, and almond and green tea–flavored ones. It really is impressive to see so many egg tart varieties in one place. In addition to these lovelies, you'll find sponge cakes, floss buns, red bean buns, pork buns, and pineapple buns—and that's only the beginning. Smoothies and bubble tea are also available, as is Eight Treasure Ice, a shave ice dessert topped with all sorts of tasty things, including red beans and black grass jelly.

Ten Ren Tea and Ginseng, 135-18 Roosevelt Ave., Flushing, NY 11354; (718) 461-9305; Subway: 7 to Main Street; tenren.com; Tea House. Ten Ren is a well-known tea and tea house brand in NYC, but the location in Flushing is one of the best. Walk in and you'll see ginseng on the right and a tea counter on the left. You can order hot and cold tea, with or without "bubbles," aka tapioca balls. If you do choose to get bubbles, rejoice in the fact that there a lot of them! They are gentle in texture and never get stuck in the straw. Plain green tea is available, as is the more elaborate taro flavor, which at Ten Ren tasted a little nuttier than in other tea houses—quite delightful. There are also a few seats along the front window where you can enjoy your tea beverage in the store. Toward the back, boxes of tea are also available for purchase, as are more valuable loose teas, like pu-erh, located on the right-hand wall in golden containers.

Yeh's Bakery/Red Leaf Bakery, 57-25 Main St., Flushing, NY 11355; (718) 939-1688; Subway: 7 to Main Street; Chinese Bakery. If I were to order an Asian-style cake, I would get it here. The sponge cake is light, perfectly sweet, and appropriately moist (this is not an American style of baking, where super-moist is often desirable). Cakes come as whole, round cakes topped with fresh fruit, or as longer, sliceable roll cakes—in this case, you can purchase them whole or by the slice, and slices are wrapped up in plastic wrap and displayed in the main counter. The green tea cake is particularly good, but taro, coconut, and rainbow are also popular. The Boston cream pie is also wonderful. On the savory side of things, you'll find warm beef curry puffs and chicken puffs, as well as a very tasty scallion roll. There's no seating here, so takeout is your only option. The bakery is located a bit south of downtown Flushing, but it's so worth the hike (or bus ride) down Main Street for their amazing baked goods.

AA Plaza, 40-66 Main St., Flushing, NY 11369; Subway: 7 to Main Street; Chinese Street Food; $. This small set of stalls is located underneath the Flushing LIRR station and is a great spot to catch a snack if you have a good-size break between trains, or even if you're just visiting the neighborhood. A variety of things are sold in this Plaza, including scallion pancakes, fried chicken, steamed pork buns, and fish balls. The scallion pancake is truly delicious, quite large, and fried up on the flat griddle, one after another. It's studded with little green scallion chunks and is served up hot in a little square paper bag. Just rip off strips of it as you eat it. It's warm, flaky, and soft all at once. The deep-fried chicken drumsticks are also tasty and cheap as all get out (at the writing of this book, two drumsticks were $1). Fish balls (spicy or not, though the spicy ones are the best) and steamed pork buns are also available at other stalls, and both are terrific. This is super-cheap street food and absolutely worth a look-see at the least.

Chestnuts King, 41-40 Main St., Flushing, NY 11369; Subway: 7 to Main Street; Chinese; $. This tiny stall on Main Street sells roasted chestnuts, and that's it. The chestnuts are from Tianjin and are roasted in the skin over little black pebbles (they actually look a little like black beans) in a mechanical roaster, and sold in quarter-, half-, and 1-pound quantities. The chestnuts are slightly sweet, very starchy, and definitely tasty. A little goes a long way.

Mongolian BBQ Cart, Kissena Blvd. near Sanford Ave., Flushing, NY 11355; Subway: 7 to Main Street; Chinese; $. Kan, the man who runs this cart, has also set up shop on Main Street near Sanford Avenue, so be aware that he does move around a bit. His specialty is meat on a stick or skewer, but he also offers sandwiches and a few other things. The lamb skewer is wonderful—moist, almost buttery lamb meat is grilled to perfection. He'll ask you if you want it spicy, and unless you really have a hard time with spicy food, I recommend you go with at least a little spice, which consists of chili powder and cumin. These two elements add wonderful flavor to the meat. On top of that, he sprinkles on some sesame seeds, which elevate the meat to new heights. That little bit of nuttiness is so excellent. Kan has a good grasp of English, and he likes to chat up his customers. If you're interested in pushing the limit past muscle meats, opt for the grilled fish ball skewer or lamb heart skewer. Spicy sauce and hoisin sauce are also available in a squirt bottle, and Kan is happy to add those to your meat if you like.

Peking Duck Sandwich Stall, Main St. and 40th Rd., Flushing, NY 11355; Subway: 7 to Flushing Main Street; Chinese; $. This is a tiny stall, jutting out from the bottom of the building that houses Corner 28 Restaurant. This sandwich consists of a circular, flat yet puffy, and very soft bun with a piece of duck placed on it. Then cucumber, scallions, and hoisin sauce are added, and the whole thing is folded in half, right in front of you. Each duck bun is $1. A few other dim sum–type items are available, too; the sesame balls are a good choice.

Xinjiang BBQ Cart, 38th Ave. or 39th Ave. & Main St., Flushing, NY 11354; Subway: 7 to Main Street; Chinese; $. The best thing on the menu is the cumin lamb skewer, which is full of delicious, spicy cumin goodness. The amount of meat is substantial and always very tender. The man who runs this cart takes a lot of care in the length of time he cooks the meat, developing a beautiful crust on it. The chicken skewer is also very good. He'll ask you if you want it spicy, and that is recommended, unless you can't handle spicy food at all. He salts the meat, then adds chili powder and cumin, and it all combines into something wholly delicious. The menu is small—apart from the above two skewers, you can get beef, chicken gizzard, lamb tendon, and chicken heart.

Zhu Ji Dumpling Stall, 40-52 Main St., Flushing, NY 11354; (718) 353-6265; Subway: 7 to Main Street; Chinese; $. This is often referred to as the "41st Avenue dumpling stall," since the actual location is on 41st Avenue, across the street from the (very nice) Starbucks (which is a cool haven during a heat wave—thank you industrial-strength air-conditioning). The food here is very cheap, but not cheaply made. One of the best things here is the serving of fried pork and leek dumplings. They are almost buttery tasting and not spicy, though you could put some hot sauce on them. There are four to an order, so it's very easy to just inhale them while standing there on the street, though there are a few stools inside on which to sit and enjoy your dumplings.

Bayside, Douglaston & Whitestone

These three communities are not accessible by subway, but Bayside and Douglaston are accessible by the LIRR, one of New York City's commuter rails. Whitestone is best accessible by car or bus. To get to these neighborhoods, one needs to do a little more planning than simply hopping on the train, but the food at these destinations is worth making the little extra effort.

Bayside is an upper middle class neighborhood in northeastern Queens. It has a suburban feel to it, thanks to all the single family houses and wide streets. Bayside history goes back to 2000 BC, when the Matinecock Native American tribe first settled there. For a long time it was home to farming, later giving up the ghost to urban sprawl in the early 20th century. Rumor had it that Bayside was going to be the next Hollywood, but that never materialized.

Whites are in the majority here, but there are sizable Korean and Chinese populations; there is also a small African-American community. There are three main drags, commercially, including Bell Boulevard, Northern Boulevard, and Francis Lewis Boulevard. For most people, accessing the food scene on Bell Boulevard is the easiest, as it's closest to the Bayside LIRR station. Bayside has some excellent bakeries and restaurants, and some really are worth the trip out east to experience.

Douglaston is an affluent suburban neighborhood east of Bayside; the two communities are separated by the Little Neck Bay and Alley Pond Park and are one LIRR stop away from each other. Douglaston, too, was the home to the Matinecock Native American tribe; in the early 19th century a man by the name of George Douglas bought the 240-acre parcel of land, and when he died he willed it to his son, William Douglas. When the railroad arrived in the area, he donated an outbuilding to serve as the station house, and with thanks the railroad named the stop Douglaston, and the community took on the name as well.

The racial demographics in Douglaston are similar to Bayside, with a majority white population and sizable Chinese and Korean populations. Northern Boulevard, one of the main commercial districts, is one of the main commercial areas, as well as Douglaston Parkway, on which the massive Fairway Market resides. There is a cluster of establishments around the LIRR station, including the swanky Il Toscano and the pub Strawberry's Sports Grill, owned by former Mets outfielder Darryl Strawberry.

Whitestone is a residential neighborhood in northeastern Queens, sitting atop Bayside and Flushing, located to the east of College Point. It's about 4 square miles in size and is home to the Whitestone Bridge (gorgeous views of it can be seen from Francis Lewis Park). The name of the area comes from the presence of a large, white limestone boulder near the river's shore. The abovementioned Francis Lewis was a signer of the Declaration of Independence and the English raided the area during the Revolutionary War, so there's a lot of early American history here.

The current racial makeup is very similar to Bayside and Douglaston, though the percentage of white residents far outpaces anything else. This group is made up of Italian Americans, Irish Americans, Greek Americans, and Croatian Americans. With that in mind, you'll find a lot of good European chow in this neighborhood.

Foodie Faves

Bon Chon Chicken, 45-37 Bell Blvd., Ste. B, Bayside, NY 11361; (718) 225-1010; LIRR: Port Washington Line to Bayside; bonchon .co.kr; Korean Fried Chicken; $. A friend once told me that he was a big fan of various East Asian styles of fried chicken, swooning over how crispy it gets while staying moist and flavorful. Bon Chon, an import from Korea, makes exactly this kind of chicken, and it is remarkably crisp, rendering it highly appealing. You can order your chicken in various configurations—just "drums" (drumsticks);

just wings; just white meat (think boneless buffalo wings, but not uniformly shaped); or a combination of drumsticks and wings. Orders come as small as three pieces (drums) or as large as 22 pieces (wings). The chicken arrives hot, lightly topped with either soy garlic sauce (which is both a bit sweet and nicely savory) or a spicy sauce (spicy but not overly hot), and very crispy. While you wait for your chicken, a bowl of cubed pickled turnip and a bowl of cabbage slaw with a ginger sauce arrive at your table, both of which are tasty and refreshing; they serve as a very nice foil to the fried chicken. To drink, there's beer and soju on the alcohol side, water and soda on the soft-drink side. There are plenty of other items on the menu, like potstickers, scallion pancakes, pork *katsu*, and edamame. But it's really the delicious Korean fried chicken that is the star of the show. As for the space, it is a bit dark, though not oppressively so, with wooden booths and seating areas; on each table is a button you can press to summon the waitstaff. The general vibe is very relaxing, too.

Golden Sparrow, 12-58 150th St., Whitestone, NY 11357; (718) 746-0206; LIRR: Port Washington Line to Murray Hill, then Q15 Bus north; Cafe; $. If you're looking for a place to relax and/or go for coffee with a friend, Golden Sparrow is the place for you. They serve Intelligentsia coffee, an excellent roaster based in Chicago, and makes tasty espresso based drinks with a fluffy steamed-milk style. The coffee is strong and delicious and goes great with their baked goods; the pecan bar is delicious, a nice combination of a buttery shortbread crust with roasted, caramelized pecan spread on top. There are a range of fun cupcakes, including red velvet; a variety of *macarons,* in flavors such as lemon, pistachio, and blueberry; and cake pops. And since they are a gelateria, too, they sell homemade gelato. Give the namesake gelato a try, the Golden Sparrow, consisting of sweet cream gelato mixed with chocolate chip marshmallow crunch cookies. It's really good! Get it in a cone, cup, or as part of a shake. Also, there are a few savory sandwich options—pulled pork, chicken, kasseri and ham, and grilled cheese. If you'd like to enjoy your food there at the cafe, there are tables in the back, some comfy chairs up front, and when it's warmer, you can sit in their beautiful back garden, surrounded by greenery, figs, and apricot trees.

Press 195, 4011 Bell Blvd., Bayside, NY 11361; (718) 281-1950; LIRR: Port Washington Line to Bayside; press195.com; Sandwiches; $. Delicious pressed sandwiches (aka panini) are the name of the game here, and the selection is incredibly wide ranging, from vegetarian to full-on meat. Each sandwich arrives beautifully plated, warm and nicely toasted, accompanied by a lightly pickled cucumber salad. It's pretty much impossible to find a bad thing on their 40-sandwich menu, but some of the highlights include combinations like tomato, fresh mozzarella, fresh basil, and their house-made maple syrup basil pesto; roast pork, ham, swiss cheese, pickles, and roasted garlic spread (essentially a Cubano); grilled eggplant, roasted red peppers, smoked Gouda, and roasted garlic spread; and the turkey, sweet onion jam, fresh mozzarella, and grilled marinated mushrooms. Unique to Press 195 is their line of pressed knish sandwiches—knishes are used in place of bread, making for something wildly different! Fillings range from grilled vegetables to steak, meat loaf to turkey. Along with your sandwich, consider placing an order for their hand-cut, twice-fried Belgian *frites,* which arrive in a paper supported by a conical metal frame. Just like the *frites* overseas, there are a variety of sauces for your dipping pleasure—the chipotle jalapeño mayo is fabulous, and not overly spicy at all but full of flavor; ketchup also comes with the fries by default. Their homemade strawberry lemonade—made from real strawberries and real lemons—is a perfect companion to all this food, too. It's wonderfully fruity and not overly sweet. The indoor seating is informal, and there's even an outdoor patio that is open during the warmer months.

Three Brothers Butcher BBQ, 40-21 Bell Blvd., Bayside, NY 11361; (718) 224-7753; LIRR: Port Washington Line to Bayside; 3brosbbq.com; Southern Barbecue; $. Only a block or two from the Bayside LIRR station, barbecue is alive and well at this friendly, informal spot in the busy Bell Boulevard commercial area. This is Southern/Mississippi 'cue and meats are smoked there on the premises. Get your fill, be it ribs, pulled pork, chicken, wings, brisket, or sausage. Their pulled pork sandwich is excellent, served either on a hero or a round roll, served with coleslaw on the sandwich and their sweet and tangy barbecue sauce. Get a piece of their light, sweet cornbread to go with it (pieces are also wrapped and piled on the counters, so you can easily grab a piece on the go). For a truly decadent treat, get an order of the smothered BBQ fries, topped with a choice of BBQ pork, beef, chicken, or chili, along with cheddar, hot peppers, and onions. Nachos come the same way. The burnt ends are also popular, with plenty of smoky flavor. Boylan sodas are the main drink option. The guys behind the counter are super helpful, friendly, and easygoing and it is a joy to engage with them either in placing an order or for casual chitchat. There are some tables along the wall, so you can enjoy your food right there. Three Brothers also serves as a butcher shop, so you can buy various cuts of meats there, as well as anything smoked they offer.

Specialty Stores, Markets & Producers

Cupcakes in Heels, 43-19 Bell Blvd., Bayside, NY 11361; (718) 415-2009; LIRR: Port Washington Line to Bayside; cupcakesinheels .com. A tiny slip of a space houses this cute little cupcake shop, whose cupcakes are named after designers—for instance, The Prada is pistachio, The Dolce is salted caramel, and The Burberry is strawberry. The frostings are very light and the cupcake itself is not too moist, nor is it overly dry, as can be the case with many cupcakes in this town. There is no seating, so the best thing to do is get your cupcakes to take out (they have nice cupcake-protecting packaging for multiple cupcakes), though if you really need to eat it there, just ask the person behind the counter for a fork and a napkin. An hour before closing you can  BOGO your cupcakes, which is a nice deal. Coffee is also served, as are bottled juices and sodas.

D'Aquila Pastry Shop, 33-31 Francis Lewis Blvd., Bayside, NY 11358; (718) 886-4800; LIRR: Port Washington Line to Auburndale; Bakery. Italian and American pastries are the name of the game here, and they do a great job with them. Their cannolis are popular, but they make a whole lot more. There are shelves of Italian butter cookies, as well as flaky Danishes and turnovers, éclairs, fruit tarts, napoleons, and cheesecake. Everything is very fresh and tasty. They also sell gelato, which is also very tasty. Long lines overtake the bakery during the holidays, so keep that in mind around Christmas and Easter.

Douglaston Greenmarket, 41st Ave. and 235th St., Douglaston, NY 11363; LIRR: Port Washington Line to Douglaston; grownyc.org/douglastongreenmarket. This well-placed greenmarket—located at the Douglaston LIRR station—is open on Sunday from 8 a.m. to 3 p.m. from early July to mid November. A terrific variety of food is for sale at this greenmarket—wild-caught fish and shellfish off the coast of Long Island, bread, local fruits and vegetables, various meats, and cheese from New Jersey. While you're there, catch a cooking demonstration, and often there are activities for kids. Note that EBT/food stamps, debit/credit cards, and WIC and FMNP checks are accepted at this greenmarket.

Greek Food Emporium, 12-52 150th St., Whitestone, NY 11357; LIRR: Port Washington Line to Murray Hill, then Q15 Bus north; Greek. This is the brick-and-mortar location (aka flagship store) of the online business of the same name. It is a lovely shop and a wonderful resource for the people of Whitestone. You'll find a lot of Greek staples—rusks, noodles, olive oil (some organic), legumes and lentils, frozen sausages (orange *loukaniko* is particularly awesome), a whole variety of fetas, including Horio, Kofinaki, and Arahova, Nescafé for frappés, cookies from Victory Sweet Shop in Astoria, bread and pitas, tinned Greek vegetables like giant beans and roasted eggplant, sardines in oil and salt, tuna in olive oil, rice, jams and preserves (including mastic paste), and a terrific olive bar where you can taste the olives before you buy them. The store is bright and cheery, encouraging you to hang out and pick up a few (or a lot of) things. A definite must-visit next time you're in Whitestone.

Joe's Sicilian Bakery, 21-216 48th Ave., Bayside, NY 11364; (718) 225-2272; LIRR: Port Washington Line to Bayside; Bakery. The most delicious Italian butter cookies are found here, which are smooth, rich, and fantastically buttery. If you feel that bakery butter cookies are ho-hum, you haven't tried the ones here—good chance you'll have a food conversion on the spot. Other delicious treats include their chocolate-frosted brownies, irresistible NY–style mini cheesecakes (plain or topped with whipped cream and strawberries), biscotti, fondant-topped black and white cookies, and flaky bow ties. In the back you'll find pizza, both Sicilian style and round NY style, which you can buy by the slice or pie. The round makes for a nice cheesy slice. They bake bread here, too, which is very popular in the neighborhood—particularly beloved is the savory sausage, pepper, and onion bread. Semolina loaves and rolls are also for sale.

Teaspoon Bake Shop, 36-41 Bell Blvd., Bayside, NY 11361; (718) 224-4626; LIRR: Port Washington Line to Bayside; theteaspoon bakeshop.com; Bakery. The baked goods at this bright, clean, and cheery American-style bakery are beyond excellent. Everything is well executed and simply delicious. Their brownies are on the fudgy side and are huge; their cupcakes—the chocolate ones especially are rich and very chocolaty—are topped with silky buttercreams, tangy cream cheese frosting, or light whipped cream; and the maple oatmeal cake is soft inside and has a fantastic caramelized top, a nice splurge for breakfast. And speaking of breakfast, they carry a whole line of muffins and scones, which go perfectly with a cup of Stumptown Coffee. But what the bakery is most famous for is their line of cake balls, similar to cake pops but without the stick. The red velvet is

the star, extremely moist and dipped in tempered dark chocolate—
a perfect combination. The peanut butter pretzel cake ball is also
a delight, a combination of smooth peanut butter and crunchy
pretzels, also dipped in dark chocolate. The bakery has a few tables
with chairs, so you can enjoy your sweet treats right there at the
bakery. Before you leave, be sure to take a gander at the amazing
decorative cakes up in the front window—they are truly creative!

Glendale, Maspeth, Middle Village & Ridgewood

The communities of Glendale, Maspeth, Middle Village and Ridgewood are located in a part of Queens that has virtually no subway access. Only along the edges is there a station or two, so this is a very car-oriented part of Queens, and good for those who like to walk a lot. There are some bus lines that run though, so that is also helpful. The majority of the residents have come from Irish, Italian, and Eastern European stock, and quite a large German population was there for some time, which gave birth to numerous German restaurants. All but one faded away, the survivor being Zum Stammtisch, which is very well regarded in New York City.

The major commercial area is along Myrtle Avenue and to some extent Cooper Avenue. The aforementioned Zum Stammtisch is there on the corner of 70th Street, with its relatively new pork store adjacent to it. The Shops at Atlas Park is another commercial destination in Glendale, located on the site of the former Atlas Terminals industrial park. Shops and restaurants make their home there, from the super-chain California Pizza Kitchen to the highly praised German restaurant Manor Oktoberfest, which has an excellent reputation for delicious Teutonic food.

Again, there is no subway service within the neighborhood boundaries, though access to the Myrtle Avenue M station is available to those in the southwestern part of the neighborhood and the Woodhaven Boulevard M/R station for those in the northeastern corner of the neighborhood. It really is easiest to travel to this neighborhood by car.

Foodie Faves

Antica Trattoria, 68-10 Fresh Pond Rd., Ridgewood, NY 11385; (718) 386-1559; Subway: M to Fresh Pond Road; anticafresh.com; Italian; $$. Terrific classic Italian food can be had at this well-regarded Italian restaurant in the heart of Ridgewood; locals consider it a true gem in the area. Dine on delicious pastas, meats, fish, and various salads and antipasti. The lasagna—complete with a meat sauce as well as béchamel, gets particularly high marks. To contrast this meaty traditional dish, give the *busiate cú li sardi* a try—a combination of sardines, young fennel, pine nuts, and raisins, all topped with toasted bread crumbs. The pizza is also very good, with a solid basic pie in the form of either the Margherita or Napolitana, and the Tre Sapori is bursting with flavors of olives, red peppers, and sausage. Their *Pesce del Giorno* (fish of the day) is worth keeping an eye on, too. For dessert, the tiramisu is excellent. As for the space, it's a bit more upscale compared to a lot of other places in the area, with white tablecloths and murals on the walls, along with antique (reproduction) lanterns alongside.

Bosna Express, 791 Fairview Ave., Ridgewood, NY 11385; (718) 497-7577; Subway: M to Forest Avenue; Balkan; $. Stop here for some of the best *cevapi* and *pleskavica* in the neighborhood, though the *pleskavica*—affectionately known as the "Balkan burger"—is the main event. It's huge and can feed two people at least, and is made from beef and lamb, which is a very traditional combination. It's served with *lepinja,* the traditional Bosnian bread, as well as lettuce, onions, and *ajvar;* you can also opt to get these toppings on the side. *Kajmak,* a kind of tart cream cheese, is available at an additional cost. The burger is just fantastic—salty, savory, and sweet from the *ajvar* and yogurt. Wash it down with a bottle of Cockta, and you're set. Get a shepherd salad, some *grah (bean soup)* or stuffed cabbage as well. The space is tiny, so takeout is your best bet.

Krolewskie Jadlo, 66-21 Fresh Pond Rd., Ridgewood, NY 11385; (718) 366-6226; Subway: M to Fresh Pond Road; krolewskiejadlo .com; Polish; $. One of the great things about this place—whose name translates to "king's feast"—is the way it's designed inside. There's lots of wood, it's cozy, and has a real European feel to it. That's emphasized even more when a soccer match is playing on the TV affixed to the back wall. One of the best parts of their menu is the $9 weekday lunch special (12 to 4 p.m.), which consists of soup, a main dish, and dessert. And believe me when I tell you this—it is a ton of food, or truly a king's feast. You will not leave here hungry. Their borschts are good but the white borscht is a real standout—it's creamy and flavored with bits of smoked pork. This is an incredibly satisfying dish. For your mains, nothing could be more classic than stuffed cabbage or kielbasa with fries. The cabbage is stuffed with a moist meat mixture, topped with a tomato sauce and accompanied by creamy mashed potatoes. The kielbasa is grilled until it gets a little crispy on the outside, is topped with

 lightly fried onions, and comes with mustard, along with fries. In addition, plates of vegetables come with your meal, too—they might be red cabbage, cucumbers, peas, or carrots. Dessert is either chocolate cake or apple cake; the apple cake is the way to go. A good Polish meal is made even better by a glass of beer, and there are a few on tap (including the fabulous Old Speckled Hen).

Spolem Cafe, 66-30 Fresh Pond Rd., Ridgewood, NY 11385; (347) 725-3379; Subway: M to Fresh Pond Road; Cafe/Coffee House; $. A hip yet unpretentious spot on Fresh Pond Road in Ridgewood, Spolem Cafe is a great place to relax with a drink and/or a light meal. They offer coffee and tea and have a bar stocked with liquor, beer (some on tap), and wine. Baked goods offered include waffles, pastries, muffins, as well as quiches; their menu keeps expanding, too. If you'd like a little extra oomph in your coffee or tea, they'll spike it for you (try the Mambo Cafe—coffee with Sambuca). They've also developed a very tasty Nutella latte—it isn't overly sweet and the coffee, chocolate, and hazelnut flavors meld together very well. Enjoy it while perusing the *New York Times,* which is free to read. There is also free Wi-Fi, so you can hang out and do some work there (or update your Facebook status). The staff is nice, friendly, and very welcoming to all. At night the lights go down, and vibe changes from a cafe to more of a bar/lounge. And if you're lucky, you'll catch some live tunes one of these nights.

Uvarara Vineria e Ristoro, 79-28 Metropolitan Ave., Middle Village, NY 11379; (718) 894-0052; Subway: M to Middle Village Metropolitan; uvararany.com; Italian; $$$. Middle Village is fortunate to have this lovely Italian restaurant in their community. The Iadicicco family has been running it since 2007, bringing regional food from southerly Campania—home to the major cities of Naples and Salerno—to the hungry masses. Wine is a big part of their work here, so wine tastings are a regular occurrence. To start your meal, consider a bit of cheese or cured meats. Meats and cheeses are

Italian, naturally. Give the speck a try, which has a long and interesting history (it has origins in Tyrol). Their gnocchi alla Romana is a house special and understandably so—the gnocchi are cooked with butter and Parmesan, making for an incredibly delicious combination. Entrees consist of pasta and meat dishes, including fettuccine Bolognese and the excellent *guazzetto di pesce,* which is mix of fish and seafood in a light white wine–tomato sauce. Happily, tiramisu is on the dessert menu, but the Drunken Pears get much love—it's hard to go wrong with a roasted pear with a wine glaze accompanied by a scoop of gelato.

Landmarks

Zum Stammtisch, 69-46 Myrtle Ave., Glendale, NY 11385; (718) 386-3014; zumstammtisch.com; German; $$. Hands down, this is the best German food in Queens, as well as having one of the most atmospheric settings of any Queens restaurant. Walk through the doors and you'll find yourself in Germany, what with the traditionally decorated walls, complete with animal heads, shelves with beer steins, and Germanic paintings. The waitresses also wear traditional dresses and say *danke* to add to the vibe. Beer is a great way to accompany your meal, and beer flows plentifully here. The barrel beers are delicious—give the Hofbräu Hefe Weizen a try, which comes in a tall, elegant glass. As far as the food goes, it's hard to find a bad thing on the menu. The German herring salad is a terrific choice for those who love fish, and it comes with beets and potatoes along with the herring; herring in cream sauce is also a great choice. For an overview of German vegetable salads, give the *Deutscher Salat* plate a try, which consists of cucumber, carrot, beet, and cabbage salads. The two and three sausage plates are classic, complete with Zum Stammtisch's terrific sauerkraut and German potato salads. Of the three sausages, the *Krainerwurst* is tops (a savory pork sausage smoked with hickory). It's also easy to cut, as it arrives on the plate cut so that it's fanned out at the top; be careful when you cut into a hot sausage, as droplets of hot fat can jump out at you after the thin casing is pierced! Apart from that, solid menu choices include the sauerbraten and the *Jägerschitzel,* a breaded veal cutlet topped with a mushroom and veal stock sauce. Daily specials are also available, and range from roast duck to goulash. For dessert, it's hard to go wrong with traditional sweets like apple strudel (get it a la mode for an extra treat) and Black Forest cake. After your meal, don't forget to stop by the neighboring Stammtisch Pork Store, which carries a number of imported German products (edible and not), sausages, and frozen dishes from the restaurant.

Atlas Park Greenmarket, Cooper Ave. and 80th St., Glendale, NY 11385; Subway: 7 to 74th Street or E/F/M/R to Roosevelt Avenue, then Q45 bus south to Atlas Park; grownyc.org/atlaspark greenmarket; Greenmarket. Located at the Atlas Park Mall, this seasonal market, which runs on Saturday, 8 a.m. to 4 p.m., from early June to mid/late December, is very popular with locals and visitors to the mall. In addition to the fresh local vegetables and fruit, you can purchase baked goods from Meredith's Bakery from upstate, as well as potted plants from Carucci Greenhouses & Farms on Long Island. Cooking demonstrations take place, and recipes are shared with greenmarket shoppers, so that they can take advantage of the wonderful seasonal produce for sale. EBT/food stamps, debit/credit cards, and WIC & Senior FMNP coupons are all accepted at this greenmarket.

Iavarone Bros., 69-00 Grand Ave., Maspeth, NY 11378; (718) 639-3623; Bus: Q18 terminus; ibfoods.com; Italian. If you're looking for an excellent selection of Italian products in the neighborhood, look no further than Iavarone Bros., located right on the corner of Grand Avenue and 69th Street. This location is part of the greater IB Foods family, a small collection of Italian marketplaces/restaurants scattered throughout Long Island, with one location in Queens, this one. They carry a whole line of fresh pastas (e.g., angel hair, lasagna sheets, ravioli, perciatelli) and prepared sauces (e.g., vodka, tomato, Alfredo), and also sell prepared food, like pizzas, pasta dishes, quiches, and chili. The shop also has a full-service deli, complete with salads, antipasti, and a meat and fish counter with cuts of chicken, beef, pork, fresh sausages, fish fillets and shellfish, all looking clean and healthy. Fresh and smoked mozzarella is also for sale, piled on top of the deli counter, as well as cured sausages and charcuterie. Sweets from Junior's are also available.

Krystal European Bakery, 66-72 Fresh Pond Rd., Ridgewood, NY 11385; (718) 418-9493; Subway: M to Fresh Pond Road; Romanian Bakery. Classic Romanian baked goods can be found here, and they do not disappoint. A few American-style desserts dot the display case, like cheesecake and carrot cake, but it's really the Romanian sweets that shine. There's fruity apple strudel, cheese strudel, sweet cheese puffs, cherry turnovers, little croissants, butter cookies, linzer tarts, and these wonderful cherry squares, consisting  of a sweet cherry filling sandwiched between two layers of pastry. In the spring they carry loaves of *cozonaci,* a traditional Romanian Easter bread. Apart from the sweet things they make, savory items are also for sale in the refrigerated case toward the back, like salami, bologna, smoked bacon, and both cow's and sheep's milk kashkaval cheese. The red pepper spread *zacusca,* the roe spread *salata de icre,* and *ciorba de miel*—a Romanian spring lamb sour soup (often made from lamb offal like heart and lungs)—are also available for sale.

Morscher's Pork Store, 58-44 Catalpa Ave., Ridgewood, NY 11385; (718) 821-1040; Subway: M to Forest Avenue; morschers porkstore.com; Butcher. The German butcher stores of Ridgewood are slowly falling away, but there are some still hanging on.  Morscher's is one of those, and is a wonderful place for meat, especially pork. Sausages, bacon, and hams hang down from the ceiling, plus there are fresh meats in the case, such as steaks, pork chops, ribs, and roasts. A number of pantry items are available here, most importantly the brown mustard that goes so well with these kinds of meats—Bauer's is the brand to look for. Last time I was in, I saw a container of whole cabbages fermenting in the traditional way, perhaps for sauerkraut or stuffed cabbages later on. German cookies, jams, and pickles also line the shelves. Pick up one of their excellent *Krainerwurst* on your way home and put it on the grill. Heaven.

Muncan Food Corp., 60-86 Myrtle Ave., Ridgewood, NY 11385; (718) 417-5095; Subway: M to Fresh Pond Road; Butcher/Meat Market. Look to Astoria for the sibling to Ridgewood's Muncan Foods—they both carry similar things, and the Ridgewood location might be a bit smaller than the Astoria location. But the same high quality meats can be purchased here—lots of cured meat and sausages, hanging from the ceiling and in the cases, mostly made with pork. If you are curious about anything, just ask for a taste and they'll give it to you; they might even make suggestions if they think you are open to them. If you are really stuck, just choose some bacon, which they excel at making; the double smoked is particularly good. And while pork is their main meat, they stock some beef and duck items. But whatever you decide, no doubt it will be simply amazing.

Parrot Coffee, 58-22 Myrtle Ave., Ridgewood, NY 11385; (718) 821-2785; parrotcoffee.com; European Grocery. Parrot is a bright and shiny specialty food store wonderland on Myrtle Avenue, not far from Forest Avenue. It's part of a local mini-chain, with locations in both Astoria and Sunnyside. From chocolates to bread, homemade phyllo delicacies to olives, they stock some of the most interesting and flavorful products around. The focus is on foodstuffs from the Balkans and Turkey. It's a great place to find bulk nuts and dried fruit; there are also some nuts already prepackaged in 1-pound bags; dried fruit is also available both in bulk and in bags. Bulk coffee is also available. The refrigerated section contains various butters, a wonderful strained goat yogurt from Greece, as well as a Bulgarian whole-milk yogurt made from the milk of grass-fed cows, and different kinds of Eastern European and Mediterranean cheeses. The freezer section contains *bureks, cevapi,* phyllo dough, various Eastern European sausages, slab bacon, hummus, and homemade dips and spreads. Parrot carries the best medjool dates around, too. They are huge.

Rego Smoked Fish, 69-80 75th St., Middle Village, NY 11379; (718) 326-2170; Not accessible by subway; Fish Market. **Hidden** away in a semi-industrial area, this tiny shop sells smoked fish (the actual smoking is done off-site in Greenpoint, southern neighbor to Long Island City in Queens) to the public on Sunday from 8 a.m. to noon. The fish available for sale at Rego Smoked Fish is excellent and you can taste anything that is open and free for the staff person to handle. In the main case are whole whitefish, sable, nova, salty lox, and a few other things; the whitefish must be purchased whole (they run around $12 each at the writing of this book), but the nova, lox, and sable, for instance, can be purchased by the pound and even by the slice; the fish is sliced by hand while you wait. The kippered salmon is baked so it is sold in chunks rather than delicate slices like the lox and the like. In the refrigerator to your left are various sizes of containers of things like pickled herring, pickled herring in wine sauce, pickled herring in sour cream, whitefish salad, cream cheese, and green olives. If you'd like to order a big platter for a party, they'll put one together for you. A platter of whitefish, nova, baked salmon, and sable for 12

people goes for $110 (they need 2 days' advance notice to plan for the order).

Ridgewood Youthmarket, Myrtle and Cypress Avenues, Ridgewood, NY 11385; Subway: L/M to Myrtle-Wyckoff Avenues; grownyc.org/youthmarket/ridgewood; Greenmarket. The Ridgewood Local Development Corporation and the Myrtle Avenue Business Improvement District produce this much-needed greenmarket in the area of NYC where Brooklyn's Bushwick and Queens' Ridgewood meet at the borough border. Young people from both communities arrive at the market space and sell fresh fruits and vegetables purchased at the Wholesale Greenmarket—a market located in Hunts Point, Bronx, where locally grown produce is bought directly from farmers. The product there is extremely fresh—likely, it is less than 24 hours old. Prospect Hill Orchards also sells fruit at this market. Working at the Ridgewood Youthmarket gives local young people from underserved parts of the city a chance to develop skills, training them to operate a farm stand and teaching them business skills. The market is open seasonally, from early July to late October and operates from 10 a.m. to 2 p.m. on Saturday.

Rudy's Pastry Shop, 905 Seneca Ave., Ridgewood, NY 11385; (718) 821-5890; Subway: M to Seneca Avenue; Bakery. The most glorious German-style baked goods are for sale at Rudy's Pastry Shop, and if you are a fan of sweets, this place is not to be missed. It's been around for 72 years and is still going strong, currently run by Antonetta Binanti. Their Danish is wonderful—the pastry is soft yet substantial, flaky and sweet. It's filled with things like cherry, apricot, and apple, and the pastry is topped with a sweet sugar glaze. The Danish is really remarkable—they rival the amazing ones I ate in the Midwest in the 1970s. Their cheesecake is also wonderful—pleasantly tangy and creamy. They make cakes as well, both in slices and in cake-pop form—give the red velvet a try. You can also treat yourself to a cappuccino or latte with your sweet thing of choice, as they now serve coffee in the back. There are some tables and chairs, too, so you can enjoy your pastries there at the shop. Additionally, they make chocolates at the shop, too—truffles, caramels, chocolate covered pretzels, and more. And they are excellent.

Stammtisch Pork Store, 69-46 Myrtle Ave., Glendale, NY 11385; (718) 386-7200; stammtischporkstore.com. Just adjacent to the restaurant Zum Stammtisch, the Pork Store stocks an excellent selection of German foodstuffs, from jams to chocolates, sauerkraut to preserved meats, spaetzle, beer, mustard, breads, Haribo candies, and more—even German toiletries. Head to the back and ascend a few steps and you'll find a meat case sporting a mouthwatering selection of German-style meats—braunschweiger, bratwurst, liverwurst, knockwurst, and much more—there are over 40 different kinds of meats! Salads and soups made in the restaurant are also available for sale. Some of the dishes available at Zum Stammtisch can also be purchased here in their frozen state, like the very popular sauerbraten. This is an excellent and much-needed resource for the area, which has lost some of its major German butchers in the past years.

Stanley's Pierogies, 54-01 Metropolitan Ave., Ridgewood, NY 11385; (718) 821-3147; Subway: M to Forest Avenue; Meat Market. Pierogies is pretty much all they sell here in this tiny shop, mostly patronized by Polish immigrants in Ridgewood. The pierogies are delicious, filled with all sorts of things, from the familiar potato, potato and cheese, or sauerkraut, to kasha, and even fruit. The blueberry pierogies are fantastic. The different kinds of pierogies are fresh and come about 10 to a package, and buying in bulk lowers the price even more, which really isn't much to begin with; at the writing of this book, each package costs $4.25.

Western Beef, 47-05 Metropolitan Ave., Ridgewood, NY 11385; (718) 417-3770; Subway: M to Metropolitan, then Q54 west; Supermarket. This Western Beef location is the corporate headquarters of the company, and the store is huge. The aisles here are wide and easy to navigate (a rarity among NYC supermarkets). The store itself stocks a large variety of ethnic foods—Dominican, Peruvian, Ecuadorian, Asian, Mexican, West Indian, and more—which is one of the things it is well known for. Their International aisle is amazing, and there is a good selection of fresh produce, including chilies and tomatillos, and an impressive selection of Carribbean and Latin American roots like red yautia, sweet batita, eddoes, and yucca, all piled high. The produce department is the home to a number of Caribbean herbs like sorrel and mauby bark, as well as dried spices popular in Latin American cooking. One of the elements in any Western Beef store is the big walk-in refrigerated meat department and this location does not disappoint. There are plenty of smaller packaged parts, but there are also some larger cuts as well, like full slabs of short ribs. Variety cuts (e.g., tongue, kidneys, liver) are also easily found here, as are soup bones and oxtails, and everything is priced really well. The fish market is very clean and the fish look very fresh, even the large fish like whole carp. Fish eggs and fish liver are also for sale. Latin American dairy products are also in full force, from Salvadoran-style cream to *queso fresco*. A deli, complete with olive bar is also present. Don't forget to pick up some bread, which is baked on the premises in their own brick oven.

Forest Hills, Rego Park, Kew Gardens & Kew Gardens Hills

Forest Hills in the 17th century was originally called Whitepot, part of the larger town of Newtown. Fast-forward to the early 20th century to the planning and development of Forest Hills Gardens (based on the garden communities in England), one of the most beautiful planned communities in America. It's easy to get to and from the area in and out of Manhattan, thanks to the E and F trains, which run express; from a Queens perspective, it takes under 15 minutes to get from Queens Plaza to Forest Hills on the E train. Main commercial areas are along Austin Street, which is populated with independent shops as well as chains. Additional shopping is found on Metropolitan Avenue, which is about a mile from the subway; Queens Boulevard, another commercial strip, is much closer. Forest Hills is also fortunate to have beautiful Forest Park at its back door as well.

Kew Gardens is a diverse community south of Forest Hills. It's also up against Forest Park to its west. To contrast that, the Jackie Robinson Parkway defines its northern border. The commercial areas are along Metropolitan Avenue, Lefferts Boulevard, Austin Street, and Kew Gardens Road.

Kew Gardens Hills should not be confused with Kew Gardens, though somewhat related, they are separate communities. Along Main Street between 71st Road and 73rd Avenue especially, there are a number of businesses that cater to the Jewish community, including bakeries, delis, sushi, doughnuts, bagels, and pizza, which are all kosher. The famous Max & Mina's ice cream shop is in this strip of businesses.

Finally, we have Rego Park, also known as "Regostan" because of the strong Bukharian community that established itself there in the early 1990s. Rego Park was named by developers Henry Schloh and Charles Hausmannafter after their "Real Good Construction Company." The area was originally part of Forest Hills but that changed because of development needs. The current commercial areas are 63rd Drive/63rd Road, Queens Boulevard, and to some extent Austin Street.

Bareburger, 71-49 Austin St., Forest Hills, NY 11375; (718) 275-2273; Subway: E/F/M/R to Forest Hills-71st Avenue; bareburger .com; Burgers/Organic; $. This local chain has its origins in Astoria, and after much success expanded outward from the neighborhood to Manhattan and Brooklyn. The food overall is organic, from the meats to the fries to the milk in the shakes and beyond. They are also known for their selection of game meats for burgers, including bison, wild boar, and elk. Vegetarians have options as well, with both a veggie burger and portobello burger to choose from. Burgers come with a choice of breads—brioche and whole grain; you can even get it wrapped in a lettuce leaf if you are avoiding gluten or grains (gluten-free patrons can also order their burger on a tapioca rice bun). When it comes to the fries, Bareburger goes beyond simple ketchup (theirs is organic) and serve the fries with dipping sauces like chipotle mayo. The serving is quite large, so sharing is definitely the way to go. Other sides include onion rings, balls of sweet potato croquettes, and a selection of Rick's Picks pickles. Shakes are delicious, and come in a variety of flavors. The dining rooms are made from repurposed materials and each Bareburger is child-friendly, so bring the whole family to feast on the American classic meal, with a healthy revamp.

Brownie & Cream, 72-40 Austin St., Forest Hills, NY 11375; (718) 480-3849; Subway: E/F/M/R to 71st Avenue; Bakery; $. This little spot opened on Austin Street in late 2011, and offers a small range of baked goods by the piece, including brownies, French *macarons,* and tiny cupcakes. They also have a half-dozen flavors of ice cream, two of which they make—the vanilla cheesecake and the coffee bean. The *macarons* are slightly larger in size than your average ones, and pack a lot of flavor within. Particularly tasty are the Nutella, espresso, and the more unorthodox red velvet flavor. The vanilla cheesecake brownie is doubly delightful, with a creamy top layer of cheesecake and a rich, fudgy brownie below. The lemon bar is also pleasantly tart, a nice departure from the usual overly sweet lemon bars. The bakery runs a number of daily brownie specials, so take a look-see at the chalkboard on the wall for what's happening that particular day.

Katsuno, 103-01 Metropolitan Ave., Forest Hills, NY 11375; (718) 575-4033; katsunorestaurant.com; Japanese; $$. Let me admit something to you—at the time of this writing I have developed a serious taste for sashimi (I blame it on the awesome sashimi at Linn in Astoria), when for such a long time I was a sushi roll kind of gal. So I am here to tell you that Katsuno serves beautiful, lovely, clean-tasting, almost buttery sashimi—it feels like it will melt in your mouth with an ever so slight lingering taste of the sea. It's like sashimi is the most natural thing to eat here. I am particularly enamored with the salmon and yellowtail—two slices come with each order and you very well may feel sad after you eat the first piece, knowing there is only one piece left. Aside from the excellent sashimi, the cold pumpkin is very good. It's made with

kabocha squash, a very dense
and meaty kind of winter
squash. It is cooked in broth,
then cooled, with a little bit of
the broth remaining at the bottom
of the bowl. It tastes savory and a
little meaty, truth be told. Delicious.

Give some of their interesting and unusual appetizers a try—cold
onsen poached egg, thinly sliced *magret* duck, and even fried
chicken. Sushi (fish on a clump of rice) and maki (fish and rice
rolled up) are both on the menu. As a lover of avocado rolls, I do
enjoy theirs. For something truly nutrient-dense—and vegetarian—
the natto roll is the way to go. *Ume* plum and shiso leaf (perilla) is
another great combination. Yellowtail, spicy tuna, and eel rolls are
also good choices. Grilled meats and noodle dishes also grace the
menu; *chirashi* (loose sushi rice topped with sashimi and vegetable)
is always a fun choice, too.

Salute 2000, 63-42 108th St., Forest Hills, NY 11375; (718)
275-6860; Subway: E/M/R to 63rd Drive-Rego Park; Uzbeki/Kosher;
$. Beautiful Central Asian food graces the menu here, and it's a
joy to eat. The Korean carrot salad (also known as *morcovcha*) is
a huge serving of thinly shredded carrots and some garlic, with
a vinaigrette that is both a little sweet and tangy, and is a must
have when eating Uzbek food. Their Salute Salad is also a lovely
mix of fresh vegetables, including tomatoes, cucumber, cabbage,
peppers, and beets marinated in a house dressing. Other meatless

Regostan—the Bukharian Community in Queens

In Rego Park, Forest Hills and Kew Gardens is a Jewish immigrant community from Central Asia known as Bukharians. Bukhara is a city in Uzbekistan, but the term "Bukharian" is used to refer to Central Asian Jewish population as a whole. Central Asia encompasses the countries of Uzbekistan, Kazakhstan, Tajikistan, Kyrgyzstan, and Turkmenistan. Their origins are in Persia (modern-day Iran) and their more recent ancestors lived along the Silk Road, a caravan path that led from China to the Middle East. The majority of the current community came to the US after the collapse of the Soviet Union in 1991. The term "mass exodus" has been used to describe their move away from the old world and here to the new world in New York City. Tens of thousands have settled in NYC. Languages spoken include Russian, Tajik, Farsi, and Uzbek.

options are the marinated mushrooms, homemade hummus, baba ghanoush, and *ochor,* which are marinated mini eggplants. If you're an omnivore and soup is your bag, give the *pelmeni* a try—this is brothy soup with little meat ravioli in it. On the bready side of things, of course get one of the round fresh Uzbek breads called *non.* The *samsa* and *cheburekeh* are filled with beef, with the *samsa* being breadier than the *cheburekeh,* which

There are a few commercial areas in Queens that are populated by businesses catering to the Bukharian community: 63rd Road in Rego Park, on 108th Street in Forest Hills, and near Lefferts Boulevard and 83rd Avenue in Kew Gardens. These businesses will often be kosher establishments, and will be closed from sundown on Friday to sundown on Saturday, in order to keep the Jewish Sabbath. The groceries sell all sorts of foods, from preserved fish to pickled vegetables, traditional breads to dried fruits and nuts. At the restaurants, you'll find a lot of the same traditional dishes— *cheburecki, mantu,* and *samsa,* which are all dumplings stuffed with meats or pumpkin; *morcovcha,* or Korean carrot salad; hummus and baba ghanoush; pelmeni, a kind of brothy dumpling soup and *lagman,* a kind of brothy noodle soup; and kebabs made with chicken, beef, and lamb (no pork because it's kosher). And, of course, the Uzbek bread called *non,* which is round and fluffy. The food is flavorful and hearty, and if you like Middle Eastern and/or Russian food and their derivatives, you will love this food.

are deep-fried triangles of pastry filled with meat. Both are delicious, as is the Uzbek *mantu,* which is a big dumpling filled with meat with a thin, dark sauce poured on it that is a little bit sweet. There are over two dozen kebab options, made with lamb, beef, chicken, veal, salmon, and vegetable (tomatoes, onion, pepper), and can be ordered as just kebabs or as part of a platter, which includes coleslaw, onions, and a side of potatoes or fries. The *lula kebab* is particularly good, made from ground lamb and beef with spices. It's juicy and very easy to remove from the skewer. Lamb is the restaurant's specialty, and the boneless chicken kebab is also excellent and comes with high praise by the staff. End your meal with a strong Turkish coffee and a piece of house-made baklava, filled with walnuts and lightly sweet.

Landmarks

Ben's Best, 96-40 Queens Blvd., Rego Park, NY 11374; (718) 897-1700; Subway: E/M/R to 63rd Drive-Rego Park; bensbest.com; Kosher; $. Ben's Best is a classic kosher deli, located in a strip mall on Queens Boulevard very near the heart of the Bukharian (Central Asian Jewish) community in Queens. Classic Ashkenazi Jewish cuisine is served here—kugel, potato pancakes, stuffed cabbage, chopped liver, kreplach, matzo ball soup, brisket, and more. The establishment is dairy-free (shellfish- and pork-free, too, of course). There's a comfy seating area in the back and you can also purchase food up front for takeout. A great meal would start with a bowl of matzo ball soup, pastrami or corned beef sandwich, with a small bit of noodle kugel or rugelach for dessert. Their sandwiches are pretty big, so this meal would definitely leave you stuffed. You can also purchase meats, chicken and tuna salads, and chopped liver by the pound.

Cheburechnaya, 92-09 63rd Dr., Rego Park, NY 11374; (718) 897-9080; Subway: E/M/R to 63rd Drive; cheburechnaya.com; Russian/Kosher; $. This standard in Rego Park's restaurant scene is a terrific source for Bukharian Kosher cuisine, a food culture that comes from Central Asia—in this case, Uzbekistan. The space is quite big and very casual, great for families. One of the nice things about the menu is that you can purchase their different offerings—*bureks,* kebabs, etc.—by the piece, so you can assemble any number of meal combinations you like and try many different things in one sitting. The *morkovcha* carrot salad is delicious. The carrots are julienned and tossed in a vinaigrette. It's light and refreshing and seriously good. Their *samcy* and *cheburecki* are great—the *cheburecki,* filled with both cabbage and meat (lamb and beef combo), are served with a kind of tomato gravy, and the combination is wonderful. The *samcy* with pumpkin is something I get every time I come here—the dough is flaky, topped with black sesame seeds, and the pumpkin filling is slightly sweet. Kebabs come in meats like lamb and beef, and lamb is very tasty; they also offer meatless kebabs. Be sure to order a bowl of their light borscht, which is fabulous. Have a Dyushes with your meal, which is a sweet pear soda from Russia. Please note that because this is a kosher establishment, they shut down early on Friday afternoon and do not open until after sundown on Saturday.

Danny Brown Wine Bar & Kitchen, 104-02 Metropolitan Ave., Forest Hills, NY 11375; (718) 261-2144; Subway: E/F/M/R to Forest Hills–71st Avenue; dannybrownwbk.com; New American; $$$$. This beloved neighborhood restaurant gained notoriety in 2010 by receiving a Michelin star, putting it on the radar of food lovers both far and near. At the time of this writing, it remains the only restaurant in Queens recognized with a star by the Michelin Guide. It is a wonderful restaurant with a welcoming, comfortable atmosphere amongst beautiful, understated surroundings. It has a menu full of excellent, well-executed dishes and an extensive great wine list, with wines by the glass, bottle, and half-bottle. While the menu changes with the seasons, some dishes have remained on the menu from the start—the Serrano ham croquettes with saffron aioli is one, and the incredibly tender and juicy organic chicken under a brick, served with potatoes and greens is a second. The burger is also a big hit and comes with perfectly cooked fries. If you'd like to come and just have a glass of wine and a little something to eat, go for one of their small plates, like gnocchi mixed with very fresh favas, asparagus, saffron, and shaved Parmesan. Or try some of their cured meat or cheese plates. Cheeses range from the ultra-creamy French Crémeux (cow) to the Spanish Idiazabal (sheep), to a lovely French Bleu d'Auvergne. Meats range from the Italian *bresaola* (beef), to a beautiful chicken liver mousse fortified with cream and cognac, to the French *rosette de Lyon* (pork sausage). Cheeses and meats can be purchased as one-offs, a mix of three, five, and six items, or on a board with condiments like cornichons, fig compote, and olives. There are usually specials—a small plate, a large plate, and a cheese—that are really worth considering; the waitstaff will tell you what they are before you order. And don't forget dessert. They do a panna cotta, a flourless chocolate cake, a crepe, and a poached pear, among others, as well as offer dessert wines. Finally, on Tuesday and Wednesday they offer a 3-course prix-fixe meal for $28.

East Ocean Palace, 113-09 Queens Blvd., Forest Hills, NY 11375; (718) 268-1668; Subway: E/F to 75th Avenue; Dim Sum; $. On the outside of the building—think 1970s anonymous brickwork—you'll see that it says "Sea Food Restaurant," and the dim sum options are friendly with shrimp. That includes shrimp *shumai,* shrimp dumplings, shrimp rice rolls, shrimp stuffed peppers. When you arrive—and often on a weekend by 11 a.m. there are already people waiting in line—they'll ask you how many in your party and note that on a list. At one point, you may be asked if you would like to share a table. Totally go for it if you are comfortable with that. It can mean getting a seat sooner than later. Sit down, and a pot of tea is almost immediately placed in front of you (ask for water if you want it). Then the carts start coming fast and furious—the service here is very efficient! You'll have a wide variety of dishes to choose from—all the aforementioned shrimp options, as well as pork buns, bok choi, turnip cakes, egg tarts, fish balls, pork buns, clams in a soy-sesame sauce (these are very good), spring rolls, rib tips, and beef noodles.

Nick's Pizza, 108-26 Ascan Ave., Forest Hills, NY 11375; (718) 263-1126; Subway: E/F/M/R to Forest Hills–71st Avenue; Pizza; $$. Some of the best pizza in Queens is right here in Forest Hills. Nick's has been around for about 20 years and is owned by the same people who run Adrienne's Pizzabar on Stone Street in Manhattan (my favorite pizza in Manhattan). Everything tastes fresh and delicious, and the pizza crust is substantial without feeling heavy or overwhelming; it has a nice bite to it. Their sauce is both sweet  and tangy—try the simple Margherita pizza to get an idea of their pizza-making skills (add some of the slightly spicy pepperoni for extra oomph). They also make a fantastic white pie. A few salads are on the menu, and the house salad—consisting of watercress, arugula, roasted peppers, and sun-dried tomatoes, all in a light honey Dijon dressing—is spot-on and a great way to start out your meal. To wash it all down, try a Fizzy Lizzie soda, made with sparkling water and fruit juice, or a Stewart's soda (black cherry, please). Coffee is also available. This place is really popular, so don't be surprised to see a line out the door, especially on weekends. Pies are sold whole only, so no slices. They are cash only, too.

Wafa's, 100-05 Metropolitan Ave., Forest Hills, NY 11375; (718) 880-2055; Subway: E/F/M/R to Forest Hills–71st Avenue; wafasfood .com; Lebanese; $. Pretty much everything here is delicious—it's virtually impossible to have a bad meal here. Both vegetarians and meat eaters alike will find plenty to eat and feel satisfied after, as the menu is full of flavorful, well-executed dishes developed by Lebanese native Wafa Chami. Their swiss chard and lentil soup is a real knockout and comes in a big portion, definitely enough for two or three as a starter. This soup is full of lemony goodness, mixed with the beautiful greens and substantial brown lentils. It's a little bit spicy, too. There are plenty of veggie-friendly options that will make a meat-eater happy, like their *mousakaha*, a mixture of eggplant, chickpeas, and pomegranate juice. Their baba ghanoush is creamy with a beautiful aftertaste, and can be scooped up with their lovely, thin pita bread. On the meat end of things, the chicken shawarma is moist and meaty with a hint of cinnamon in the mix. The *shish tawook,* a dish of charbroiled chicken breast that has been marinated in lemon juice, olive oil, and garlic, is also excellent. Be sure to have some tahini sauce and, if you like your food spicy, hot sauce brought to the table, which are essential elements of the meal. For dessert, try a combination of a piece of baklava and strong coffee. Prices are extremely reasonable, so both your belly and pocketbook will walk out of Wafa's very happy.

Specialty Stores, Markets & Producers

A & R International Food Delicatessen, 63-46 108 St., Forest Hills, NY 11375; (718) 459-3956; Subway: M/R to 63rd Drive;

Russian/Uzbeki Deli. If you're looking for ingredients to make Russian, Uzbeki, or Georgian food, there's a good chance you'll find what you need here at this large, bright, well-organized deli in the northern part of the kosher business strip along 108th Street. Pantry items and a good selection of fresh deli items are all for sale. Dried fruits and nuts—pale, hard apricots and conventional dried orange apricots, golden and black raisins, as well as hazelnuts, Turkish pistachios, and almonds (roasted and raw)—can all be bought in bulk, and at decent prices. Cheeses such as fetas, kashkaval, blue cheese, imported soft Russian-style cheese, and both cured meats and roasted deli-style meats can also be purchased by weight. There's a selection of imported candy and chocolates in the back, and you'll find other sweet things in various places around the store, including kosher marshmallows. Also in the back is an area with bulk pickled vegetables—tomatoes, cabbage, and cucumbers, as well as whole pickled herring. Prepared salads are also in the refrigerated case, including creamy mushroom salad, bright red zucchini salad, and *morkovcha* carrot salad. Smoked fish also makes an appearance, naturally, and can be purchased at the deli counter. Breads are up front by the store entrance, including both the traditional round Uzbeki *non* bread and the long, textured Persian *barbari* bread. There's even a small steam table in the front of the store with various chicken and fish dishes to choose from. Next to that are *piroshky, samsas,* and other savory and sweet pastries.

Aigner Chocolates, 103-02 Metropolitan Ave., Forest Hills, NY 11375; (718) 544-1850; Subway: E/F/M/R to 71st Avenue/Continental; aignerchocolates.com; Chocolatier. Founded in 1930, this chocolate shop is the retail side of a 2-story factory located behind the shop. It has remained in the family all this time, with the grandson manning the store. Their family has origins in Austria and Denmark. A whole range of delicious chocolate treats sit on the shelves and behind the counter—truffles to caramels, butter crunch to thin mints, flat pieces of chocolate, and beyond. The Austrian red licorice is sweet, fruity, and chewy all at the same time. They do produce chocolate novelties, like animal- and object-shaped chocolate lollipops (think horses and trains), and package up gift boxes appropriate for baby showers/births, Mother's Day, Christmas, and Valentine's Day. You can purchase chocolates by the pound or even by the piece.

Andre's Hungarian, 100-28 Queens Blvd., Forest Hills, NY 11375; (718) 830-0266; Subway: M/R to 67th Avenue; andresbakery.com; Hungarian Bakery. Many sweet delights can be found here at this little Hungarian bakery that has been serving Forest Hills and Rego

Park for close to 35 years. There's a range of cakes on the shelves—the multilayered Dobosh torte, Sacher torte, creamy vanilla and chestnut roulades, hazelnut triangles, and more. They also make wonderful apple strudels—apple, cherry, cheese (as well as cherry and cheese together), poppy seed, and even cabbage. You'll also find great rugelach, creamy and tangy cheesecake, tangy apricot *pite* (a square of layered fruit puree and cake), and poppy seed or walnut *floden* (a short layered cake). Try their little sweet almond macaroons topped with tart raspberry jam and covered in white chocolate—they are quite flavorful and sweet, so a little goes a long way. They also prepare some savory traditional dishes for take out, including veal goulash, chicken paprikash, stuffed cabbage, and cucumber salad. This is a great option if you are on the go. And if you just want something to snack on, their flaky cheese biscuits are perfect, with sharp cheesy goodness. The place smells terrific when you walk in, too, making it a serious challenge to walk out of there empty-handed. On top of it all, everything here is kosher.

Bonelle Pastry Shop, 108-30 Ascan Ave., Forest Hills, NY 11375; (718) 575-1792; Subway: E/F/M/R to 71st Avenue/Continental; Bakery. The first thing you notice when you walk into this little bakery is the heady aroma of butter, sugar, and cinnamon. This place is the real deal. The offerings are classic—croissants, both plain and filled, pecan triangles, red velvet cake, rainbow cookies, blueberry crumble cake, fruit tarts, and cinnamon rolls. The cinnamon raisin rolls with icing and almonds are huge, but do not skimp on flavor, taste, or texture—they are flaky, sweet, and delicious, a real treat. They also produce a line of Italian butter cookies that have pure butter flavor and a delightful crumbly texture. Bonelle is an old-time favorite in the neighborhood, and the high quality of their products is the reason they are held in such esteem.

Carmel Grocery, 64-27 108th St., Forest Hills, NY 11375; (718) 897-9296; Subway: E/M/R to 67th Avenue; Middle Eastern Market. This little market is located among a whole variety of Kosher shops that cater to the local Bukharian community. There is a lot packed into this small space, too. Dried fruits, nuts, and seeds (think squash, watermelon, sunflower, etc.) are plentiful, along with a nice olive and pickle bar, complete with pickled cucumbers and peppers, and a red-tinged green olive that belies its spicy nature. Frozen foods include *sambousek* dough (used to make the triangular meat pie popular in the Middle East), and premade *bureks* (give the cheese-olive a try). Israeli, Turkish, and Greek tinned products are also for sale, like *zacusca,* eggplant paste, *foul mudammas,* and giant beans. Dried beans are also available. You'll also find Israeli cookies and spices, pita and lavash, halvah and dates. Up at the front there is a counter of prepared foods and other things that need refrigeration, like smoked salmon, mackerel, and a few Israeli cheeses. They make some fresh spreads, like eggplant and onion, baba ghanoush, Romanian eggplant, and *shoug,* a spicy spread for sandwiches. At certain times of the year, fresh sour green apricots are also for sale, a very popular item among the locals.

Woodhaven

Located in central western Queens, Woodhaven is bordered by Brooklyn's Cypress Hill to the west, beautiful Forest Park to the north, Ozone Park to the south and Richmond Hill to the east. I am telling you this because Woodhaven, a working-class neighborhood, gets lost in the shuffle. A lot of Queens residents haven't even heard of it. It was settled in the mid-18th century, before the Revolutionary War; in the 19th century racetracks—the Union Course and the Centerville—found their way to Woodhaven, as well as manufacturing amid the farmland. These days the neighborhood—apart from the commercial area along Jamaica Avenue—feels a bit like a sleepy suburb. The homes tend to be rowhouses and pretty little detached houses. Look down any of the side streets off of Jamaica Avenue and you'll see a lot of gorgeous old homes.

In the earlier part of the 20th century, the population was mostly made up of those of European descent—Irish, Italian, German, and Polish. There are vestiges of those groups here and there—a Polish

Cheese of the World, 71-48 Austin St., Forest Hills, NY 11375; (718) 263-1933; Subway: E/F/M/R to Forest Hills/71st Avenue; cheeseoftheworldforesthills.com; Cheese Shop. In general, Queens doesn't have a lot of dedicated cheese shops. Sure, at various independent markets they'll carry cheeses, but they are mixed in with a lot of other products. So it's nice that Forest Hills has a shop dedicated to cheese. Here you'll find cheeses made from cow, goat, and deli here, a German deli there. Nowadays there are many Latin Americans, African Americans, and Asians in that mix, and they've brought their food with them. It's a very diverse community.

The majority of that food is found along Jamaica Avenue in the form of restaurants, delis, bakeries, and markets. There are a couple of spots that have been here for decades—Schmidt's Confectionary and Manor Deli. They are the real old timers of the neighborhood food scene and worth a visit (note that Schmidt's is not open from late June through September). They hark back to an earlier, simpler time. Representative of the newcomers is Mama Mecna's, an excellent Filipino restaurant, one of the newer gems in the neighborhood.

While you're in the area, check out Forest Park if you have time. It is the third largest park in Queens, after Flushing Meadows–Corona Park and Alley Pond Park, and serves the recreational needs of a large, diverse population. Frederick Law Olmstead, co-designer of Central Park and Prospect Park, designed Forest Drive, the park's main drive. Forest Park is a gorgeous green space in the borough, and definitely worth a visit.

sheep's milk, as well as cheeses made from mixed milk. They even carry a few raw cheeses (though they are aged, as NY State law states that raw cheeses must be aged over 60 days), like the lovely Basque cheese Idiazabal; it goes very well

with *membrillo*. Cured meats can be purchased here, from prosciutto di Parma to *jamón ibérico* to sopressata; Alps Provisions charcuterie is also available. They also carry a variety of olives, as well as additional pantry items like jams, sauces, and crackers.

Eddie's Sweet Shop, 105-29 Metropolitan Ave., Forest Hills, NY 11367; (718) 520-8514; Subway: E/F/M/R to Forest Hills–71st Avenue; Ice Cream. Charming doesn't begin to describe this place—it is seriously old school. Originally opened in 1909, it is a real institution in Forest Hills. They serve house-made ice cream here, as well as homemade syrups and whipped cream . . . oh, the whipped cream! This isn't the stuff made from vegetable oils and such and squirted out of a can, but it is the real deal, whipped from real cream. It adds so much to your hot fudge sundae, which is fabulous. The sundae itself is a big delicious mess, but they give you a plate under your sundae glass to catch the overflowing hot fudge sauce and melting ice cream. You can also get milk shakes, floats, and egg creams, all to be enjoyed on their decades-old wood-topped stools, which have been here since the beginning, up at the counter. There is seating in the back as well. At the entrance is a candy counter, where you can buy all sorts of sweet candy treats. Eddie's is just across the street from a movie theater, so it's a great place to stop into after your flick is over.

La Boulangerie, 109-01 72nd Rd., Forest Hills, NY 11375; (347) 644-5606; Subway: E/F/M/R to Forest Hills–71st Avenue; French Bakery. On a side street off of busy Austin Street is a lovely French bakery that provides Forest Hills with wonderful French classic baked goods. Their croissants are excellent, as is the *pain au chocolat,* and the raisin roll is simply spectacular. Puffy round-topped brioches, apple tarts, and cupcake-size *gâteaux bretons* are also for sale. The classic *croque monsieur* is available, and they make chicken soup daily. Inside the bakery there are some tables and chairs, so you can enjoy your bounty of deliciousness right there and then (maybe with a cappuccino or cafe au lait), or take it home—they put your goods in those old-fashioned waxed paper bags to keep things nice and fresh.

Max & Mina's, 71-26 Main St., Kew Gardens Hills, NY 11367; (718) 793-8629; Subway: 7 to Main Street, then Q44 bus; maxand minasicecream.com; Ice Cream. Known for their crazy flavors like pizza, lox, garlic, gefilte fish, and ketchup, Max & Mina's churns out creamy, premium ice cream, which also happens to be kosher, since they are smack dab in the middle of a staunchly Jewish neighborhood. Apart from the more extreme flavors, familiar ones fill up the menu—hazelnut, peppermint stick, rum raisin, dark chocolate, chocolate chip cookie dough—as well as slightly more unusual like Merlot, chocolate banana, chocolate beer, Cheerios, buttercream, and pancake chip. Shakes and malts are also available. Enjoy your ice cream at the store at one of their tables, or even sitting on an Adirondack chair by the window! There are photos, articles, posters, comic books, and bumper stickers everywhere. The place is a real sensory experience.

Mendy's Royale Kosher Bake Shop, 72-22 Main St., Kew Gardens Hills, NY 11367; (718) 544-8736; Subway: 7 to Main Street, then Q44 south; Kosher Bakery. So many great sweet things are for sale here, it's hard to know where to start. They make beautiful loaves of *mandelbrot,* some covered in chocolate. Their babkas are very popular, as are the Danishes filled with fruit or with chocolate. Italian-style cookies are also a big hit here, as are the large hamantaschen; there are whole cakes as well. There are some dairy sweets but those are kept separately from the others. This is the nicest bakery in this strip of kosher businesses and definitely worth checking out.

Queens Bazaar, 94-02 63rd Dr., Rego Park, NY 11374; (718) 459-5536; Subway: E/M/R to 63rd Drive; Central Asian Grocery. This shop is full of Central Asian delights, and then some. Dried seeds, nuts, and fruits are located throughout the store, to be purchased in bulk. Particularly tasty are the jumbo Samarkand apricots—dried apricots with the pit left inside. They are delicious, but be careful not to chomp down hard on the apricot or you'll break a tooth on the pit. Pale organic Russian dried apricots, Iranian raisins, and Samarghandi *aluche*—a kind of sour cherry—are also found here. A selection of loose olives, each kind in its own deep bucket, can be mixed and matched for quite a low price. Queens Bazaar carries a wide range of Sabra products, too. The round Uzbeki bread called *non* can be purchased here as well.

R & O Family International OlgaR, 93-07 63rd Dr., Rego Park, NY 11374; (718) 896-6800; Subway: E/M/R to 63rd Drive; Bukharian/Russian. This is one of a number of little markets that sell products to the Central Asian community in Rego Park. Here, there are plenty of pantry items and ingredients one might need to cook Uzbeki or Georgian food, as well as fruit preserves and "chilly sauce" (spicy). Homemade salads made with potatoes, cabbage, and peas are in to-go containers in a refrigerator in the back; house-made pickles can also be found there. Meats, cheese, and the traditional Uzbek round bread called *non* can also be purchased at this market.

Trader Joe's, 90-30 Metropolitan Ave., Rego Park, NY 11374; (718) 275-1791; Subway: E/F/M/R to 71st-Continental, then Q23 bus to Metropolitan Avenue, or M to Metropolitan, then Q54 bus east on Metropolitan; traderjoes.com. This is Queens' only Trader Joe's location, and is best accessible by car, but it is possible to get there with a subway-bus combo (see above). It's located in a strip mall populated by big box stores—Michael's, Bob's Discount Furniture, Staples, and the like—and contains a parking lot. As in most TJs, great deals on cheese, pasta, chocolate, sauces, frozen foods, bread, juice, beer, and more abound within. Produce is also for sale, including citrus, onions and garlic, cucumbers, tomatoes, blueberries, avocados, and organic strawberries in season. As someone who has been shopping at Trader Joe's for close to 30 years (I was introduced to their awesomeness at a young age), it's been fun to see the quality of their produce get better and better over the years. I also love seeing things like soy-free dark chocolate, 100% grass-fed ground beef, aged raw-milk cheeses, Kerrygold butter, shade-grown/organic/fair trade coffee beans, organic citrus, unsulphured dried fruit, raw nuts, and other seriously healthy things that are also delicious. Their selection of gummi vitamins is impressive (seriously, they have five or six different kinds), and they carry a variety of supplements. Dog and cat food can be purchased here, too, which is a good thing for your furry friends. Unlike most of the NYC Trader Joe's locations, the crowds are manageable—even on a weekend—and the lines aren't at anaconda length; the experience is more like that at a suburban Trader Joe's. The staff and especially the cashiers are super-nice and always greet you with a smile. It's pleasant to shop here and you'll save a lot of dough as well.

Street Food

Los Chilitos Taco Cart, Continental/71st Ave. between Austin St. and Queens Blvd.; Subway: E/F/M/R to Forest Hills–71st Avenue; Mexican; $. This little Mexican food cart boasts a regular clientele, and there are regulars—the food is really good. The truck offers a familiar roster of Mexican treats—tacos, quesadillas, *cemitas* and *tortas,* tostadas, *clacoyos* (aka *tlacoyos*), gorditas and *sopes.* Since gorditas are more difficult to find, it's worth giving them a try. The two halves of the thick masa disk are griddled until they have a nice crust going on, and are filled with lettuce, cheese, sour cream, and *chicharron*. As for the tacos, the chicken is delicious with very simple, classic flavors. The chicken is cooked until it has a bit of a crust on it, but keeps its tenderness, and is topped with cilantro, avocado sauce, and onions. The spicy pork is also very good. The variety of taco fillings is extensive, from the conventional carnitas to the meatless huit-lacoche to the less common *oreja* (ear). While you're waiting for your food, you'll notice there are a couple of containers— one is filled with fried dried chilies (a tasty snack for chiliheads) and another is filled with roasted peppers. There are red and green sauces, and the red sauce in particular has quite a kick; it's spectacular both in heat level and its crazy, intense reddish-brown color.

Jamaica, South Richmond Hill, Ozone Park & Fresh Meadows

Heading further east into Queens are the communities of Jamaica, South Richmond Hill, Ozone Park, and Fresh Meadows. Jamaica is the home to a stable African-American community, though it is also home to one of the largest Salvadoran communities in NYC. South Richmond Hill is known for its Sikh community, the largest in NYC, too. Ozone Park, known for its proximity to JFK airport and the Aqueduct Race Track, is a mix of peoples—Irish, Polish, and Germans established the community, with Asians and Hispanic people finding their way there later. Fresh Meadows, located along Union Turnpike, is a little more affluent than the other three neighborhoods in this group, and is known as the home to a planned community originally developed for WWII vets. It's also quite close to St. John's University.

In Jamaica, you'll find a lot of fast food, but restaurants specializing in Carribean/West Indian food are there, too. As mentioned above, it is also home to a large Salvadoran community, so *pupusas* and other Salvadoran taste treats are easy to find. In South Richmond Hill, both Indian and West Indian food abounds, and it is home to one of NYC's rare Surinamese restaurants. This is the place to find amazing roti and aloo pies, as well as refreshing *sorrel* drink too, three West Indian specialties. You'll also find shops that specialize in ingredients to make West Indian food right at home, too. Ozone Park is where Dallis Coffee is based, one of the oldest coffee roasters in NYC. Finally in Fresh Meadows, you'll find great pizza, superb Italian baked goods, and because of the substantial Jewish population in the area, kosher spots as well.

Foodie Faves

Acquista Trattoria, 178-01 Union Turnpike, Fresh Meadows, NY 11366; Subway: E/F to Kew Gardens–Union Turnpike, then Q46 bus; acquistany.com; Italian; $$. I was first directed to this place by a friend who is active in local politics, then by another couple of locals, and their recommendations did not fall on dead ears. After eating here, I was quite impressed—the food was terrific!

First, their slices are very good. This NY slice has a nice balance of cheese and sauce, and is awesome totally unadorned, even though oregano and pepper flakes are available to add. The crust has a nice crunch to it, too. And even though it's a sit-down trattoria, at lunch you can come in and just have a slice and something to drink (Pellegrino Limonata is always a good choice). On the subject of pizza, they make "baby pizzas," which are small pizzas—this is a small, personal-size pizza, which is nice because if everyone wants pizza but not with the same toppings, they can all get their very own pizza. Problem solved. Their pastas are excellent, all homemade, even the gnocchi, which just about melt in your mouth. Their *quattro formaggi* gnocchi is nice and creamy (but not overly heavy). The *penne alla vodka* is very good, especially with the addition of asparagus. But before the pasta arrives at your table, you are presented with a basket of delicious toasted focaccia topped with rosemary and a plate of olives swimming in slightly spicy olive oil. It goes without saying that the focaccia dipped in the olive oil is pure heaven for those who like that sort of thing. In addition to pastas and pizza, enjoy meat dishes, sandwiches (heroes and panini), calzones, and a tasty selection of antipasti. The tiramisu is the perfect ending to a meal, too.

El Comal, 148-62 Hillside Ave., Jamaica, NY 11418; Subway: F to Sutphin Boulevard; Salvadoran; $. The menu here boasts quite a variety of foods, but the *pupusas* are the real draw. *Pupusas* are a wonderful import from El Salvador, and super-delicious. Made from masa, they are filled with seemingly pedestrian things like cheese, beans, and pork, but like with many great dishes out there, the sum is greater than its parts. It's easy for a place to prepare the *pupusa* ahead of time and then slap it on the grill to heat it up, but the cooks at El Comal make every *pupusa* to order; getting your food out to you might take a little longer as a result, but it is so worth it. You can get yours filled with cheese, pork, pork and cheese, beans, or chicken. They are cooked on the *comal* (griddle) and come to your table accompanied by a tangy *curtido* (theirs is not spicy) and a cup of mild salsa. The cheese *pupusas* are very simple, filled with melted white cheese; you're lucky if some of the cheese will ooze out while the *pupusa* is cooked, resulting in delicious griddled cheese bark. The pork *pupusas* are filled with nicely seasoned pounded pork and is also very good. Be sure to eat your *pupusa* with the cabbage and carrot *curtido,* a traditional accompaniment. Wash it all down with a bottle of Boing!, Country Club (raspberry), or Jarritos. If you're looking for dessert, *tres leches* cake and flan are both available. And if you are interested in eating beyond the *pupusas,* there is a steam table on one side of the restaurant, sporting things like *carne guisado,* fried chicken, and a beautiful container of fresh guacamole. NB: If you need to use the restroom, you'll need a key, available up by the register.

Mama Meena's Family Restaurant, 94-20 Jamaica Ave., Woodhaven, NY 11421; (718) 696-8882; mamameenas.com; Filipino; $. At Mama Meena's, everything is on the high end of the tasty

ROCKAWAY BOARDWALK

The most exciting and—dare I say—hip part of the Rockaways food scene is the part that is connected to the rest of Queens through Jamaica Bay and Broad Channel. The eateries operate seasonally in the summer, opening along with the beaches on Memorial Day weekend and closing down sometime in September.

The A and S (Shuttle) trains take you down there and connect to the Beach 90th Street, Beach 98th Street, and Beach 105th Street stations; Rockaway Park-Beach 116th Street is the terminus of the line. That being said, it can be a little confusing, especially if you've never been there before. Here's the deal:

The A train splits into two lines at the Broad Channel Station; at this point, you'll want to make sure you are on a Rockaway Park–bound A train, and it only runs during morning and evening rush hours, which are 6:30 to 8 a.m. and 5:15 to 6:45 p.m. If you are not on the right A train during those times, you'll need to switch to an S train (Shuttle) at Broad Channel. That train runs all the time.

Here are the highlights you'll find at the Rockaway Boardwalk, going east to west:

86th Street Vicinity

Rippers, Boardwalk and Beach, 86th St., Far Rockaway, NY 11693; Subway: A or S to Beach 90th Street. This is the place for burgers and fries on the Boardwalk, and they are served in squishy potato buns, too—total bonus. Meat is from The Meat Hook, meaning it's expertly butchered from humanely raised animals. There are veggie burgers, too, hot dogs, and fresh juices.

96th Street Vicinity

DiCosmo's Homemade Italian Ice, 95-19 Rockaway Beach Blvd., Far Rockaway, NY 11693; Subway: A or S to Beach 98th Street; dicosmos.com. These are Italian ices with the reputation of being good enough to go up against the Lemon Ice King of Corona.

Lobster Joint, Boardwalk and Beach 97th St., Rockaway Park, NY 11694; Subway: A or S to Beach 98th Street; lobsterjoint.com. If you're craving a lobster roll, stop here.

Motorboat and the Big Banana, Boardwalk and Beach 96th St., Far Rockaway, NY 11693; Subway: A or S to Beach 98th Street. Attention *Arrested Development* fans: frozen chocolate-covered bananas are for sale here. Get some fried chicken and/or seafood to go with that banana (the fish sandwich is a winner).

Rockaway Taco, 95-19 Rockaway Beach Blvd., Far Rockaway, NY 11693; (347) 213-7466; Subway: A or S to Beach-98th Street; rockawaytaco.com. Head here for expertly made fish tacos, something of a unicorn of tacos in NYC.

106th Street Vicinity

Caracas Arepa Bar, 106-01 Shore Front Pkwy., Rockaway Park, NY 11694; (718) 474-1709; Subway: A or S to Beach 105th Street; caracasarepabar.com. Homemade Venezuelan food is the name of the game here, which means stuffed arepas (pork, beef, and cheese, to start). They also sell beautifully fried *maduros* (sweet plantain) showered with cotija cheese, and empanadas.

Steve's Ice Cream, 106-01 Shore Front Pkwy., Far Rockaway, NY 11693; Subway: A or S to Beach 105th Street. Get a scoop or two, a root-beer float or even a beer float, shakes, and ice cream sandwiches. They do Blue Bottle pour-overs, which is rather poetic, seeing that this is the former location of Blue Bottle Coffee on the Boardwalk.

scale, and that starts right away with drinks. They serve a melon drink made with shreds of cantaloupe, a sweet melon syrup, shave ice, and optional evaporated milk (the milk can lighten up the sweetness). It comes with a straw and a spoon so you can dig into it with a spoon for quicker intake (and crunch on that ice if you like) or let it melt on its own schedule and the drink will last throughout your meal. There are a variety of appetizers on the menu, and a couple are noted as "MM's Special." The Lumpia Shanghai is one of the most fun appetizers around. It's really finger food—very small fried egg rolls served with a slightly sweet and not overly spicy chili sauce. Beyond the apps are noodle, vegetable, beef, chicken, fish, seafood, and pork dishes; many of the vegetable dishes are not vegetarian, though. However, in the MM's Special Grill section, there is *inihaw na talong,* which is grilled long peeled Japanese eggplants served with raw tomatoes and scallions, with a side of shrimp paste. On the opposite end of the scale is the classic pork adobo. The pork arrives in its beautiful, dark, savory sauce, which is nicely soaked up by the white rice. The pork shreds easily with a fork, so no knife is needed. The adobo dish can also be made with chicken, too. If you'd like to have something a little more brothy, the Chicken Tinola is a great choice. It's a mild yet flavorful chicken soup made with ginger, lemongrass, green papaya, and pepper leaves. You'll also find chunks of green chili—seeds and ribs included—floating around in there. For those milkfish fans, don't worry—there are a few dishes on the menu that utilize this popular fish. Deboned, it comes simply battered and deep fried, or consider having it cooked with vegetables in vinegar. For dessert, there's flan, ice cream, and *turon* (fried sweet plantain), but the *halo halo* is the way to go. It can come with ice cream or not (but get the ice cream—coconut, *ube,* or mango), and is made with shaved ice, red and white beans, tropical fruit jelly, and milk. It's a traditional and refreshing way to end the meal.

Singh's Roti Shop and Bar, 131-18 Liberty Ave., South Richmond Hill, NY 11419; (718) 323-5990; Subway: A to Ozone Park–Lefferts Boulevard; singhsrotishopnyc.com; West Indian; $. The rotis here are gigantic—like three times the size of your head. They are delicious—flaky and buttery and they definitely keep their integrity. You can order them with things like chicken, goat, duck, and potatoes. Other dishes like jerk chicken, chicken curry, crispy pork skin, and black pudding are also on the menu. For sweets, you'll find cassava cake and the West Indian version of *gulab jamoon*—yes, the spelling is slightly different and the pastry is different, too. They are drier—not soaked in syrup but covered in a sugar glaze. They are like little torpedo-shaped doughnuts. Often there is a line of people waiting to order, but the line moves quickly. This gives you time to make up your mind as to what you want, and that is a big help because sometimes it's a real challenge to choose which delicious dish is going to end up in your belly. (Spoiler: It's all really good so no matter what you choose, it will be the right thing.)

Warung Kario, 128-12 Liberty Ave., South Richmond Hill, NY 11419; (718) 322-4774; Subway: A to Ozone Park–Lefferts

Boulevard; Surinamese; $. It's uncommon to find a restaurant dedicated to the cuisine of Suriname, so dining at Warung Kario is a real treat. The food is presented in a steam-table setup for both lunch and dinner. If you'd like try a bunch of different things, the staff will put together a plate for you, or you can choose the dishes you prefer. Some of the elements you'll find are stewed chicken cooked with galangal, soy sauce, and *kecap* (both sweet and salty); *bami goreng* (stir-fried noodles); *nasi goreng* (fried rice); kidney beans; and steamed greens like bok choi. There is a sambal made of shredded potato, chicken liver, and gizzard that is a very good condiment. Don't miss the *bacabana* (a breaded and fried long slice of plantain that is served with a rough peanut sauce) and the *lumpia* (filled with vegetables and chicken). Most of the food is prepared spicy, since that's what the local community wants, so be aware. Also, the only meat they serve is chicken, since there are both Hindus (who don't eat beef) and Muslims (who don't eat pork) that patronize the restaurant; it is also a halal establishment.

Landmarks

Lulu's Italian and American Bakery, 185-26 Union Tpke., Fresh Meadows, NY 11366; (718) 454-4300; Subway: E/F to Kew Gardens–Union Turnpike, then Q46 bus; lulusbakeryshop.com. For some of the best Italian cookies and pastries in Fresh Meadows, a stop at Lulu's is mandatory. Their selection is varied, excellent, and everything fresh as can be. Here, you'll find buttery Italian cookies (yes, they use real butter), breakfast pastries (muffins, turnovers), cupcakes, cheesecakes, whole cakes, and a selection of mini pastries of all kinds, which makes for an easy way to try a bunch of different things. It's a rarity to find the elusive hazelnut cannoli in this town, but Lulu's has it, and it's fantastic. The cream is studded with mini chocolate chips, chopped hazelnuts, and the shell is lightly glazed with chocolate—the whole thing is crazy delicious. Their cream puffs are also very good and some are filled with luscious chocolate cream. The tiramisu is creamy and boozy. Other standouts are the cheesecakes, lobster tails, fruit tarts, and red velvet cupcakes, but really, it's hard to go wrong here with any choice. If you'd like to sit down and enjoy your sweets, there are a few tables available in their bright and airy bakery. Their iced coffee is also very good (get it with half and half for extra richness) and totally hits the iced-coffee spot New York City residents hold dear.

Schmidt's Confectionary, 94-15 Jamaica Ave., Woodhaven, NY 11421; (718) 846-9326; Subway: J/Z to Woodhaven Boulevard; Chocolate Shop. **When you step into this Woodhaven institution, it's like going back in time. There's a warmth to the place, thanks to the vintage display cases, wooden details, and stained glass windows in the back. It's also been around for over 80 years. The display cases are filled with milk and dark chocolates—caramels,**

maple creams, coconut royals, chocolate-covered orange peel, marshmallow jelly bars, peppermint patties, peanut butter cups, and that is just the beginning. The chocolates taste and look homemade, taking on a rustic appearance, and the chocolates are displayed on the parchment paper they cooled on in the back. On the subject of temperature, the shop is only open from about late September until late June—they  are closed during the summer because it's just too warm to make chocolates the way Margie Schmidt, the founder's granddaughter, would like. Consequently, toward the end of the season the pickings are somewhat slim; in, say, November or December, the cases are sure to be full of chocolates.

Specialty Stores, Markets & Producers

Dallis Brothers Coffee, 100-32 Atlantic Ave., Ozone Park, NY 11416; (718) 845-3010; Subway: J/Z to 104th Street; dallis broscoffee.com. This is delicious coffee. The Russian-born Dallis Brothers started the company in 1913, and they delivered coffee door to door throughout Queens and Brooklyn. As the years went by, they grew, expanded, automated certain things, and were eventually acquired by Brazilian Octavio Cafe. The Dallis name remains and they continue to do work in Ozone Park. Tours of the facility are held the first Saturday of each month, incorporating a bit of local history, a tour of the facility, and a coffee tasting. Tours are $10. They have one request, "Due to the tasting component we ask that all participants keep perfumes and colognes at home."

E & J Banana Country, Inc., 120-01 Liberty Ave., South Richmond Hill, NY 11419; (718) 641-5253; Subway: A to Ozone Park–Lefferts Boulevard; West Indian Market. A really nice selection of West Indian products, as well as produce, can be found here. On the shelves are ground spices, masalas (including the Trini *amchar masala*) and curry mixes; Indo-West products like hot lime pepper, Guyana hot pepper sauce, and Guyana burnt sugar; sauces like the popular green seasoning, *kecap manis,* and *casareep;* coconut milk; dhal snacks; rice, beans, and grains; and raw sugar and chow mein. There's also salted fish like hake and cod, and smoked fish like herring; tubs of variety cuts in brine, like pork tail and snouts, salted beef, and mackerel; small cakes of bulk tofu in water. Produce includes conventional items like apples and oranges, as well as Hatian mangoes, okra, celery leaf, bitter melon, hot peppers, sorrel flowers, and *phooi* (aka Indian spinach). There's a fish store next door as well that sells live crabs, shellfish, and fish.

Hetman of Woodhaven, 84-24 Jamaica Ave., Woodhaven, NY 11421; Subway: 85th Street-Forest Parkway; Polish Deli. This small Polish deli serves what is left of the Polish community and has a nice selection of products on the shelves and in the meat case.

There are plenty of noodles, some grains, teas, and jams. Polish beer is also for sale on the shelves. Sausages like *domowa, lesna,* and *kabonos* are in their meat counter, as is *mortadela, baleron,* and Hungarian smoked bacon. Cheeses like Muenster, and smoked *ramzes* and *krolewski* are also for sale. Keep an eye out for a big bucket of whole fermented pickles up front, which is also the place for bars of E. Wedel chocolates, a very popular chocolate brand in Poland; I recommend the semisweet bar, called Jedyna. This is their oldest bar, having been produced for almost 90 years.

M&M Natural Fruits, 80-44 Jamaica Ave., Woodhaven, NY 11421; (718) 480-1531; Subway: 85th Street-Forest Parkway; Grocery. There is a surprising variety of items for sale at this little market in central Woodhaven, serving the South Asian community primarily. Here you'll find packages of Kalizira rice and sweet rice, *chira* (a kind of pounded rice from Bangladesh), buckets of legumes and dhal (*kala-chana,* pigeon peas, *motor-dhal,* red lentils, yellow split peas, etc.), green mango pickle and olive pickle, rice noodles, cassava flour, jars of various pickled vegetables, cans of coconut milk, eggplant paste, jars of Madras curry, tinned sardines, fermented fish sauce, canned star gooseberry, various spices (including *kalonji*) and spice mixtures, and *misri.* They even have tins of Australian grass-fed butter (Anchor brand), which apparently is very popular. They have pans of Safir Bakery baklava from Brooklyn, which is excellent, so be sure to pick some up on your way out.

Manor Delicatessen, 94-12 Jamaica Ave., Woodhaven, NY 11421; (718) 849-2836; Subway: J to Woodhaven Boulevard; manordeli.com; German Deli. It's heartening to find old-time places like Manor Delicatessen—which has been around for over 90 years—in a city that is constantly changing. It's about the only German deli remaining in the area. They are known for their salads, including potato salad (both mayonnaise-based and the vinegary German style), macaroni salad, coleslaw and seafood salad. The German potato salad is light and tangy. They make a number of salads and wraps, grilled sandwiches, soups, as

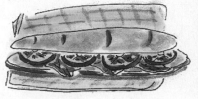

well as hot dinners. Their roast beef is prepared in house, and you'll find they have four different roast beefs, each with a different level of rareness, which is something you don't see a lot of these days. Their bratwurst on a bun with mustard and sauerkraut is a deal at $5 a pop, and they have trays full of kosher pickles. Pick up some of the German meat cakes, which are made with pork, beef, and onions. They make a terrific red velvet cake, too. The staff is super-friendly and happy to answer any questions you might have. It's also conveniently located pretty much under the Woodhaven Boulevard stop on the J train.

Sybil's Bakery, 132-17 Liberty Ave., South Richmond Hill, NY 11419; (718) 835-9235; Subway: A to Ozone Park–Lefferts Boulevard, then the Q112 bus; West Indian. The bakery case is filled with delicious and high-quality Caribbean baked goods; really, they are some of the best in the area and have a wonderful, clean flavor overall. The familiar Jamaican beef patty is for sale, and they have smaller meat patties as well. Top picks include the flaky cheese scone, and the cassava cake tastes beautifully of almond and coconut. Other West Indian delicacies are also available—black cake, pine tarts, carrot cake, cheese pies, and more. There is a selection of Caribbean sodas, and of course their tasty sorrel drink. Take your goodies and sit outside on a sunny day—despite the busy nearby roads, it's a nice place to sit and relax.

Recipes

Chana Dhal with Ghiya (Bottle Gourd)

This recipe comes from Anne Noyes Saini, cocreator of the popular NYC food site City Spoonful. She is a resident of Queens and is passionate about the borough's immigrant food cultures, especially South Asian, as her husband's family is from India. Below is one of her favorite dishes, and one she makes often. All the ingredients can be purchased at any well-stocked South Asian market, like the ones in Jackson Heights or South Richmond Hill.

This is a popular dish in the North Indian state of Punjab. It's not considered fancy food—that is, what you might serve to guests—but rather it's a simple stew you would eat at home with rice.

Ghiya (bottle gourd) is something like a cross between a pumpkin and a zucchini. It's a very healthy vegetable, which I love because it's a great absorber of the flavors of anything cooked with it—even as it imparts its own subtle flavor to anything cooked with it.

Chana dhal is the yellow lentil kernels contained within the outer skin of a chickpea (two kernels per chickpea). Of all the Indian daals, it has the richest, heaviest flavor.

Yield: 4 servings

½ *ghiya* (bottle gourd), chopped into small cubes
1 cup *chana dhal*
4 cloves of garlic, diced
1 thumb-size piece of ginger, diced

¼ teaspoon turmeric powder
1–4 green chilies, diced (depending on your tolerance for spicy food)
¼ teaspoon ground coriander seeds

½ teaspoon salt (or more, to taste)

3 cups of water

1 tablespoon canola oil

½ teaspoon cumin seeds

1 small red onion, diced

2 plum tomatoes, diced

Handful of chopped cilantro (optional)

In a pressure cooker or deep-sided pot (preferably with a heavy bottom) add: the ghiya, dhal, garlic, ginger, turmeric powder, chilies, ground coriander seeds, salt, and water.

PRESSURE COOKER: If you're using a pressure cooker, seal the cooker but don't put on the weight initially. Turn the heat up to high until the cooker starts to hiss and emit steam, then add the weight and leave the heat on high until the cooker again starts to hiss. At this point, turn the heat down as low as possible and set a timer for 10 minutes. After the 10 minutes are up, turn off the heat and leave the cooker to cool off until no steam is emitted when you press on the weight.

CONVENTIONAL POT: If using a conventional pot, bring everything to a vigorous boil; then turn the heat down to medium for 30–60 minutes, put on the lid, and stir occasionally, adding water as needed. When the ghiya is translucent and very soft and the dhal is so soft that the individual kernels start to disintegrate and mush together, the dish is finished.

While the dhal and ghiya are cooking, add the canola oil to a small saute pan, turn heat up to medium and, when the oil is hot, add the cumin seeds.

When the cumin seeds are fragrant and "dancing" slightly in the oil, add the onion and cook until the onion is totally soft, translucent/brown, and almost mushy—so that all the water and crispness have been cooked out of the onions. (If the onions start to burn, lower the heat as needed.)

Next add the tomatoes and cook until the individual tomato pieces break down into a mushy paste and all their water has been cooked away. Turn off the heat.

Add the tomato mixture (in Hindi, we call this mixture a tarka *or* chaunk—a *cooked mixture of spices and seasonings that add flavor to* dhals *or other dishes) to the* dhal *and* ghiya*. Stir thoroughly and simmer the combination on low heat for about 10 minutes to let the flavors meld.*

OPTIONAL: *At the very end of the final simmer, before turning off the heat, add the chopped coriander leaves and stir gently.*

Chef's note: I like to let the finished dish cool for about 20–30 minutes (which allows the flavors to further blend); then I bring it back to a quick simmer before serving it piping hot over basmati rice.

Courtesy of Anne Noyes Saini, cocreator CitySpoonful.com

Ceresnova Bublanina
(Slovak Cherry Cake)

This recipe comes from Judith Klein Rich, founder of the popular food blog Fooditka, and one of my fellow writers at We Heart Astoria. She is also in love with Queens—Astoria, in particular, where she lived for many years. Her blog features many dishes she develops herself, and she shares traditional dishes as well. I happily credit her for introducing me to the magic of bryndzové halušky—potato spaetzle with sheep's milk cheese and bacon—at Koliba, the best Czech/Slovak restaurant in Queens. She came to this country as a child from Slovakia, and never gave up her love of the food of her birth country. This is a delightful, delicious cake and well worth making.

This airy cherry cake has been enjoyed in my family on many occasions. Whether for birthdays or casual get-togethers, we always grace the table (and our guests' tastebuds) with bublanina. Even our American friends love it and have fun pronouncing the whimsical name. Say it—"hoob-lah-NHI-nah."

Yield: 1 cake

- 1¼ cups milk (whole milk is best)
- ⅔ cup powdered sugar
- 5 eggs, separated
- ¼ cup of unsalted margarine or butter, melted
- 1½ cups all-purpose flour, plus extra for cherries
- 1 teaspoon baking powder
- ½ cup white bread crumbs (extra fine)
- 2 cups pitted cherries (preserved wild cherries are better because they have more flavor, but make sure to drain them well)
- Powdered sugar, for dusting

Preheat oven to 370–375°F. Combine milk, sugar, egg yolks, and melted butter and mix well.

Whisk together the dry ingredients—flour, baking powder, and bread crumbs. Add to wet ingredients.

Beat the egg whites to form stiff peaks. Gently fold into the batter. Spread onto a greased 9 x 9-inch baking pan, lightly dusted with flour.

Toss pitted cherries in some flour and fluff up with your hands. Take the cherries and place them into the batter in a symmetrical pattern (or asymmetrical if you prefer). They soak into the batter quickly so work fast.

Bake for 30 minutes or when it passes the clean-toothpick test. Let cool, cut into squares, and dust with powdered sugar.

Courtesy of Judith Klein Rich, founder of Fooditka.com

Caponata

I can't tell you how happy I am to be able to share this recipe with you. It comes from my friend Laura Mello, who helps to manage the Hellgate CSA in Astoria (and is also one of its original members) as a coordinator and farmer liaison. She is also an amazing home cook with great technique; she once taught me how to cook a steak properly. Hearing about this caponata from her is one of my earliest memories of my time in Astoria—it really is legendary. And way delicious. It is best made in the summer, when eggplants are plentiful and in season, available through your CSA, local greenmarket, or produce stand.

I've been serving this caponata to my husband's family for about 10 years now. His Uncle Sal says it rivals the best caponatas he's had in Sicily. The key is patience—the recipe does take a long time, but it is worth it.

Yield: about 16 cups

2 large eggplant, peeled and cut into small (½–1 cm) dice

Salt

1¼ pounds celery stalks

Olive oil

2 large onions, sliced into thin slivers

6 ounces capers, rinsed

½ cup pine nuts

½ pound pitted Castelvetrano or other good-quality, brined green olives, roughly chopped (13–14 ounces olives with pit is about ½ pound pitted)

1 (28-ounce) can whole tomatoes with juice

¼–⅓ cup red wine vinegar, plus balsamic vinegar to taste

1 tablespoon sugar

Put the diced eggplant into a strainer, sprinkle generously with salt, toss, and set aside for an hour or two to draw out some of the water. This will make it less bitter and firmer, so it will absorb less oil. (You can skip this step if you wish.)

To prepare the celery, cut each stalk into three strips lengthwise and slice each strip into very thin pieces. Set aside.

Heat very large pot (at least 5 quarts) over medium heat. Cover bottom of pan with olive oil and add onion. Sauté for a few minutes and add celery. Sprinkle lightly with salt. Cover for about 5 minutes to let celery steam. Remove lid, lower heat, and continue to cook until onions are translucent and celery has softened (the heat should be low enough so the onion does not brown), about 10 minutes. Add the capers, pine nuts, olives, and tomatoes with their juice, crushing or tearing the tomatoes into pieces. Continue cooking, stirring occasionally, for about 30 minutes. If the onion starts to brown, reduce heat. Remove mixture from pan into a bowl and set aside.

Rinse salt from eggplant and toss to drain most of the rinsing water. Cover bottom of pan with olive oil again and add ⅓ to ½ of the eggplant. Sauté each batch for about 15 minutes, adding more oil if the pan starts to get too dry.

When last batch of eggplant is done, combine all the cooked eggplant and the onion-celery mixture in the pan. Lower heat to simmer and cook for up to several hours, stirring about every 15 minutes. Put the cover on for a while from time to time. Turn off heat and cool to room temperature.

If you can, do the above the day before you plan to serve the caponata, and continue in the morning, or just before serving. Heat caponata again and cook for another 30–60 minutes at a simmer. Stir in vinegars and sugar. Cook gently until vinegar is almost completely absorbed. Taste and adjust seasoning if necessary.

The caponata is best when served at room temperature.

Recipe by Laura Mello

Mexican Panzanella

I was asked to do a cooking demonstration at the Socrates Greenmarket (Astoria) in the summer of 2011, and I created this recipe as a result. It was extremely popular with the attendees, as it's fresh, full of robust flavors, and filling. It's best made in the summer when tomatoes, cucumbers, peppers, and corn are all in season, readily available at the greenmarket or produce stand. The ripe tomatoes really do a good job of softening the bread.

Serves 6–8

- 1 small loaf of crusty yeast bread (Italian-style is good), preferably stale
- 4–5 large tomatoes, cut into large dice
- 2 ears of corn, kernels removed
- 1 red pepper, seeded, cut into medium dice
- 1 large cucumber, peeled and seeded, cut into small dice
- ½ red onion, cut into small dice
- 2 cloves garlic, pressed
- salt
- ¼ cup chopped fresh cilantro
- Cotija cheese, crumbled (to taste)
- 1 avocado, chopped (optional)

Vinaigrette

- ⅓ cup olive oil
- 3 tablespoons apple cider or sherry vinegar
- ½ teaspoon cumin
- 1 teaspoon crushed Mexican oregano
- ¼ red pepper flakes
- ¼ smoked paprika
- Juice from ½ small lemon
- Salt and pepper
- Honey, to taste

Chop the bread into 1-inch cubes. If you are using fresh bread, toast the cubes in the oven or toaster oven for 5–10 minutes.

Combine the tomatoes, corn, red pepper, cucumber, onions, and garlic in a large bowl. Add a little salt to draw out the vegetable juices. Let rest for about 5 minutes.

Meanwhile, chop the cilantro. Add that to the vegetables when they are done resting.

Add the bread cubes and lightly toss. Let rest while you make the vinaigrette.

For the vinaigrette, whisk together everything except the honey. When everything has come together, add a little bit of honey. Taste the vinaigrette and adjustment seasoning as needed.

Add half the vinaigrette to the bread and vegetables and lightly toss. Wait a minute. See how much vinaigrette is absorbed by everything, then add enough to achieve your preferred texture. Let rest for a few minutes. Add the cotija cheese and toss lightly. Taste the mixture and season with salt and pepper to your preference. Top with avocado, if using.

Recipe by Meg Cotner

Gouda Grilled Cheese with Black Bean Hummus & Pickled Jalapeños

This is one of the most popular sandwiches at The Queens Kickshaw, home of great coffee in Astoria, and myriad grilled cheese sandwiches. The gouda sandwich is a wonderful combination of salty, spicy, tangy, sweet, and savory. The recipe is in multiple parts, and each element is integral to the sandwich. Believe me, once you taste it, you will be counting the days until you can eat another one.

Makes 1 sandwich

Black Bean Hummus

2 (15-ounce) cans black beans, drained and rinsed
½ cup lime juice
⅓ cup tahini paste
1 tablespoon ground cumin

2 cloves garlic, peeled
Extra-virgin olive oil
Salt and freshly ground black pepper

Puree the black beans, lime juice, tahini paste, cumin, and garlic in a food processor. Add extra-virgin olive oil as needed until the hummus is creamy. Season with salt and pepper. Yield: 1 quart. (Note: Leftover hummus can be kept for other uses and will last for a few days. Try serving it with blue corn chips.)

Pickled Jalapeños

2 pounds jalapeños
5 cups apple cider vinegar
6 tablespoons kosher salt
6 tablespoons granulated sugar
4 tablespoons whole coriander seeds

4 tablespoons black peppercorns
6 cloves garlic, peeled
4 bay leaves

Using gloves to protect your hands, slice the jalapeños width-wise in ¼-inch rounds. Set aside in a large container. Combine the vinegar, salt, sugar, coriander seeds, peppercorns, garlic, and bay leaves in a large saucepan and bring to a boil over high heat. Once the brine has boiled, reduce the heat and simmer for 5 minutes. Remove from the heat and pour over the sliced jalapeños. Let cool, and then refrigerate.

Sandwich

1 tablespoon guava jam
2 (¾-inch) slices brioche bread
1 tablespoon black bean
    hummus, recipe above
5 slices pickled jalapeños,
    recipe above

2½ ounces Gouda cheese
    (sliced or shredded)
1½ teaspoons clarified butter

Preheat the oven to 500°F. Smear the guava jam on one slice of brioche, and the black bean hummus on the other slice. Be sure to cover the surface entirely to ensure the bread does not burn while in the oven. Place the pickled jalapeno slices on one side, and divide the cheese over both halves. Place cheese-side-up in the oven for 5 minutes.

Remove from the oven and place the halves together. Pat half the butter on one side of the sandwich and griddle it on medium heat until nicely browned. Repeat on the opposite side. Let the sandwich cool for about 30 seconds to set, and then slice in half.

Courtesy of Tia Keenan, The Queens Kickshaw (p. 54)

Appendices

Appendix A: Eateries by Cuisine

The restaurants in this book are arranged by cuisine here—some places are appropriate for more than one category, so we've included them wherever they are a good fit. If a place is a food truck or food cart, as opposed to an actual restaurant, that is also indicated. Cafes have indication as to the roaster they use for their coffee beans, because that matters to a lot of people. Some regional indications are also notated.

American
Astor Room (Astoria), 16
Queens Comfort (Astoria), 54

Argentinian
El Gauchito (Elmhurst), 207
La Esquina Criolla (Elmhurst), 213

Bangladeshi
Haat Bazar (Jackson Heights), 182
Kababish (Jackson Heights), 160

Barbecue
Butcher Bar (Astoria), 83
John Brown Smokehouse (Long
  Island City), 38
Three Brothers Butcher BBQ
  (Bayside), 285

Belgian
Wafels & Dinges (truck)
  (Astoria), 110

Comfort Food
El*Ay*Si (Long Island City), 30
Queens Comfort (Astoria), 54

Cuban
El Sitio (Woodside), 116
Fatty's (Astoria), 31
Rincon Criollo (Corona), 225

Diner
Jahn's (Jackson Heights), 177

Eastern European
Bohemian Hall and Beer Garden
   (Czech/Slovak) (Astoria), 69
Cevabdzinica Sarajevo (Bosnian)
   (Astoria), 24
Djerdan (Bosnian) (Astoria), 28
Koliba (Czech/Slovak)
   (Astoria), 71
Ukus (Bosnian) (Astoria), 64

Ecuadorian
Hornado Ecuatoriano/Pique y
   Pase "Pepin" (truck) (Jackson
   Heights), 196

Egyptian
Kabab Cafe (Astoria), 70
Mombar (Astoria), 72

Filipino
Engeline's Restaurant
   (Woodside), 117
Ihawan (Woodside), 119
Krystal's Cafe and Pastry Shop
   (Woodside), 121
Mama Meena's Family Restaurant
   (Woodhaven), 335
Tito Rad's Grill & Restaurant
   (Sunnyside), 130

French
Cafe Triskell (Breton) (Astoria), 22
Fresca La Crepe (Woodside), 118
Tournesol (Long Island City), 77

Gastropubs
Alewife (Long Island City), 14
Sparrow Tavern (Astoria), 60
Sweet Afton (Astoria), 62

German
Zum Stammtisch (Glendale), 296

Vesta (Astoria), 65
Via Trenta (Astoria), 66

Namaste Tashi Delek Momo
Dumpling Palace (Jackson
Heights), 170
Tawa Food (Jackson Heights), 173
Woodside Cafe (Woodside), 132

New American
Alobar (Long Island City), 14
Danny Brown Wine Bar & Kitchen
(Forest Hills), 316
El*Ay*Si (Long Island City), 30
Fatty's (Astoria), 31
LIC Market (Long Island City), 41
Quaint (Sunnyside), 126
Sage General Store (Long Island
City), 57
Salt and Fat (Sunnyside), 127
Sparrow Tavern (Astoria), 60
Stove (Astoria), 61

North African
Harissa (Moroccan/Algerian)
(Astoria), 34
Kabab Cafe (Egyptian)
(Astoria), 70
Little Morocco (Astoria), 43
Mombar (Egyptian) (Astoria), 72

Pakistani
Kababish (Jackson Heights), 160

Paraguayan
I Love Py (Sunnyside), 120

Peruvian
Cevicheria El Rey (Jackson
Heights), 155
Costa Verde (Corona), 206
El Chivito D'Oro (Jackson
Heights), 156
Urubamba (Jackson Heights), 175

Polish
Krolewskie Jadlo (Ridgewood), 294

Progressive European
Bear (Long Island City), 18

Pubs/Bars
Donovan's Pub (Woodside), 136
Dutch Kills (Long Island City), 29
Gaslight, The (Sunnyside), 134
Hell Gate Social (Astoria), 35
Molly Blooms (Sunnyside), 135
PJ Horgans (Sunnyside), 134

Sweet Afton (Astoria), 62
Terazza 7 (Jackson Heights), 174

Salvadoran
El Comal (Jamaica), 334

Spanish
La Rioja (Astoria), 39

Steak House
Christos (Astoria), 25

Surinamese
Warung Kario (South Richmond
   Hill), 339

Taiwanese
King 5 Noodle House/Nan Bei Ho
   Corp. (Flushing), 253
Ku-Shiang Taiwanese Restaurant
   (Flushing), 255

Tibetan
Gangjong Kitchen (Jackson
   Heights), 159
Lali Guras (Jackson Heights), 161

Lhasa Fast Food (Jackson
   Heights), 162
Phayul (Jackson Heights), 170
Potala Fresh Food (cart) (Jackson
   Heights), 198

Thai
Arunee Thai (Jackson
   Heights), 155
Ayada (Elmhurst), 204
Chao Thai (Elmhurst), 205
Leng Thai (Astoria), 40
Ploy Thai (Elmhurst), 216
Sripraphai (Woodside), 136
Thailand's Center Point
   (Woodside), 129
Wave Thai (Astoria), 66
Zabb Elee (Woodside), 133

Turkish
Turkish Grill (Sunnyside), 131

Uzbeki/Bukharian
Cheburechnaya (Rego Park), 315
Salute 2000 (Forest Hills), 311

Venezuelan
Arepas Cafe (Astoria), 15
Patacon Pisao #2 (Elmhurst), 216

Vietnamese
Joju (Elmhurst), 211

West Indian
Singh's Roti Shop and Bar (South
   Richmond Hill), 339

Wine Bar
Claret Wine Bar (Sunnyside), 114
Crescent & Vine (Astoria), 27

Appendix B: Specialty Foods, Dishes & Markets

As in the previous appendix, regional indications are notated in parentheses.

Artisanal Markets
Queens County Market
 (Sunnyside), 147

Asian Products
Chong Hat Market (Korean)
 (Jackson Heights), 181
Family Market (Japanese)
 (Astoria), 88
H Mart (Korean)
 (Flushing), 269
Han Ah Reum (Korean)
 (Woodside), 140

Hong Kong Supermarket (Chinese)
 (Elmhurst), 231
Indo Java Market (Indonesian)
 (Elmhurst), 232
Inthira Thai Market (Thai)
 (Woodside), 141
Jmart (Chinese) (Flushing), 271
New Long Cheng Market (Chinese)
 (Woodside), 143
Pacific Supermarket (Chinese)
 (Jackson Heights), 190
Phil-Am Foods (Filipino)
 (Woodside), 146

Sunnyside Meat Market
(Sunnyside), 149
Western Beef (Ridgewood), 305

Candy
Fa Guo San Candy Shop USA
(Flushing), 268

Cannoli
D'Aquila Pastry Shop (Italian)
(Bayside), 287
La Guli (Italian) (Astoria), 92
Lulu's Italian and American Bakery
(Italian) (Fresh Meadows), 340
Terrizzi Pastry Shop (Italian)
(Astoria), 104

Ceviche
Cevicheria El Rey (Jackson
Heights), 155
Costa Verde (Corona), 206

Charcuterie/Cured Meats
Alps Provisions (Astoria), 79
Dave and Tony Salumeria
(Astoria), 87
Muncan Foods (Astoria), 96

Rosario's Deli (Astoria), 99
Sorisso's (Astoria), 104
Stammtisch Pork Store
(Glendale), 304
Sunnyside Meat Market
(Sunnyside), 149

Cheese
Cheese of the World (Forest Hills),
324
Rosario's Deli (Astoria), 99
Titan Foods (Astoria), 105
Trader Joe's (Rego Park), 329

Chocolates
Aigner Chocolates (Forest Hills), 321
Schmidt's Confectionary, 341
Trader Joe's (Rego Park), 329

Cholados
Las Americas Bakery (Elmhurst), 186
Pecas Y Mas (Sunnyside), 146

Coffee Beans
Baruir's Coffee (Sunnyside), 138
Dallis Brothers Coffee (Ozone
Park), 342

Parrot Coffee Market (Astoria), 98
Queens Kickshaw, The (Astoria), 54
Sweetleaf (Long Island City), 63
Trader Joe's (Rego Park), 329

Delis
A & R International Food
   Delicatessen (Forest Hills), 319
Manor Delicatessen
   (Woodhaven), 345
Nile Deli (Astoria), 97

Dumplings
Best North Dumpling Shop
   (Northern Style) (Flushing), 244
Chinese Food Cart (Cantonese)
   (Elmhurst), 236
Henan Feng Wei Restaurant
   (Henanese) (Flushing), 250
Lao Bei Fang Dumpling House
   (Elmhurst), 214
My Sweet Home Dumpling House
   (Flushing), 257
Nan Xiang Dumpling House
   (Shanghai soup dumplings)
   (Flushing), 257
Savor Fusion Mall (Various), 260

Sifu Chio (Hong Kong)
   (Flushing), 261
White Bear (Flushing), 265

Empanadas
El Riconcito de Tito (Colombian)
   (Jackson Heights), 157
Empanadas Cafe (Corona), 209
La Esquina Criolla (Argentinian)
   (Elmhurst), 213
San Antonio Bakery #2 (Chilean)
   (Astoria), 58

European Products
A & R International Food
   Delicatessen (Forest Hills), 319
Euro Market (Astoria), 88
Hetman of Woodhaven
   (Woodhaven), 343
Parrot Coffee Market
   (Astoria), 98
Slovak-Czech Varieties (Long
   Island City), 102

Fresh Juice
Elmhurst Mex Grocery Juice Stand
   (Elmhurst), 229

Fresh Start Organic Market
(Astoria), 89

Appendix C: Food Events, Festivals & Celebrations

Queens is the home to a number of immigrant communities, many of which celebrate their culture's special days or seasons with food. There are also celebrations of specific neighborhoods and the borough itself. The following are some of the food events and festivals held each year in Queens.

February

Lunar New Year Parade, Queens Crossing Mall, 39th Ave. and Main St., Flushing; and Korea Village Open Center, 150-24 Northern Blvd. at 150th St., Flushing; Subway: 7 to Main Street. Every year in late January or early February (depending on how the dates on the lunar calendar fall), the East Asian community celebrates the movable Lunar New Year, also known as the Chinese New Year, though the lunar year is recognized in multiple Asian cultures. Depending on which animal in the Chinese zodiac (*Shēngxiào* in Chinese) represents the year at hand, that animal is showcased during the parade, which is the highlight of the celebrations that day. The parade winds its way along streets in the central business district, along 39th Avenue, Union Street, Sanford Avenue, and Main Street. The parade ends near Queens Crossing Mall and that's were the food is, along with cultural performances. The Korean community also celebrates Lunar New Year at the Korea Village Open Center, a space dedicated to Korean culture, and will have Korean food on hand, along with dancing, games, and music. Of course, after the celebrations, the neighborhood is your oyster, and most restaurants will be celebrating the new year with delicious food offerings on their menus.

April

Songkran Festival, Wat Buddha Thai Thavorn Vanaram, 76-16 46th Ave., Elmhurst; Subway: M/R to Elmhurst Avenue. This Southeast Asian festival celebrates the Buddhist New Year, usually occurring mid-April. In Thailand, it happens at the hottest time of the year—the end of the dry season—so water plays an important part of the celebration, with people throwing water at each other (though, this custom is not so common in Elmhurst). The festivities take place at the Wat Buddha Thai Thavorn Vanaram (a *wat* is a Buddhist monastery). While there, you'll no doubt spy the numerous sand *stupas,* which look like the beginnings of multiple sand castles (complete with colorful flags), but they are not—they have to do with the idea of cleansing and a new start to the new year. Of course when the wet season starts, the *stupas* will be washed away, and any baggage along with them. Food is a big part of this festival, and there is a whole array of dishes. Contributing an offering is a good idea, so plan to bring something (cash) to complete this part of the celebration. All are welcome.

May

Cinco de Mayo Festival, Flushing Meadows Park; Subway: 7 to 110th Street or Willets Point. Mexicans and Americans alike happily celebrate May 5, the day that commemorates the Mexican army's triumph over the French at the Battle of Puebla in 1862; May 5 is not Mexican Independence Day—that would be September 16. Each year on the first Sunday in May, the Cinco de Mayo Festival comes to Flushing Meadows–Corona Park, with festivities taking place near the Queens Theater and Unisphere. Tens of thousands of people attend this event, enjoying music, dancing, and of course, food— you'll be able to chow on tacos, quesadillas, burritos, and more, while soaking up the vibrant Mexican culture you'll be immersed in.

Greek Festival, St. Demetrios Church, 30-11 30th Dr., Astoria; (718) 728-1718; Subway: N/Q to 30th Avenue; saintdemetrios astoria.com. You can't miss seeing evidence of the presence of this festival each spring, because the carnival rides—the Ferris wheel especially—are visible from the elevated subway tracks as you pass by. While this festival is grouped in with many of the other more common summer street fairs in Astoria, it rises above the pack in part because of the amazing food—crazy delicious lamb gyros, souvlaki, moussaka, sweet *loukoumades,* icy frappés, and more. The festival has also been operating for almost 40 years. Now that's staying power. Enjoy traditional live music as well, and the aforementioned carnival rides.

Indonesian Food Bazaar, Masjid Al-Hikmah parking lot, 48-01 31st Ave., Long Island City; (718) 721-8881; Subway: M/R to 46th Avenue; masjidalhikmahnewyork.org. A number of these charity bazaars are held during the summer time, at the mosque that serves the Indonesian community in this part of Queens. The bazaar happens once a month, May through August, and takes place rain or shine. The food here is some of the best Indonesian you'll find in all of New York City—satays, soups, tempeh, meats (no pork), vegetables, drinks, and desserts. The vendors are happy to answer any questions you might have and are delighted to show off their culture's food. Keep an eye on the mosque's website for announcements of dates for the bazaars throughout the warm, summer months; they will break for Ramadan if it falls during the summer. Each bazaar lasts from 9 a.m. to 4 p.m. Pro tip: Show up around 11 a.m. when the food is abundant and the temperatures aren't too hot (that blacktop on the parking lot can really heat up).

Queens Taste, Caesars Club at Citi Field, Flushing Meadows–Corona Park; Subway: 7 to Willets Point; discoverqueens.info/

queenstaste. Produced by the Queens Economic Development Corporation, this annual food-tasting event brings together a solid selection of Queens restaurants and food producers to show off their best stuff, whether it's long-standing trusted dishes or new menu items/products. It's a great way to get a sense of food in the borough, and a convenient way for these vendors to get feedback from many people in one fell swoop. The event is ticketed and open to all; media representatives can contact them to get a press pass.

June

Burmese Food Fair, Long Island City Aviation High School, 45-30 36th St., Long Island City; Subway: 7 to 33rd Street; blog.moegyo .org. This is one of the most anticipated food festivals in Queens, and while serving up some of the best Burmese food in the City the proceeds go to support the Moegyo Humanitarian Foundation, which provides humanitarian aid when and where needed and currently works to "help orphans and disadvantaged children in poorest parts of Myanmar." Food offered at the fair ranges from appetizers to main dishes to desserts, like *samusa thohk,* a kind of vegetarian samosa salad; *ohn-no kout swel,* chicken and coconut soup with egg noodles; and *thar kwai yai,* sticky rice in coconut milk sauce. The *yaykae thote* is a fabulous shaved ice dessert, too. Pay for dishes at the different stands with tickets that you buy at the table as you enter the building (each ticket equals $1). Each year the fair lasts from 12 to 4 p.m.

Dine Astoria Week, centralastoria.org/dine-astoria. First produced in 2012, this week strives to promote Astoria's dining scene
by partnering with a selection of local restaurants that offer affordable prix-fixe lunches and dinners (not including tax and tip).
Cuisines run the gamut, from Indian to Mexican, Greek to Croatian,
German to Thai. As with Queens Restaurant Week, this is a great
opportunity to try a new restaurant or support your favorites in the
area. A few restaurants offer a free beverage or ice cream, too.

Taste of LIC, Gantry Plaza State Park at the waterfront, 4-74 48th
Ave., Long Island City; Subway: 7 to Vernon-Jackson or G to 21st
Street; chocolatefactorytheater.org/home.html. A plethora of Long
Island City food businesses participate in this fundraiser for The
Chocolate Factory, an Obie Award–winning theater and performance
space in Long Island City, Queens. For the size of the neighborhood,
the participation is extensive—over 50 restaurants, bars, caterers,
bakeries, and food shops arrive to share their creations with the
community. Keep an eye out on the Chocolate Factory's website for
a link to the event (the URL changes each year) and a list of the
participants. Since this is a fundraiser, it is a ticketed event, with
price levels that afford more perks the higher you go, including
after parties and opportunities to hang with the movers and shakers
of the western Queens food world; if you are media, you can request
a press pass to attend the expo of edibles. The views of the East
River and neighboring Manhattan are pretty sweet, and Gantry Park
has received a series of beautiful upgrades in the recent past, so
take some time to enjoy the stunning sights westward.

July

Cheesemonger Invitational, Larkin Cold Storage, 47-55 27th St., Long Island City; Subway: 7 to Hunters Point or G to 21st Street; cheesemongerinvitational.com. If you love cheese, this is the place for you. It's only been around for a few years, but it's become a very popular event in this short time. Cheese shops from around the world come to compete in a variety of activities, from the intellectual side of cheese (testing of cheese facts and general cheese knowledge) to having a developed palate for cheese (blind tasting), to skill in cutting and wrapping cheese, and how to plate it properly. Industry experts are the judges. For observers and attendees—who are allowed in for the finals of the Invitational—refreshments are provided, and for $50 it's all-you-can-eat cheese, beer, wine, and cocktails.

Junta Hispana, Flushing Meadows–Corona Park, near the Unisphere, Flushing; Subway: 7 to Willets Point; juntahispana.net/events/new-york. If you are looking for a festival in which to immerse yourself in Hispanic culture, Junta Hispana is the one for you. Not to mention it's free to attend. Twenty Spanish-speaking countries are represented, with the opportunity for attendees to learn about the culture and traditions of each country, through music and dance performances, traditional crafts, and of course, food (check out the information booth representing each country to learn even more about them). Myriad authentic taste treats are accessible at the traveling food market known as "Mercado Rodante," located in the event plaza. The event takes place rain or shine.

Peruvian Independence Fair, Dutch Kills Park, 37th Ave. at 27th St., Long Island City; Subway: N/Q to 36th Avenue; fipeny .com. Located in Dutch Kills—a part of Long Island City just south of Astoria—this is the main festival in Queens celebrating Peruvian history. Peru's independence was proclaimed by José de San Martin in July 28, 1821. The festival in Queens includes music and dance from that country, including the Afro-Peruvian community. The food of the various regions—coastal, highlands, and forests—is showcased. Admission is free.

August

Hong Kong Dragon Boat Festival, Meadow Lake in Flushing Meadows–Corona Park, Flushing; Subway: 7 to Willets Point, then to a special event bus; hkdbf-ny.org. Since 1990, the Dragon Boat Festival has taken place at Flushing Meadows–Corona Park and has blossomed into quite the athletic event; it's now one of the largest dragon boat festivals in the country. It celebrates the fifth month of the lunar calendar. At the event, East Asian arts and culture are represented by live dance and music performances, as well as booths near the main stage area showcasing folk art and crafts. There is a whole food court involved—look for things like skewers of fish balls, lo mein, chicken curry, and shaved ice. Admission to the event is free, and you pay for food; it happens rain or shine.

September

Queens County Fair, Queens County Farm Museum, 73-50 Little Neck Pkwy., Floral Park; (718) 347-3276; Subway: E/F to Kew Gardens–Union Turnpike, then Q46 Bus (eastbound on Union Tpk.) to the Little Neck Parkway stop, cross Union Turnpike and walk north on Little Neck Parkway 3 blocks to the museum entrance; queensfarm.org. The Queens County Farm Museum, with origins in the year 1697, is the only working historical farm in New York City, and its 47 acres are the longest continuously farmed land in New York State. Each fall they hold a traditional county fair with live-stock competitions, as well as competitions in vegetables, baking, and canning. There's a pie-eating contest, a Bavarian garden, and food vendors during the weekend. The corn maze (aka maize maze) is pretty awesome, too. It lasts for a weekend, during the hours of 11 a.m. to 6 p.m., and admission is $8 adults, and $5 kids 12 and under.

Queens Restaurant Week, discoverqueens.info. For 10 days to 2 weeks, restaurants around the borough of Queens serve up special 3-course prix-fixe meals for $25; the Queens Economic Development Corporation is behind the promotion. This is a great opportunity to try out food at restaurants and in neighborhoods where you might not usually go, especially when it's a restaurant that is normally a bit spendy. It's a great way to support some of your favorite restaurants as well. The interest from local restaurants has grown over the years, and some years over 100 restaurants have participated.

Usually at the start of Queens Restaurant Week a kickoff event occurs, with free food and drink available to those in the area at the time. Keep an eye out on the website for more information as the week approaches.

October

Apple Festival, Queens County Farm Museum, 73-50 Little Neck Pkwy., Floral Park; (718) 347-3276; Subway: E/F to Kew Gardens–Union Turnpike, then Q46 Bus (eastbound on Union Tpk.) to the Little Neck Parkway stop; queensfarm.org. Cross Union Turnpike and walk north on Little Neck Parkway 3 blocks to the museum entrance. From 11 a.m. to 4 p.m. immerse yourself in the world of the apple— the fruit New York State excels at like nobody's business. Enjoy a variety of apples on their own, some delicious freshly pressed cider, and gawk at (as well as eat) the country's largest apple cobbler, baked right there at the farm. Additional food vendors will be on hand to feed you, and you can even enjoy a hayride. This is a great event for children—I know when I was a kid, apples were a favorite (hello, Bintz's Apple Mountain in Michigan). Admission is free.

Diwali Mela, 74th St. between Roosevelt Ave. and 37th Ave., Jackson Heights; Subway: 7 to 74th Street or E/F/M/R to Jackson Heights–Roosevelt Avenue. Diwali, known as the Festival of Lights, is one of the key festivals for Hindus, so you can imagine that it is celebrated with gusto in Jackson Heights' Little India. Food stalls line the street, serving up savory chat and traditional sugary Indian sweets. The celebration lasts from 1 to 6 p.m., and there is music and dancing to accompany your eating and general festive attitude.

Taste of Sunnyside, Sunnyside Community Services ground floor Ballroom, 43-31 39th St., Sunnyside; Subway: 7 to 40th Street; (718) 606-1800; sunnysideshines.org; tasteofsunnyside.com. This "restaurant festival," hosted by the Sunnyside Chamber of Commerce and Sunnyside Shines Business Improvement District, showcases a couple dozen restaurants from all over Sunnyside. There are two "seatings," which essentially means there are two start times; this is done to alleviate the intense crowding that is all too familiar at events like this. That being said, there is a risk that food could run out during the second seating, so it's best to purchase a ticket for the first. Tickets are quite affordable; at the writing of this book, tickets are $25.

November

Queens Uncorked, The Foundry, 42-38 9th St., Long Island City; Subway: 7 to Queensboro Plaza; ediblecommunities.com/queens. It's unclear whether or not this event will continue into the future, but it's worth your while to keep your eye on the Edible Queens website in the fall to see if it is indeed happening. At its core, this is a wine and food pairing event, but it is also a fund-raising event; proceeds from the ticket sales go toward whatever needy cause Edible Queens deems worthy (the amazing GrowNYC has been a recipient). It takes place at The Foundry, a beautiful spot in

Long Island City that's perfect for parties. Restaurants, food artisans, wineries, and wine shops participate, creating a smorgasbord of tasty awesomeness. Ticket prices are quite reasonable for the quality of the food and wine being presented; at the writing of this book, tickets are $40.

Appendix D: Community Supported Agriculture (CSA) in Queens

A CSA, which stands for **Community Supported Agriculture,** is a way to access fresh, seasonal, organic and/or ecologically grown food grown by local farmers. A group of people get together, led by an administrative team called the Core Group, and purchase "shares" in a farm; their "dividends" take the form of whatever food is harvested by the farmer. It's a way to get high quality, healthy produce at an affordable price. At most CSAs both vegetables and fruit are available, and with some CSAs one can purchase meat, dairy, grains, maple syrup, and other value-added products.

Some CSAs also accept food stamps or offer low-income shares to those in need. Contact the individual CSA for possible details.

To participate in a CSA you must be a member (those who partake in a CSA are called "members"), and that requires applying for membership, which entails a small administrative fee. CSAs are extremely popular in Queens, so get on the wait-list as soon as possible for the CSA of your choice—you can do that by e-mailing the CSA or filling out the appropriate form on their website. Here is a list of Queens CSAs, the main farms they use, and their websites.

Astoria

Astoria CSA
Farm: Golden Earthworm
astoriacsa.com

Harvest Astoria CSA
Farm: Norwich Meadows
harvestastoria.com

Hellgate CSA
Farm: Green Thumb
hellgatecsa.net

Douglaston

Douglaston CSA
Farm: Golden Earthworm
justfood.org/csaloc/queens

Flushing

Flushing CSA
Farm: Golden Earthworm
facebook.com/flushingcsa

Forest Hills

Forest Hills CSA
Farm: Golden Earthworm
foresthillscsa.com

Tuv Ha'Aretz CSA
Farm: Golden Earthworm
foresthillstuvcsa.com

Glendale

Glendale CSA
Farm: Garden of Eve
glendalecsa.com

Hollis Hills
Hollis Hills CSA
Farm: Golden Earthworm
hollishillsjc.org/affiliates/
  hollis-hills-csa

Jackson Heights
Farm Spot CSA
Farm: Golden Earthworm
farmspot.org

Tierra a Mesa 90th Street CSA
Farm: La Baraja
justfood.org/csaloc/queens

Long Island City
Long Island City CSA
Farm: The Farm at Miller's Crossing
liccsa.wordpress.com

Ozone Park
Ozone Park CSA
Farm: Norwich Meadows Farm
ozoneparkcsa.wordpress.com

Sunnyside
Sunnyside CSA
Farm: Golden Earthworm
sunnysidecsa.com

Woodside
Woodside CSA
Farm: Nolasco Farm
woodsidecsa.blogspot.com

Index